Technical Aid to FOOD INDUSTRIES

Edited & Compiled by
G.T. Kale
R.C. Bhutiani
N.V.R. Iyengar
V. Balu
A.N. Sankaran

BIOTECH
2007
Biotech Books
Delhi - 110 035

ISBN 81-7622-173-2

Published by : **BIOTECH BOOKS**
1123/74, Tri Nagar,
DELHI – 110 035
Phone: 27382765
e-mail: biotechbooks@yahoo.co.in

Showroom : 4762-63/23, Ansari Road, Darya Ganj,
NEW DELHI - 110 002
Phone: 23245578, 23244987

Printed at : **Chawla Offset Printers**
New Delhi – 110 052

PRINTED IN INDIA

INTRODUCTION

THIS volume contains the proceedings of the Third Symposium which was organized by the Central Food Technological Research Institute, Mysore, in 1953, and inaugurated by Shri K. D. Malaviya, Deputy Minister, Natural Resources and Scientific Research, New Delhi. While the first two Symposia dealt with 'Food and Population' and 'Development of Food Industries in India', this Symposium was specially organized to establish further contacts with the food industries to know their problems and to devise ways and means of giving them necessary technical aid. The Symposium was attended by representatives of the Ministries of Food and Agriculture of the Central and State Governments, of Food Industries Associations and a large number of private Food Industries, which has lent a special value to the proceedings of this Symposium.

The papers published in this book describe the present state of the Indian Food Industries and the technical problems facing them. The first 12 papers deal with the general subject of technical aid to the Industry and lay stress on the problems involved in the improvement of quality of processed food products. These are followed by accounts of the technical problems of individual industries or groups of allied food industries. The industries dealt with are biscuit and bakery, breakfast foods, flour and barley milling, confectionery, Indian sweets, cocoa and chocolates, fruit and vegetables, gelatine, cold storage and deep freezing, oil milling, fish and the typically Indian Industry —*Pan Supari*. The various contributions emphasize generally the need for a liaison between agri-horticultural authorities and the food processing industry, for cheaper and good quality raw materials, utilization of indigenous materials required in processing techniques, fabrication of equipment required for small- and large-scale industries and adoption of modern scientific methods.

Our grateful thanks are due to the Council of Scientific and Industrial Research, New Delhi, and particularly to Dr S. S. Bhatnagar for encouraging us in our efforts to hold this Symposium at the Institute and sanctioning the publication of the proceedings. Grateful thanks are also due to all those who prepared papers and participated in the discussions.

Thanks must also be expressed to the members of the staff of the Institute who co-operated enthusiastically and particularly the members of the Division of Information and Statistics who were mainly responsible for the organization of the Symposium and publishing its Proceedings.

One of the main objects of the Five-Year Plan is to achieve substantial industrial development during 1951–56. The Programmes of Industrial Development have set targets for the production for a few major food industries (sugar, vegetable oil, vanaspati and salt) to be achieved during the period. The Indian Food Industry comprises about 40 different small- and large-scale industries having an annual turnover of about 1,500 crores of rupees. These industries require to be developed on modern scientific lines, the benefits of which will accrue not only to the industries themselves but also to the public and the national exchequer. It is hoped that the conclusions and the recommendations of the Symposium, which are summarized in the Appendix, will indicate the complexity of the problems and the lines on which effective help should be rendered to the Industry.

V. SUBRAHMANYAN
Director

CONTENTS

LIST OF PARTICIPANTS

Government Departments

SHRI B. BANERJEE, Ministry of Food and Agriculture (Food), New Delhi.

SHRI P. H. BHATT, Ministry of Food and Agriculture, New Delhi.

SHRI L. K. HANDIQUE, Department of Agriculture, Assam, Shillong.

SHRI B. P. MASCARENHAS, Department of Industry and Commerce, Government of Mysore.

SHRI P. B. MATHUR, Department of Industries, Government of Uttar Pradesh.

SHRI V. A. MEHTA, Ministry of Industry and Commerce, New Delhi.

SHRI G. B. MOHANTY, Department of Fisheries, Government of Orissa.

SHRI V. SANE, Government Hill Fruit Research Station, Government of Uttar Pradesh.

SHRI P. V. SURYA PRAKASA RAO, Government Fruit Products Research Laboratory, Kodur, Government of Madras.

SHRI M. S. SWAMINATHAN, Department of Food Supplies, Government of Mysore.

United Nations Organization

DR F. B. CARBASIUS WEBER, Food Technologist, F.A.O., with the Government of Uttar Pradesh.

MR DICK V. FAGAN, Extension Specialist with the Government of Mysore.

Universities and Institutions

DR H. C. BIJAWAT, National Chemical Laboratory, Poona.

PROF. S. K. EKAMBARAM, Maharaja's College, Mysore.

DR S. V. GOVINDA SETTY, Medical College, Mysore.

SHRI B. M. LAL, Indian Institute of Science, Bangalore.

DR B. N. LINGARAJU, Medical College, Mysore.

DR Y. NAYUDAMMA, Central Leather Research Institute, Madras.

DR R. RAJAGOPALAN, Indian Institute of Science, Bangalore.

Food Industries Associations

1. Shri Ahmed Mohideen, Confectionery Manufacturers' Association of India, Calcutta.
2. Shri K. M. Pavaiah, Coorg Orange Growers' Co-operative Society, Ltd., Mercara.
3. Shri R. B. Rao, Federation of Biscuit Manufacturers' of India, Delhi.
4. Shri P. J. Roy, All-India Vanaspati Manufacturers' Association, Bombay.
5. Shri L. J. De Souza, All-India Food Preservers' Association, Bombay.

Food Industries

Shri S. N. Bali, Messrs Harry Ferguson of India, Ltd., Bangalore.
Shri K. P. Bhargava, Messrs G. G. Industries, Agra.
Sardar N. S. Chadha, Messrs C. R. Ice-Cold Storage, Agra.
Shri G. W. Chandiramani, Messrs Sheile & Co., Bangalore.
Shri N. M. Chauhan, Messrs Parle Products, Bombay.
Shri D. K. Dutt, Messrs Sreekissen Dutt & Co., Calcutta.
Messrs Farrukhabad Cold Storage Ltd., Farrukhabad, (U.P.)
Mr W. Fehr, Messrs Larsen and Toubro, Ltd., Bombay.
Shri B. N. Gopalakrishnan, Messrs United Breweries, Bangalore.
Shri S. N. Gundu Rao, Messrs The Ravalgaon Sugar Farm, Ltd., Ravalgaon, Bombay.
Mr R. C. Heath, Messrs Harry Ferguson of India, Ltd., Bangalore.
Shri F. K. Irani, Messrs Chamundi Breweries, Mysore.
Shri H. R. S. Iyengar, Messrs The Ravalgaon Sugar Farm, Ltd., Ravalgaon, Bombay.
Messrs M. S. Jaipur Biscuit Factory, Jaipur.
Shri K. T. Kalaya, Messrs 'Kushal' Products, Ltd., Coorg.
Shri S. F. Karaka, Messrs Volkart Brothers, Bombay.
Shri M. K. Krishna Chetty, Messrs Asoka Betelnut Factory, Coimbatore.
Shri K. Lakkappa, Messrs Mysore Sugar Co., Ltd., Mandya.
Sardar Man Mohan Singh, Messrs Frick Co., (U.S.A.), New Delhi.

SHRI P. MUKHERJI, Messrs Kisan Cold Storage and Refrigeration Service, Ltd., Patna.

DR H. A. B. PARPIA, Messrs Pure Products & Madhu Canning Ltd., Bombay.

SHRI C. V. PAUL, Messrs Earl Brothers, Bangalore.

SHRI N. B. PODUVAL, Messrs A. Boake Roberts Co., Ltd., Madras.

SHRI I. J. PURI, Messrs Kissan Products, Ltd., Bangalore.

SHRI T. RAMA AIYANGAR, Messrs The Metal Box Company of India Ltd., Calcutta.

SHRI S. V. RAMAN, Central Tea Board, Bangalore.

SHRI S. RANGANNA, Messrs Earl Brothers, Bangalore.

MR M. N. REID, Messrs Reckitt and Colman of India Ltd., Calcutta.

SHRI N. R. SATHE, Messrs The Sathe Biscuit & Chocolate Co., Ltd., Poona.

SHRI C. S. SRINIVASAN, Messrs The Mettur Chemical and Industrial Corporation, Ltd., Mettur Dam.

SHRI M. R. SHANMUGAM, Messrs Imperial Chemical Industries (India), Ltd., Madras.

SHRI K. V. SOMANNA, Messrs Consolidated Coffee Estates Ltd., (1943), Coorg.

SHRI N. THANDAVAN, Messrs A. P. V. Engineering Co., Ltd., Calcutta.

MR C. E. WOOTTON, Messrs T. Stanes and Co., Ltd., Coimbatore.

* * * *

Distinguished Guest

DR (MISS) SUSHILA NAIYAR, Minister for Health, Delhi.

* * * *

A number of other visitors and guests were also present.

MESSAGE

FROM DR S. S. BHATNAGAR, F.R.S.,

Director, Scientific and Industrial Research and Secretary, Ministry of Education and Ministry of Natural Resources and Scientific Research, New Delhi

THE scope and importance of food industries in India have been rapidly increasing during recent years. Particularly during the last war, considerable expansion took place and manufacture of several new lines was initiated. It is necessary to consolidate the progress then made and improve the quality of Indian products so that even with the change of sellers' market to buyers' market, the output of Indian industry continues to command respect in markets at home and abroad.

One of the main functions of the Central Food Technological Research Institute, Mysore, is to assist food industries to improve their standards by undertaking investigations on problems which have a collective bearing on particular aspects. Whether such problems should be referred to the Institute by individual concerns or should be presented by associations of different sectors of food industries is one aspect of the relations between industry and the Institute to which this Symposium would give thought. What arrangements should be made to test the laboratory conclusions on a large scale is another point for consideration. There may be many more.

The Central Food Technological Research Institute has already been helpful to food industries in several ways. With time, the utility of the Institute will become more and more evident. I am sure that by providing a forum for exchange of ideas, the Symposium will give a lead and help us in bringing the Institute and food industry still closer. This will enable them to appreciate each other's difficulties and requirements. I wish the Symposium all success.

New Delhi

WELCOME SPEECH
BY SHRI M. SHANKARAIYA

SHRI MALAVIYAJI, DELEGATES, LADIES AND GENTLEMEN,

I HAVE great pleasure in welcoming you all to this Symposium and to this beautiful city of Mysore. As you are aware, this is the third Symposium to be held under the auspices of the Central Food Technological Research Institute. This pleasant task of welcoming you was to have been done by Dr V. Subrahmanyan, Director of the Institute, but in his absence due to his deputation abroad, I speak here this morning in the capacity of a Member of the Local Advisory Board of the Institute. Many of you have come from distant parts of the country at considerable sacrifice of leisure or convenience, and have also been good enough to prepare papers for presentation at the Symposium. On behalf of the Institute, I have the privilege to welcome you all very sincerely and thank you for having accepted our invitation.

This Symposium is specially planned to discuss the problems and difficulties of our young food industries. The fruits of your labours and the results coming out of this Symposium will, I hope, ultimately benefit the vast millions of this country whom I here represent as a consumer. This is a very representative gathering comprising the producer, the scientist, the administrator, the statesman, the manufacturer and the merchant, and, if I may say so, it is a gathering of which the scientists and the manufacturers tend to form the most important groups. Yet, the consumer, in the end, is the most important factor of all. Without production, there would be no need for science; without the consumer, however, there would be no need for production. It is perhaps well to dwell on this aspect for a moment and keep in mind the wishes of the ultimate consumer, during the deliberations we have before us.

In foreign countries, they have their own research institutions for food industries. They have followed closely and kept pace with the markets all over the world. During the World War II, a number of food industries were started in this country, and we are aware that these have various difficulties apart from that of foreign competition. Our industries have practical difficulties in getting technical aid and this has been remedied to a great extent by the starting of this Institute. As you know, after the Independence, several National Laboratories were started and I might add that in Delhi circles these are often referred to as Nehru-Bhatnagar effect. This Institute in Mysore is making progress day by day; many important results have been obtained within the short period of 3 years. Industries will have to take full advantage of these researches and produce good and delicious food articles for the common man, at cheap rates. Discussions at this Symposium will help expedite the translating of scientific findings into practical results and will also bring about a closer co-operation between this Institute and the industry and ultimately the consumer. It is from this point of view that the Symposium will have far-reaching consequences in building up the food industy in our country.

It is a great pleasure and privilege to have as our President, Pandit Malaviyaji. As a keen student of science and a technologist, he will be able to appreciate the problems of the Industries better, and as Deputy Minister of Scientific Research and Natural Resources he will try to appreciate and understand the difficulties of the Industries and help them as far as possible. As an ardent Congress man, fired with patriotic ideas, the call of the nation attracted him and he participated in the freedom movement of the country. He worked for the amelioration of the poor from the very beginning and has been a staunch follower of the Father of our Nation, Mahatma Gandhi. In him, we have found a great help for this Institute. But for his support and encouragement, this Institute could not possibly have made so much progress that it has. His varied experience and ability will serve as a source of inspiration to this Symposium, and while welcoming him and all of you again, I now request him to declare the conference open.

THE URGENT NEEDS OF THE INDIAN FOOD PRESERVATION INDUSTRY

By

L. J. de Souza

(*Secretary, All-India Food Preservers' Association*)

The author has brought out points for the Industry to be recognized as essential and strategic. Canneries by their regulated purchases at predetermined prices will not only save wastages, particularly during glut periods, but also will encourage the grower to increase his production and improve its quality. Further, the Q.M.G.'s Department Canteen Stores Department together are the largest consumers of canned foods which are required as much in peace as in war. The author enumerates the difficulties that face the industry and retard its progress and makes suggestions about the steps that the Government should take for the development of this industry.

Many and urgent are the needs of the Indian Food Preservation Industry. It was therefore a very timely thought on the part of the organizers of the Symposium to draw attention to the subject. It is earnestly hoped that something positive and useful will result from these discussions.

Before we examine the needs of the Food Preservation Industry in India, it is necessary to examine the present status of the industry. As one intimately connected with the industry from its very birth in India and, therefore, all too familiar with the trials and tribulations of the pioneers who with vision and faith dared to start the industry in India, I must affirm that this pioneer effort has not received much support and sympathy of all concerned. The industry has not yet been recognized as being *essential and strategic*.

It will thus be obvious that the first point to decide is whether the industry is *essential and strategic*. If our reply is in the affirmative, then the solution of the difficulties that I am going to put more land under cultivation, we should have by now faced a terrible situation on the food front. Our national limitations, however, have obviously put a limit on our capacity to give more food to our people and to make up for the deficiencies in the ordinary sense. The rapid year-to-year increase in our population requires additional tapping of about a million acres of land every year for food-crop cultivation. If all this, together with the basic need in the increase in land under cereals, is taken into account, then according to the conventional method of cultivation and depending on cereals alone for our food, we must immediately spend incalculably very large sums of money. This is certainly not available to us. Is it not, therefore, logical to conclude that our scientists and food technologists have to take up the challenge to find out a short-cut to the ultimate goal of providing adequate quantity of food for the nation? I strongly believe that food technology can give an answer to this apparently insoluble problem. Howsoever people might ridicule the idea, the fact remains that the scientific knowledge can alone solve the riddle by processing unused food materials, using waste products for converting them into edible forms and by increasing the general nutritive level of our national diet. This scientific knowledge can also be exploited for increasing our cereal production by improving the present agricultural methods of handling seed, soil and water. What I mean to say is that whether it is increase in yield of food crops per acre of land or the addition of new food to our national diet, we will require the aid of scientific knowledge and that of food technology. So long as the rock basis of our efforts lies in increasing our food and nutrition, I am not concerned whether the manifestations of various forms of these efforts differ from each other. It may be in improving our fields for getting more yield per acre of land or it may be in using cheaper and unused food for blending them to usable and delicious food or it may be discovering new food or creating new food from hitherto unused or unknown sources. Owing to conservative food habits of man, it may be that food technologists who are engaged in creating new food and in increasing our total food quantity are laughed at today.

But tomorrow they will undoubtedly be considered as the saviours of humanity.

We are not known as a hard-working people. Climate alone is not responsible for this national defect. Insufficient food and low nutritional value of our food are perhaps mainly responsible for our incapacity to put in more work. Besides this, the rapid increase in our population also seems to be due mainly to our unbalanced and incomplete diet. It is up to you, therefore, to fill this tragic gap in our nation's requirement. I know food habits are most difficult to change, but your contribution coupled with suggestive and educative propaganda by the Government can break the inertia of superstition and prejudice, thereby upgrading the entire environment in which the nation is living today. I am sure when you sit down to grapple with the issues in an objective manner you will deal with all those practical problems that require solution. The Central Food Technological Research Institute, Mysore, is indeed doing commendable work in this connection and the scientific workers of this institute, headed by Dr Subrahmanyan, have already contributed a number of food articles like the new synthetic food—a mixture of tapioca and groundnut, sometimes hesitantly called synthetic rice, synthetic curd and other products from waste fruits. What is required is a quick follow up of efforts. I am glad that Dr Subrahmanyan has gone abroad to follow up the work in connection with synthetic rice. If all goes well, we can depend on the efforts of the Central Food Technological Research Institute to start large-scale trial experiments of this food from next summer. I hope, by that time, all doubts against this food will have been removed and there will be a universal acceptance of this nutritive and palatable food. It is said that we should not call this new food by the name 'rice'. I do not understand the logic. After all, a large majority of our people live on rice and have a psychological affinity for this word. Anything in the shape of rice, therefore, is more likely to be accepted by them provided, of course, the food value and the taste of synthetic rice are fully established. If it is so, I do not understand why advantage of the magic word 'rice' should not be taken by those whose interest lies, not in personal benefits, but in solving the critical food situation. Besides this synthetic food, we are likely to get soon a nutritious drink also which can very reasonably be likened to milk or curd. It will also be relevant here to mention the nutritive improvement proposed to be effected in vanaspati ghee by compulsory provision of adding vitamin 'A'. I need not mention in any detail the long standing controversy on the subject of vanaspati ghee. But, I consider it my duty to express my agreement with scientists that opinions expressed so far against vanaspati ghee in general are not based on reason or fact. I have every hope that the little prejudice which is still lingering in the minds of a section of our people will disappear soon and that they will accept the vanaspati ghee as a healthy and nutritive substitute in absence of adequate quantity of animal ghee. It should be clearly understood now that vegetable ghee does not contain any harmful thing and is not injurious to health. However, I will freely admit the possibility of adulteration of animal ghee with vanaspati ghee. Government are making serious efforts to prevent such an adulteration; for, animal and vanaspati ghee must be separated from each other and whatever quantity of pure animal ghee is produced in the country, should be made available to the people who want it. But, is it not a fact that pure animal ghee is a rare thing to find in the market today and can any one say that this adulteration will stop by putting a ban on the manufacture of vanaspati ghee? The only logical conclusion of such a ban will be more and more adulterants like dirty and poisonous *charbies* found in the market. Besides all this, I have to submit also that pure vanaspati ghee is perhaps far more beneficial and dependable than impure and adulterated ghee. The latter, as you know, is the rule of the day. Why not then accept vanaspati ghee and be happy about it? I am sure your Conference will consider all this and many more problems which in the totality of circumstances will go to extend and enlarge our food industry. For instance, we should have cheaper and more nutritious biscuits, both for the poor as well as for school-going children. Similarly, for the working class—be it farmer or mill worker—cheap and ready energy food has to be provided. In this connection, I will strongly advocate the use of food yeast blended with cereals and vegetables in palatable and presentable forms. Fruit canning and preservation industry has also to be developed in such a way that it would make available cheaper and nutritious products, and at the same time, it assumes a decentralized pattern so that fruits grown in out-of-the-way corners could be prevented from being wasted and be made available to people after preservation and keeping.

The Japanese method of rice cultivation, in my opinion, is also a matter of great importance which needs a reference in this Conference. There seems nothing special about it, but as this method requires simple treatment of soil and manure and handling of very cheap appliances and as by pursuing this method the yield of rice per acre of land increases 3–4 times, and further, as this method effects an appreciable saving in seed, I would earnestly draw the attention of all scientists engaged in agricultural technology to do their best to convert this proposition from theory into practice. Of course, I presume that they will give consideration to all aspects of the question.

Let me, in the end, conclude by pronouncing my unshakeable faith in the work and the worth of scientists and technologists. The urgency and seriousness of the situation demands of them to develop a realistic and purposeful approach to the various problems facing the country. What is needed today is a calm, dispassionate and discord-free atmosphere in which our scientists pursue their efforts so that the work of research and discovery of new techniques prospers in an intensely practical way and ensures the scientists a victory in the race which destiny has set out for them.

I must apologize to you for this frank observation and express my gratitude for the patient hearing that I have received this morning.

RECENT ADVANCES IN THE DEVELOPMENT OF FOOD INDUSTRIES IN INDIA

By

V. A. Mehta

(Ministry of Commerce and Industry, New Delhi)

In this article, the progress made by Indian food industries during the past few years as a direct result of the work of the Development Wing of the Ministry of Commerce and Industry, New Delhi, is described.

THE problem of the development of food industries has been engaging the serious attention of the Government of India since 1946. At present, the Development Wing of the Ministry of Commerce and Industry is looking after the development of all food industries (except fruit and vegetable products) and particular attention is being paid to the improvement of quality as well as the quantity of production in respect of a large number of food products.

Some of the recent advances in respect of the development of food industries are as follows:

VEGETABLE OIL INDUSTRY: Vegetable Oil Industry is a Scheduled Industry under the Industries (Development and Regulations) Act. The Ministry of Commerce and Industry received 284 applications for registration from large oil mills out of which 202 have been registered. The present policy of the Government of India is to discourage the setting up of new oil mills, particularly in areas where there are shortages of oil seeds and surplus oil-milling capacity. However, the crushing of cotton seeds and copra is being encouraged. A modern cotton seed oil factory has been recently developed at Hubli having a capacity of 12 tons a day. This unit is going into production very shortly and is equipped with hullers and delinting equipment. They propose to produce refined cotton seed oil as well as linters.

The refining of vegetable oils is being particularly encouraged.

There are a number of oil mills in India which follow the standard process for oil refining, namely chemical bleaching and alkali refining. A recent advance has been a scheme to start continuous alkali refining. This process was first started in 1933 in the U.S.A. The emulsion of oil and lye is passed through high speed centrifugal separator in which the oil is first separated from the soap stock. The time of contact of the oil with alkali is very short so that the hydrolysis of neutral fat is minimized. The loss of neutral oil in the soap stock is stated to be reduced by about 30 per cent as compared with that in the Batch process.

The Ministry of Commerce and Industry have recently sanctioned the setting up of about 12 Solvent Extraction Plants in different parts of the country in order to remove the residual oil from oil-cakes which are used for manurial purposes. *This is an important achievement of the year* 1952. The total quantity of oil cakes which will be utilized for this purpose has been limited to 2,00,000 tons per annum. It has been decided that only efficient and economic solvent extraction plants would be imported and installed.

The Government of India are also encouraging the crushing of copra in India and the present policy regarding the import of cocoanut oil has been framed accordingly. Along with the import of cocoanut oil, the import of 50 per cent copra has been made compulsory so that the latter could be utilized in the Indian mills. The Government are also encouraging the export of refined oils instead of oil seeds so that the idle capacity could be utilized. The use of non-edible oils for industrial purposes is being advocated so that more edible oils could be diverted for human consumption. The utilization of minor oil seeds for the extraction of oil, as for example *pungam* oil, *neem* oil, etc. is also being encouraged.

BISCUIT INDUSTRY: During the year 1952 (January–December 1952), India produced 12,321 tons of biscuits in about 120 organized factories. As the present installed capacity is more than the country's demand, the Government of India are not encouraging further expansion of the biscuit industry. The existing units are, however, being encouraged to modernize.

Some of the well-known biscuit manufacturers in India have started the addition of anti-oxidants in order to improve the keeping quality, appearance, uniformity, flavour and palatability of their products. Lecithin and propyl gallate are commonly used as anti-oxidants.

Emulsifying agents like glycerides are also being used by a few biscuit manufacturers in India. The function of these emulsifying agents is to distribute homogeneously the oil-soluble ingredients throughout the product in very fine particles. It may be added that a few ice cream manufacturers in India have also started the use of these emulsifying agents. The ice cream, thus produced, is stiffer in texture and suitable for serving in cones or with sticks. The manufacturers of chocolate in India are also now using emulsifying agents to prevent the 'fat bloom' in chocolates.

CONFECTIONERY INDUSTRY: There has been a remarkable improvement in the quality of sugar confectionery produced in India during the past two years. This is due to the modern plant and equipment installed in a number of factories in India. Two or three factories possess continuous vacuum cookers that permit large outputs of boiled sugar products. One factory has installed a micro-film automatic continuous sugar cooker. As the name suggests, syrup passes in a film on to hot tubes and reaches a high temperature in a few seconds. Improved types of film cookers have recently been placed on the market in the U.K., in which film cooking and vacuum cooking have been combined.

A number of confectionery manufacturers in India have started the marketing of vitaminized confectionery. The total production of confectionery during 1952 (January–December 1952) was 10,004 tons.

MEAT PRODUCTS: A modern factory has been installed in Delhi for the production of canned and uncanned piggery products like bacon and ham. This firm is run by an industrialist who took special training in the line in Europe.

AERATED WATER INDUSTRY: A number of aerated water factories in India have now installed automatic plants and are producing carbonated beverages of good hygienic quality. The main difficulty in this industry had been the inferior quality of indigenous soda water bottles. The Glass Directorate of the Ministry of Commerce and Industry has paid particular attention to this subject and very good soda water bottles are now being manufactured in India.

A number of miscellaneous type of good products are being produced in India, *e.g.*, Breakfast Foods like Corn Flakes and Oat porridge, liquid and powder glucose, and Dry Baker's Yeast of very good quality as certified by the Army Authorities.

CASHEWNUT INDUSTRY: The Cashewnut Industry has recently received a great impetus, thanks to its dollar-earning capacity. This industry requires to be mechanized with particular reference to shelling, roasting, etc. In the year ending March 1952, India exported 21,000 tons of cashew kernels worth Rs 889 lakhs of which 14,000 tons were sent to the U.S.A. and the rest to other countries.

WHAT AN INDIAN FOOD INDUSTRY NEEDS

By

N. R. Sathe

(*Sathe Biscuit and Chocolate Co., Ltd., Poona*)

Industries form a major part of the nation's wealth and the industrial development of the nation depends upon scientific knowledge, abundance of raw material at hand and efficient machinery. India is an agricultural country and she can build up big food industries provided that proper assistance to procure efficient machinery and facilities of transport are made available. Questions such as the quality of raw materials, manufacture of machinery in India, public support, and foreign capital are also dealt with in this article.

THIS year by organizing a symposium on 'Technical Aid to Food Industries,' the Central Food Technological Research Institute, Mysore, has rendered the 'First Aid' to food industries. The subject is very important and deserves exhaustive survey. This has given us an occasion to meet the top men in different food processing concerns, Government officials and heads of technical institutions with whom we can have open discussion, which will help to solve a number of common problems facing most of the Indian industries.

Science explains why an article resting on three supports is in a state of equilibrium. In the same way, the stability of an industry depends upon three basic supports, viz., the technical knowledge, efficient machinery and Government aid to secure proper type of raw material, healthy atmosphere and better transport.

TECHNICAL KNOWLEDGE: Technical knowledge does not mean a trade secret, but the art to understand the secrets of the manufacturing trade. In India, most of the food industries are running on the old established phenomenon of trade secret, and hence no improvements have been possible, as the industry lacked scientific background. In all the modern, advanced countries, all the processing stages have been brought on scientific lines by a critical study of the processes involved. They are progressing rapidly. Why our industries do not develop is, perhaps, due to lack of research facilities. Every food factory must have a small research laboratory, headed by a technically trained person. He should be able to solve his own problems, and then only, the assistance from Government laboratories will help him as clues in crosswords to solve his problems and improve the products.

At the occasion of the last Symposium, it was proposed that the Central Food Technological Research Institute, Mysore, should render every possible technical assistance to food factories, so far as the production and quality control were concerned. This is not enough. Industry demands something else, equally important. It is true that technical knowledge is the brain of the industry, but it cannot function without good machinery, equipment and Government support.

Industry forms a major part of the national wealth and every nation is trying to build its own industries with all the possible means. India should not lag behind in this race of industrialization. It is said that India is an agricultural country, and hence, not much industrially developed. This is somewhat a lame excuse because there are many countries which are mainly agricultural but which, during the last twenty years, have come up to such a stage as to manufacture common machinery required for their own requirements. The reson why India lagged behind can be attributed to the British Rule, which did not give scope for industrial development of this country, lest it might affect the interests of the British manufacturers. India is now free, free to have her own industries best suited to her conditions. Since long, India has been designated as a Golden Land. This cannot be taken in its real sense, but it leads one to think that India is well off with all the agricultural and mineral resources, which will bring in wealth and prosperity, if properly explored. In India, there is considerable scope for food factories to develop, provided that attempts are made in the proper direction.

INDIGENOUS INDUSTRIES: Sugar, milk and milk products, canning of fruits and vegetables, preservation of fish, biscuit and confectionery can be considered as some of the basic food industries which, except for machinery and a few chemicals, are not dependent on foreign countries. In India, we mainly lack efficient machinery and we have to import such machinery from other countries until we are in a position to manufacture it locally. The amount spent on machinery can be readily recovered if the plant is worked at its full capacity.

(1) GOVERNMENT SUPPORT: No industry can thrive without Government support. Take, for instance, our chocolate factory. It is equipped with up-to-date machinery and trained staff. Yet, it is entirely at the mercy of the few Government heads who decide the fate of industry by merely changing import trade policy and other restrictions from time to time. Government should have a fixed policy, properly thought out and well-planned. As a matter of fact, Government should encourage indigenous industries, remove the handicaps in their way, and study critically their real difficulties. The defects and drawbacks in indigenous products can very well be removed if the industries were properly guided by Government. We are much grieved to see our own Government helping foreign imports and condemning at the same time indigenous products saying that indigenous products are not up to the foreign standard. A glance at the industrial development generally will reveal that improvements are only possible if there are public and Government sympathy and support. Even in industrially developed countries like England, Germany, etc., the demands of industries carry higher priorities over the local civil requirements, whereas in our country, which is young in the industrial field, the industries are mostly neglected, thus hampering the progress. This state of affairs is probably due to the view taken by the Government that industrialists are of the capitalist mentality. They are liable, therefore, to be in the bad books of the authorities who are representatives of the masses. At times, it may happen that the individual whim of the authority concerned decides the fate of a number of industries, which have invested

crores of rupees and where thousands of workers are getting their livelihood. In any case, this view or attitude is incorrect and detrimental to the larger interests of the country. If industries do not develop, there will be unemployment, shortage of goods, reduced income and therefore still lower standard of living. Higher incomes and higher standards of living are only possible in a country where industries are in a prosperous state.

(2) Selection of the Raw Material: Take, for instance, the case of the biscuit industry which requires a special type of flour to turn out quality goods. Quality goods can only be manufactured out of quality raw materials. But here, no choice is left to the manufacturer in the selection of the right type of flour, and he has to be satisfied with whatever stuff is made available to him.

Fat or shortening forms another important raw material for the bakery industry. Pure butter is insufficient for meeting the growing demand of the civil population and the rigid restrictions on the manufacture of hydrogenated products of higher melting point required for the biscuit industry have greatly affected the bakery industry. After great struggle of the biscuit manufacturers and a number of representations, the hydrogenation factories have been recently allowed to manufacture hydrogenated product up to 41°C. M.P., but still the other restrictions are allowed to remain. Hydrogenated products of the desired quality should be made available to biscuits and other industries, who demand high melting fats to improve their products. The manufacture of such fats is permitted in other countries and such foreign products are freely imported and consumed in our country. There is a real and urgent need for allowing indigenous manufacture to produce fats having a high melting point as required by the food processing industries. Similar difficulties are also experienced regarding other ingredients.

(3) Transport Facilities: In India, transport is a very difficult problem. There are no good roads and conveyances to move costly agricultural produce from farms to marketing centres. Quick and efficient transport is absolutely essential to move foodstuffs from one centre to another without delay and deterioration

in transit. Either motorable roads, ferry warfs or quick railway transport should be available. Cold storage at marketing centres is absolutely essential. At present, considerable quantities of valuable foodstuffs go to waste mostly for want of proper storage and quick means of transport.

(4) FOREIGN COMPETITION: The flow of foreign capital into this country has also been a controversial subject. There seems to be no question about the necessity of foreign capital, but the dispute is only on the method of allowing it. If it comes as loans, either private or through Government, it should always be welcome. If it comes in the form of a portion of capital for industries, which are totally new and beyond the reach of Indian capital and 'know how'—for instance the oil refineries—that is equally welcome. But, when it comes to compete with the already existing industries like Biscuits, Chocolate, Confectionery, Soap, Toilet and Cosmetics, etc., it is detrimental to Indian interests and the Government must take precautions and carefully examine proposals from foreign ventures to establish themselves in the country.

Recently, a new handicap has come to add up to the already existing ones mentioned above. Day by day, the labour is becoming more and more irresponsible, mainly due to the Government's attitude towards employer-employee relations. False, alluring and misguiding propaganda by labour leaders is making the relations between the labour and the employer more and more tense. Labour should be first trained to be more honest and sincere, and then the right share may be made available to them.

The above is a brief review of the difficulties existing in the way of the development of food industries in India. Unless there is response from all sides to remove these handicaps, it will be hardly possible to bring Indian industries to the level of those established in foreign countries.

PRESIDENTIAL ADDRESS

By Shri K. D. Malaviya, Deputy Minister for Natural Resources and Scientific Research, New Delhi

I AM grateful to the organizers of this Symposium and to technologists who are present here today, for the opportunity given to me to associate myself with their deliberations. As a layman, I must aspire to learn in this surrounding and in return I may only be expected to carry forward your message to our people, who need food and nourishment, today, so urgently.

As is needed these days, such symposia should be more directly and realistically concerned with the immediate needs of the people and as such should open out new ways and means not only to create more food from the soil, but also reveal to us vast untapped food reserves and new sources of human nutrition, whether they are from the soil or from the waters of the ocean, lakes and rivers, or from the air itself. The Symposium on *Technical Aid to Food Industries* should, therefore, be planned in such a way that the urgent problems of the Indian food industries could be approached in an objective manner. Specific problems facing the different food industries of our country, whether they are fruit preservation or biscuit or bakery or meat and fish processing or discovery of new synthetic food, should all be investigated from a practical point of view and keeping always in mind the urgency of the situation.

Let me refer here to the impact of urgency felt by us all. You all know about the overall deficiency in respect of our food and I need not enter into a discussion about the attempts that have so far been made and are being made to step up our food production. Indeed, we have put in great efforts, in the last five or six years, to solve the food crisis and although it is right that the greatest incentive to more land going under cultivation in an agricultural country like ours has been due to an abnormal growth in its population, yet no reasonable man can deny that, but for the efforts of the Government—both Central and State—

to enumerate will become easy, and the proposals for their overcoming equally easy of implementation. For, to support and develop what is essential for the nation, what is of strategic importance to the country, must be solved with courage, even at the cost of some sacrifice.

The very fact that we should gather here to ask ourselves the question what and how technical aid should be rendered to the Food Preservation Industry lends ample support to the fact that there is need for this industry. When all over the world this industry is generally accepted as a *sine qua non* for the success of any plan for feeding the nation, when it is considered as an *indispensable* ally of the horticulturist, the stock farmer, the poultry farmer and the fisherman alike, there is enough justification for developing food industries on sound and scientific lines.

It is well known that the wastage of fruit and vegetables during the production seasons is anywhere between 25 and 50 per cent. The wastage in our fishing industry is as high as 35 per cent or more. Even in the production and storage of cereals, the wastage is avoidably high. It is clear, therefore, that the very first step in our attempts to solve our great problem of food is to utilize and preserve as much as we do produce. I have stated on several occasions that to ask people to *grow more* or produce more is to invite them to *waste more*.

Secondly, the only incentive that the farmer or the fisherman requires to produce more is a *ready market* and a *fair price* for the fruit of his labours. By providing him this double incentive it may be asserted that there will be no need of coaxing the farmer to grow more.

The one and only agency that can offer this incentive is the Preservation Industry. The canneries by their regular purchases at predetermined rates will not merely save wastage, particularly during glut periods, but will thereby encourage the grower to increase his production and also improve its quality. The Preservation Industry, therefore, can contribute powerfully and effectively towards a permanent solution of our greatest problem today—*Food*.

Having thus realized that the Preservation Industry is *essential*, let us for a moment see how it is also *strategic*. 'The Army marches on its stomach' is as true a saying today as it was in the days of Napoleon, who may rightly be considered the father of the Canning Industry, in the sense that it was he who first recognized its value and encouraged its development. During the World War II it was demonstrated beyond any doubt that the food supplies of the Armed Forces had to be made available in easily transportable form, and also packed scientifically to supply the required nutrients in a handy and readily consumable form. *Canned foods* were the answer to this need, and none ignores the fact that during the war period the Canning Industry, in America in particular, made tremendous strides.

In India, too, the need was equally felt. Though foreign canned food was available to the Indian Forces, the needs of the forces of the producing countries were greater, and therefore the Government of India had to make its own arrangements in this matter. It approached the few canneries that were in production. These, however, were not prepared for a large output because they were not technically and mechanically equipped for the purpose. But the industry rose to the occasion, and contributed its mite in the important task of feeding our forces. And, there should have been no need of emphasizing the need of developing the industry, as the Government were the first to feel this need. The industry naturally expected that the Government would take steps to help the industry to stabilize itself on a strong foundation.

As soon as the period of shortage created by the War ceased, the industry was relegated to the limbo. The result was that it had to struggle to take its rightful place in the matter of supplying canned fruits and vegetables to the Army. It is, however, gratifying to state that the departments concerned accepted the industry's claim, and the industry now supplies almost the total requirements of our Army. However, it may be mentioned that Canteen Stores Department still continues to think that our Army officers must have foreign preserved foods. The Q.M.G.'s Department and C.S.D. together are the largest consumers of canned foods, and this proves that these foods are required as much in peace as in War. The development of the Preservation Industry thus is a necessity and therefore deserves the same attention as the Ordnance Factories do. The industry is therefore obviously a *strategic* industry.

Having thus come to the conclusion that the Preservation Industry is both essential and strategic, it remains to be seen how its development and progress can and should be fostered and aided by the Government. 'Our food problem must be placed on a war footing,' said the Prime Minister in one of his inspiring broadcasts. If we understand the implications of this statement aright, it means that the establishment and development of the industry must be one of the primary concerns of the Government. Red tape and financial consideration should not be allowed to hinder the progress of an essential and strategic factor for the good of the nation. And, even if it involves considerable sacrifice on the part of the nation, measures to develop the industry must be adopted unhesitatingly. For, this industry cannot be built to order when the need arises. Its establishment and development must be necessarily slow and orderly. The time, therefore, to plan the regulated and controlled development of this industry of vital importance is *now*.

Having established the importance of the industry, and also the imperative and immediate need of adopting effective measures for its development, we now proceed to see what are the steps that the Government must take for the purpose.

Numerous are the difficulties that face the industry and retard its progress. What we today call the Indian Preservation Industry, or more properly the Preservation-by-Canning side of the industry, was born in 1938–39. Since then, its growth has been steady. But its present stage of development, it must be stated, is entirely due to the faith and courage of a small band of preservers who have worked and fought vigorously to place the industry on a sound footing at the cost of tremendous sacrifices. But the industry is now facing a critical situation, and unless the Government comes to its rescue, the industry will face a serious set-back.

The claims put forth by the industry have been modest, but not always have they been received by the Government with the consideration they deserved. If, on the one hand, there has been a show of sympathy, on the other hand, there has been gross neglect of the basic needs of the industry. Even the recommendations of the Tariff Board, inadequate and faltering as they were, were not accepted by the Government.

The most urgent needs of the industry are:

(1) Exemption of machinery and equipment from Customs Duty.

(2) The supply of tinplate of the requisite quality, in sufficient quantity, at the proper moment, and at cheaper prices.

(3) Supply of sugar at lower price, and in proper time.

(4) Lower railway freight tariffs, both for the transport of raw materials to the canneries and finished goods from the canneries to the consuming centres.

(5) The supply of raw materials of good quality, and in adequate quantities at reasonable rates.

(6) The regulation of imports, in some cases total ban, *as a measure of protection.*

(7) Customs tariff protection against foreign competition.

(8) And last but not the least, official support to indigenous canned foods.

To enable the manufacturer to mechanize and to modernize his factory, it is necessary that the equipment should be allowed free of duty.

The question of tinplate deserves special attention. The indigenous tinplate made available by the Government to the industry is of inferior quality, and is also more expensive as compared with the prices paid by canners in Australia, America and even South Africa. The foreign canner thus enjoys a double advantage: better tin-containers and at very much lower prices, in some cases as much as 50 per cent. The question of a good and cheap container is of vital importance to the industry. India is not self-sufficient in tinplate, and therefore already imports a large percentage of its requirements. All that the industry asks for is that the imported tinplate may be allotted to the Preservation Industry and the indigenous one may be given to such others for whom the quality of tinplate is not of paramount importance. The price, of course, has to be lowered, by exempting the imports from custom duty, and its supply subsidized when necessary.

The price of sugar is unreasonably high and the sugar industry can well afford to lower it. In Australia, for example, the Government assures sugar to canneries at the world's lowest market rate. This is done by creating a fund to subsidize the supplies to the factories. The fund is built up through contributions from the sugar industry and the Government. Today, the Australian canner pays less than half of what an Indian canner pays for sugar. The Government is subsidizing the export of sugar. Why not make this subsidized sugar available to the industry and enable it to export the same in the form of chutneys, preserves and canned fruits?

The need for lowering the freight tariff needs no emphasis. If the preserved foods are to be made available to all parts of India, then the cost of transport must be cheap enough to make this possible. At present the cost of transport is anywhere between 12½ and 20 per cent of the selling price of a can of fruit or vegetables. This is abnormally high. It is also necessary to facilitate transport of fruits and vegetables from the producing centres to the manufacturing centres. The transport should be quick and cheap. Here again, the Government can act without affecting its revenues to a great extent. But so far, there has not been much response from the railway authorities.

The imperative need of cooperation between the Government, Horticulturists and the Industry needs no mention. The canneries cannot give you an 'A' grade product from a 'B' or 'C' grade fruit or vegetable. Not only has the *quality* to be improved, but the *quantity* too has to be adequately regulated. The establishment of contacts between the grower and the canner should be the task of the Horticultural Departments concerned. The question of making these products available at suitable price levels is also within the domain of the Government agencies.

The last three items are inter-related. Once it is accepted that the development of the indigenous preservation industry is essential, and even strategic, there should be no difficulty in regulating the imports *as a measure of protection*. Other countries have done it and there is no reason why India cannot or should not accept the same procedure. The question of customs tariff protection must be linked up with a clear, well-defined import policy. To grant a small tariff protection and allow imports in unlimited quantities is to nullify the effect of the protection.

There are cases when the import should be banned, except for a small token quantity to serve as a standard for the indigenous manufacturer. In this category, I unhesitatingly place Tomato Ketchup, Tomato Juice and Tomatoes Peeled, and Canned Green Peas, whether garden fresh or dehydrated and processed. These two products are being manufactured in the country in large quantities and of good quality. There is no reason whatever for their import.

Before concluding, may I appeal to the Central Food Technological Research Institute and all the institutions engaged in food research to extend their cooperation to the industry, because without the development of the industry the fruits of research will not be made easily available to the nation. And, finally, may I add that all endeavour should be directed towards INCREASING our food supplies.

SOME TECHNICAL PROBLEMS OF FOOD INDUSTRIES SUPPLYING FOODSTUFFS TO DEFENCE SERVICES

By

B. Banerjee

(*Ministry of Food and Agriculture, New Delhi*)

The development of Indian food industries has resulted mainly from the encouragement given to them by the Ministry of Defence and other Ministries of the Government of India. Major problems of the fruit and vegetable canning, biscuit, flour-milling, hydrogenated oil, dairy products, chocolate and yeasts industries vis-à-vis *the requirements of the Army are described in this paper and suggestions put forth.*

In this note, some of the technical problems of various Indian industries concerned with the production of foodstuffs for the Army are discussed. The technical aid rendered to these industries by the Ministry of Food and Agriculture and the Ministry of Defence are also referred to. Many of the food industries have expanded due to the encouragement received by them from the Ministries of Food and Defence. In fact, the Indian canning industry developed mainly due to the technical advice it received at all stages for preparing canned foods for the Army. The Technical Branch of the Ministry of Food and Agriculture has a laboratory attached to it which examines development samples from various food industries. This branch gets representative samples from various industries and recommends their products if the samples are found to conform to Army specifications. There is also a Committee called the Technical Standardization Committee (Foodstuffs) comprising officers from the Ministries of Food and Agriculture and of Defence. The function of this Committee is to draft Army specifications for foodstuffs and their packaging, and recommend changes in existing specifications in the light of the experience gained in the manufacture of foodstuffs for the Defence Services. This Committee invites comments from the industry while drafting or changing specifications and, at the same time, helps industries by giving them technical advice when they experience difficulty in conforming their products to the Army specifications.

CANNING: The most important problem facing the canning industry at present is that of heat treatment. Heat processing of canned foods ensures the destruction of spoilage organisms, besides making the food palatable and digestible. These factors are affected both by under-processing and over-processing of foods. Scientific adjustment is therefore necessary so that the spoilage organisms are destroyed without detriment to palatability and nutritive value of the product. The rate of heat penetration depends on the consistency of the contents of the can and takes place rather slowly in the case of solid foods where heat transfer is by conduction. The penetration is rapid in liquid or semi-liquid foods where heat transfer takes place by convection. Before a process can be standardized for any canned food, the rate of heat penetration to the lowest heating portion of the can should be found out. For adequate heat penetration in all parts of the retort, the canner should try automatic thermostatic control arrangement. Here is a field where the Central Food Technological Research Institute can play an important role in providing the industry with data on adequate processing of fruits, vegetables and other foodstuffs for canning.

It has recently been claimed that High-short Temperature Process gives the product a better colour, flavour and texture than an equivalent process at low temperature. The quality of the product is the same either in small or in large containers irrespective of heat exchange phenomena. The method has a wide margin of safety between adequate sterilization and over-processing. Sterilization of the product in a continuous flow heat exchange type pressure cooker permits measurement and control of the actual temperature attained by the product in a process. It also provides for efficient use of steam and cooling water in the various operations. It is suggested that necessary investigations may be undertaken to see as to what extent our canning industry can be benefited by it.

The Central Food Technological Research Institute may also study the nature of all organisms found in canned foods and specify the types which are harmful.

Biscuit: The Ministry of Food and Agriculture purchased large quantities of biscuits for the Army. The Technical Standardization Committee has recently modified the specifications for biscuits with a view to procuring for the Army better quality biscuits and, at the same time, bringing the biscuits more in line with the requirements of the civil trade. But, the quality of biscuits perhaps needs further improvement as regards aroma, keeping quality, flavour and nutritive value. It is necessary to conduct experiments and produce biscuits which will remain fit for consumption during long periods of storage under varying conditions. It is known that unsaturated fatty acids in the fat are responsible for giving off-flavours in stored biscuits due to oxidation. It is necessary to counteract this difficulty by the use of suitable anti-oxidants. It is understood that the Central Food Technological Research Institute, Mysore, has already taken up the investigation of this problem. As the properties of the shortening affect the keeping quality of the biscuits, the Ministry of Food and Agriculture made a special provision to enable the biscuit industry to use vanaspati of melting point 41°C instead of 37°C. As a result, the industry has partly overcome its difficulty in regard to the keeping quality of biscuits.

Flour Milling: At present, *atta* required for the Army is made by grinding wheat in roller mills. The percentage of extraction of *atta* is so high, that the *atta* contains phytic acid which interferes with calcium absorption in the system. Therefore, mills have been advised to fortify the *atta* for the Army with 'Creta preparata'. This is now being done with the help of a Horse Shoe Mixer.

It has been stated that the flour supplied by Indian flour mills is not suitable for the manufacture of high-grade biscuits. It is in the interest of the flour milling industry to conduct some research work on this subject for giving the biscuit industry the grade of flour required.

Another important problem is the infestation of *atta* and flour during the interval between production and consumption. The problem of disinfestation of mills and godowns by fumigation is already attracting the attention of millers. This is a subject which requires special study and it is hoped that the flour-milling industry will make full use of the findings of investigations in this line. The Director of Storage and Inspection in the Ministry of Food and Agriculture and the Pest Control Section in the Ministry of Defence will be of help in this matter.

HYDROGENATED OIL: The Army purchases large quantities of hydrogenated oil. The Vanaspati Research Planning Committee sponsored by the Ministry of Food has already reported that no deleterious effect is produced on health by hydrogenated oil. It is now commonly used as a cooking fat. Now that synthetic vitamin A is available, vanaspati can serve as a carrier for increasing the supply of vitamin A to the population. Some time ago, the Ghee Adulteration Committee of the Ministry of Food and Agriculture recommended the fortification of vanaspati with synthetic vitamin A so that its nutritive value may be increased. This recommendation has recently been accepted by the Government. In some foreign countries, the fortification of margarine with vitamin A has already materialized and margarine is now available with a vitamin A content even superior to that of natural butter. Similar fortification of vanaspati with vitamin A should be the aim of the Indian vanaspati industry, especially as there is apparently no possibility, in the near future, of the vitamin A requirement of our population being met from milk and butter. As raw materials for the manufacture of vitamins are available in India, it is for the industry to come forward and produce the vitamins which are badly needed in our country.

The Controller of the Vegetable Oil Products has directed that any factory which claims its product to be vitaminized should invariably show on the label the names of the vitamins added, and that no manufacturer can claim a product as vitaminized unless the quantity added is not less than 300 I.U. of vitamin A and 50 I.U. of vitamin D per ounce. In the case of vitamin

D which is being added to vanaspati by some factories, difficulties are being experienced in its estimation, since at present there is no recognized chemical, physico-chemical or even microbiological method for the estimation of vitamin D in foodstuffs. The biological method is very costly and time-consuming; there is a great need for a simpler process for the estimation of vitamin D and it is hoped that the Central Food Technological Research Institute would do the needful in this matter.

Dairy Products: The Army purchases a good deal of milk powder, milk condensed sweetened, and milk tinned evaporated unsweetened. But none of these is manufactured in India, and hence, the Army requirements of these products have to be imported from Australia, Holland and the U.S.A. The Indian industry has not so far come forward to manufacture these products. The Army is greatly interested in spray dried milk powder, but so far, no spray-drying plant for milk powder has been established in the country and this subject deserves the serious attention of the industry.

Chocolate: Chocolate is a good combination of nutritive substances like cocoa, cocoa-butter, sugar and milk. It is really a concentrated nutritive food. It was included in the Emergency Pack of the U.S.A. Army. The main difficulty facing the industry in India is the supply and high prices of the cocoa bean which is not grown in India, and as such, has to be imported. It is necessary that all the processes, beginning from the crushing of beans, should be carried out in the factories. Moreover, blending of nibs from different sources is necessary to impart the right flavour to the finished product. The processes of refining and the tempering of chocolate are very important and they require special study. The Defence Services may require chocolate as an Emergency Pack, but the difficulty is that normal type of chocolates *melt* at a high temperature in summer and this cannot be accepted by the Army. Such chocolate bars which would not melt at high temperatures should be manufactured. Further crushed roasted groundnuts may be incorporated in order to improve the protein value of the chocolate.

Yeast (Baker's and Pressed): The Army is interested in dried

Baker's Yeast. But this type of yeast is not at present manufactured in India. It has been reported that one firm has been successful in its experiments in producing Baker's Yeast in dried form, but no regular plant has been set up for the manufacture of active dried yeast. Of course, the firm is producing and supplying compressed wet yeast, but it has not undertaken the manufacture of dried yeast, which is so badly needed in our country. The industry is, therefore, requested to explore the possibility of manufacturing Dried Yeast in India. A large quantity of dried yeast is imported into the country for civil use.

QUALITY OF PRODUCTION IN FOOD INDUSTRIES IN INDIA

By

Girdhari Lal

(*Central Food Technological Research Institute, Mysore*)

In this paper, the author has reviewed the present status of the Indian Fruit and Vegetable Industry and has put forward valuable suggestions for improvement of the quality of its products.

It is well known that the economic prosperity of a nation, especially today, lies in the utilization of all its potential resources for industrial development. The scientist, the technician, the economist and the industrialist has each an important role to play in shaping the future set-up of the industrialization of this country, leading to a planned production of quality products. During the past quarter of the century, much headway has been made in industries like iron and steel, cloth, sugar, etc., although even in these, much remains to be accomplished in the matter of their quality as compared with their imported counter-parts. The Indian food industries which form the subject of this talk are comparatively of recent origin, and so, have yet to go a long way in establishing themselves in this country because of severe foreign competition, which is partly traditional and now partly due to international obligations. It may be realized that quality in production is one of the essential requirements for the assured success of any industrial venture. In India, the prejudice with which the consumer views indigenous processed goods is proverbial. This, till lately, had a historic background which need not be dilated upon here; let us forget the past and forge in anew by efforts that will obliterate this age-long prejudice against goods of Indian origin.

Any industry, for its proper development, presents, in general, a variety of problems, viz., (1) quality of production—this covers all the scientific and technological aspects of the manufacturing processes, besides ensuring the procurement of proper raw materials; (2) State aid, *i.e.*, tariffs, subsidies, preferential freight rates, establishment of extension service and the like; (3) establishment of industrial associations; (4) planned production; and (5) economics of production.

As indicated in the title, it is intended in this article only to present certain salient features of only one of the above items, namely, Quality of Production, with special reference to food industries in India. My only claim to speak on the subject lies in my close association with the fruit and vegetable preservation industry of this country for over two decades.

I. Factory Organization

General Management

The over-all management of a food factory is the major factor governing the ultimate quality of products. At the moment, one is constrained to remark that managements, in general, have their eye only on profits. No doubt, factories must make profits, but they must deliver the best goods too, not cheap stuff of low quality. With the advance of scientific knowledge on production, perhaps some of the enlightened managements are not sacrificing quality for cheapness. I wish this were a general case both in the interests of the trade and of the chemists and the technicians employed therein. This must come to pass sooner or later—better sooner than later—if free India is to progress and prosper. The obligation of the profession of chemists in this regard is greater than the stake of the trade. I address myself, therefore, in particular to that great fraternity, the fraternity of chemists to which I have the privilege to belong. I say to them 'Do not compromise on quality in products.' Only on such pure foundations has been built the industrial edifice of other countries. Shall India which won her freedom by political integrity, jeopardize it by professional dishonesty? Let the management play its role and give the rightful place to its chemists and the production managers.

In the above direction, the obvious grievance of the management, in some cases, may be the non-availability of properly trained chemists and technicians. But this problem is for us all to solve. The Government are already doing their best to get properly trained technical personnel under a large number of schemes of foreign aid and unless a good gesture is shown by the managements in properly utilizing the services of such trained hands, no real headway could be made in the production of quality goods. It is hoped that the enlightened administrators of various industries would not take my remarks amiss, but would help themselves and, in the long run, our country, which could raise its head with pride amongst the foreign nations in the matter of quality of our products.

Factory Management

Under this head, I mean to deal briefly with a variety of problems which face the factory in its day-to-day running. This concerns mainly the regular supply of materials of the right quality including container and packaging materials. In addition, the factory management is also responsible for planned production, *e.g.*, the factory stores should never run short of essential raw materials. To elaborate, in the case of, say, a fruit and vegetable preservation factory, the availability of proper raw materials of fruits and vegetables of the desired quality should be ensured throughout the production season for which arrangements have necessarily to be made well in advance for periods ranging from six months to one year. So also is the case in regard to the containers and packaging materials. This aspect of the factory management is sometimes lost sight of, with the result that occasionally chaos results at the actual time of production. Obviously, therefore, planned production with assured supply of adequate raw materials of the right quality at the right time would go a long way to help in the production of quality goods. It is certain that if this is accomplished, which must be accomplished especially in our food industries, we will be contributing a lot in enhancing the quality of our production. It is realized that raw materials of right quality, say for instance, in the fruit and vegetable industry, are not available at some centres. The grower, the Government, and even the factory management must all cooperate in ensuring that fruits and vegetables of the right quality shall be grown. It is known to most of us that in foreign countries the factory management plays much greater part in this respect than other organizations, *i.e.*, the Government and the farming establishments, by making cash advances to the grower to get the right quality of raw materials at the right time. It is to be hoped that the fruit industries management in our country will start doing likewise, if they are not already doing so. I am well aware that other food industries, especially the farinaceous ones like bakery, biscuits, etc., are functioning under limitations imposed by various controls. Perhaps, a sympathetic attitude of the Government in this regard to release the right type of materials in adequate quantities would help to step up the quality of production.

Another important function of the factory management is to train and build up an arsenal of skilled labour, as most of the processes in our present food industries are worked by hand labour. We cannot afford as yet, situated as we are, to put up plants for gigantic production as they have in countries like the U.S.A., and Europe. Our resources in all directions are limited; for the moment, therefore, we have to be content with laying out plants of a semi-commercial scale and so we cannot reduce labour. This is a very important part of the factory management peculiar to India, which, if properly handled, would contribute a great deal to the ultimate quality of production. Thus, labour has to be properly trained, disciplined and handled to ensure satisfactory production.

Chemical control of the manufacturing processes

This aspect of the problem, as related to quality production, is perhaps the most important and which unfortunately has not properly assessed in our food industries. Certain recipes picked out from the literature on the subject mostly in the original form, but occasionally in a modified form are being followed. Strict chemical control of the various processes at different stages is not rigidly practised, which naturally results in products of indifferent quality or indefinite purity. These egregious differences exist between batches, let alone between consignments, leaving the consumer often to guess what product would be like tomorrow with his grocer. Here, the chemist has to play a major role by effecting proper and rigid control at the various stages of the manufacture of a product. He should not just mind his pay, but must have his say in the quality of products being offered to the consuming public. Chemists may come and chemists may go, but industry goes on for ever is never true. Manufacturers should confide in their chemists, who will take care of the Bank balance. If chemists come and go, it naturally interrupts the continuity of work under the particular conditions of environment. This is not healthy for the chemists, much less for the management. If a mutual good will could be created between these two, which is bound to happen in due course, we may visualize in this collaboration a bright future for the quality of production in our food industries.

Research in the factory

Any food factory worth the name must have a small research laboratory attached to it, where newer methods of manufacture can be evolved and older ones improved upon. Then again, in this laboratory, scientific and technological researches can be conducted on the evolution of new products. The huge research organizations in foreign food factories are perhaps too good to be true for our food industrialists. Some of the best pieces of biochemical findings have come from the Glaxo Laboratories, for instance. Any piece of academic research has in it the germ of an industrial venture. This, England learnt from the days of Faraday. Here, in India, we nag at academic work. It is time we gave up this outlook. If a start is made with a small research unit attached to our food factories, much headway could be made in improving the quality of the products. It should not be forgotten that the huge research organizations which one sees attached to food factories in foreign countries were not started in a day. There also, a start was made by small units which gradually grew with the development of the factories. Thus, the importance of these research units in any food factory can hardly be overestimated. Even a very small beginning can help to overcome so many day-to-day difficulties experienced in a food factory, where one has to tackle all types of raw materials, perishables included. A thorough investigation of the day-to-day problems in a factory in such a unit is therefore highly essential for the production of quality goods. I may just mention as an illustration that during my visit to Palestine in 1946, I saw the research laboratories of Messrs Assis & Co., Ltd., Tel Aviv; these scientists have made quite a few contributions to science. This is how we should start planning research units in these food factories in our country which, besides stepping up quality in production, would be adding new categories of products from time to time.

II. Role of Government-Sponsored Food Research Laboratories

At present, there is one National Laboratory for food technological researches established in India, namely the CFTRI at Mysore. There are several State Laboratories doing work on various aspects of food and food technology besides a few in some universities. The primary functions of these laboratories are briefly discussed below:

Fundamental and Applied Research

All food technological problems are closely associated with fundamental and applied research which cannot be divorced from one another with any advantage. In India, as perhaps in other countries, the politician wants quick results of applied nature in the interests of the common man. This will eventually restrict the activities of the Indian food research laboratories on the fundamental side. Anyway, that appears to be the unwritten law peculiar to our country based on the adage 'He who pays for the piper calls for the tune'. But you will enjoy the piper most when he plays his best and you will probably pay him more then. Scientists want to be left alone to their bench but certainly that is not going to help, at least not them, unless they come forth with results of immediate benefit to the common man. It is not enough to achieve the results, but oftentimes he has to propagate them. Be this to the discredit of the management, scientists in India have to strike a balance between fundamental and applied research in a manner that brings quick results. This is virtually the policy of the Government-sponsored laboratories in this country at the moment. The researches undertaken are done for the benefit of the industry and for the common man. Let industries therefore look round and gauge the findings of these laboratories for possibilities of enhancing the quality of their production.

The above is a very intricate problem and it is mainly for this reason that this Symposium has been held in which distinguished industrialists are taking part today. It is a matter for serious consideration by us all to find ways of establishing close collaboration and liaison between the food industries and the Government-sponsored laboratories. Our deliberations during the course of these two days, I hope, will have much to say on this aspect. On our part, we are trying and will try our best to disseminate as much information as possible through our monthly Bulletin, the 'C.F.T.R.I. TECHNICAL BULLETIN', which, I am sure, you are already familiar with.

Technical aid and collection of reliable statistics and information

Dealing with this aspect of the subject I will illustrate the functions of the food laboratories in this country, based on the activities of this Institute in this regard. For the benefit of food industries in this country, a special Division known as 'Information and Statistics Division' in this Institute is dealing with the above aspect in collaboration with the respective specialists in the different lines. Primarily, the activity of the I & S Division at this Institute is for the benefit of the industry. A large number of technical enquiries being received are either answered straightaway in cases where information is available or after carrying out the necessary *ad hoc* research work. The Processing Division is carrying out a programme of investigation for and on behalf of the Indian Coffee Board. The industry can take still greater advantage of such facilities as exist in this Institute. Lack of full appreciation on the part of the industry in this direction may be due probably to the fact that this Institute is only in the third year of its existence. I want to assure you that we are always prepared to help wherever possible by correspondence, by visits, if desired by the industry, and also by undertaking short- and long-range technological problems on behalf of the industry. In giving advice of a particular nature or in solving time-consuming technical problems or in arranging for personal visits, there may be a few hurdles from the view-point of the industry. That is, they have to pay for it; Government wants payment; in most cases the charges are nominal. Personally, I would favour free advice whenever it can be rendered for a period of about 5 years, till our infant food industries get established. But, it would be in the fitness of things if these industries come to our help even at this stage when the financial resources of this country are very limited because of the vast obligations and commitments of the Government particularly after the partition of the country. Perhaps, the cottage and other small-scale ventures in this line may be exempted, but we expect a good gesture in this respect on the part of the well-established food concerns. I may be pardoned for this slight digression from the subject at this stage, as this aspect had to be dealt with while dealing with the functions of this Institute in regard to advisory work.

Absence of reliable statistics is one of the greatest handicaps for any planned production in any industry. For instance, no reliable data are available on the production of fruits and vegetables on which the manufacturers can base their production programmes. Then again, no data are available for the manufactured goods consumed in the country and exported outside in respect of any food industry. Such a state of affairs is highly detrimental to the interests of our growing food industries.

Efforts are being made, however, in this Institute, to publish from time to time and make available as much information as possible in this direction collected from as many sources as possible. It is realized that, placed as we are in Mysore where the only technical library we could consult is our own, full justice is not being done to this subject at this stage and also due to lack of appropriate staff which again is due to the tightness of the Government finances. Perhaps, some well-established food factories could generously donate adequate sums of money from time to time to help further expansion of the restricted research facilities available here at present. It is hoped that the part played by the food industries in other countries in sponsoring research and other related activities will be a worthy example for our business magnates to emulate in the interests of the national cause.

Training of Technical Personnel

It is well known that our country lacks adequate facilities for training of technicians and chemists for not only the food industries, but for all other industries in the country. The need for training such personnel who are essentially the backbone of any industry has been stressed time and again by various Committees of the Government and the Industry. Government plans are in hand for establishing such educational and technological institutes for training technical persons in the different branches. Such broad-based schemes again involve finances. To tide over the interim difficult period, every effort is being made by Government to utilize foreign technical aid in the form of studentships and fellowships, which are now freely available for students of science for getting training in fields of applied research. For many reasons the general policy of the Government, however, at present is not to burden the National Research Institutes with having to give this specialized technological training. But time will not be far when, as already mentioned above, special technological institutes will be set up for training technical personnel in India for the various industries. A beginning in this respect has already been made in the establishment of the Indian Institute of Technology, Kharagpur, where specialized training in various subjects is imparted. This expanding Institute and the Institutes of similar nature which may come up in future, will help a great deal in providing technical personnel to the various industries. In regard to food industries, we have at this Institute one year Post-graduate Diploma Course in Fruit and Vegetable Technology, a course which came to us as a legacy from the former Indian Institute of Fruit Technology. The Fruit and Vegetable Preservation Industry has shown its appreciation of this course by absorbing diploma holders in its staff. Efforts are being made for enhancement of the duration of this course to two years with a view to enlarging its scope and producing personnel of better calibre.

Laying Standards of Quality

There are practically no Food Laws in this country on a nation-wide basis as in other countries, except in certain States of India. Even where they exist, it is doubtful if they operate as they should. This is a subject to which we must all give our thought. It has been receiving the attention of the Government for some time past. A Food and Drugs Act is under consideration of the Government and the formation of a Central Food Laboratory is contemplated. It is thus a matter of great satisfaction that some beginning is being made in this respect of the control of quality in food and food products in this country. I need hardly emphasize the importance of laying down standards and specifications which, if rigidly enforced, would definitely help a great deal in improving the quality of our products. At present, on our food products which we manufacture for export purposes, like mango chutney, curry powders, canned fruits, squashes, etc., no control is exercised by the Government to adjudge their standard. The result has been disastrous in some cases, because some of the manufacturers who exported their products in recent times suffered a great set-back as their products were not found to be of a uniform standard and also not up to the standards laid down in other countries.

In the line of fruit products, due to the efforts of some of the pioneering research workers and of the All-India Food Preservers' Association which contributed voluntarily in the form of payment of a cess on their production, the Fruit Products Order was promulgated a few years ago. I need not go into the past history of the working of this Order, but now there is a genuine effort on the part of the Government and the Industry to bring this Order into full force and to enforce that the quality of production shall conform to a specific level, to help the industry establish itself on right lines. As most of you may be knowing already, the analytical side of the F.P.O. Organization has been entrusted to this Institute and we can assure the industry that things will be judged entirely on merits.

In the end, I will appeal to all those engaged in food industries to work in close collaboration with the scientific institutes that the Government have sponsored in the line in various centres of the country, in order that the level of quality of production may go up and thus put the Indian food industries on the World Map. Let your patience be not taxed by the slow progress of the scientific research which is its inherent character in any line in any part of the world. Science will ultimately triumph as it has always done in this country as in other countries. Then, we shall have food industries comparable in size and quality to the best in the world like 'The Heinz,' the 'Huntley Palmers' and so many others of the West which started with humble beginnings, much in the same way as our food industries.

IMPORTANCE OF STANDARDS FOR THE INDIAN FOOD PROCESSING INDUSTRY

By

H. A. B. Parpia

(Messrs Pure Products and Madhu Canning Ltd., Bombay)

Indian food processors are facing considerable difficulty as a result of the lack of proper standardization of products. Sub-standard products prejudice the consumer against Indian processed foods and damage the reputation of the industry as a whole. It is time that the Departments of Agriculture, Research Institutions and the Industry get together not only for laying down proper standards for which suggestions are made in this paper, but also for putting them into practice. This would considerably improve the quality of our products required both for home and foreign markets.

THE Central Food Technological Research Institute, Mysore, should be complimented on for the timely organization of this valuable Symposium.

The Indian Food Processing Industry has developed to a stage when the co-ordination of technical information has become necessary for further advance. As a result of the help received from the Government in the form of a tariff wall against the import of foreign processed foods, the industry at home has been able to keep its head above water. If the cost of some of the major raw materials were at the world market level, we could have been able to export many of our products. In spite of the fact that our can prices are about 66 per cent higher than those in other food processing countries, we have been able to develop an export market for our indigenous products.

The demand for processed foods at home has kept up to a fair level. The customer is getting more and more quality-conscious. This can be seen from the fact that a certain class of consumers still prefers imported goods. On the other hand, the Government has recently increased the import quota for foreign canned foods, the explanation given for this step being that it would force the Indian food processors to improve the quality of their products. This must have been done by the Government after full consideration of the consumer interest and, as such, needs appreciation, but one doubts if this action could bring about the contemplated improvement without the existence of any quality standards. A more correct way of improving the quality of Indian products would be to provide the industry with proper technical aid in the form of developing a system of standards and setting up proper machinery for their implementation and constant improvement. Thus, the local consumer would be assured of standardized canned goods and the reputation of Indian products at home and abroad could be improved.

The development of standards for processed foods cannot be materialized within a short period. We cannot completely transplant foreign standards here, because our conditions are different from those in other countries. The work will need intensive study of several well-established foreign standards and further investigation of problems peculiar to the Indian situation. Considering these factors, it would be advisable if the work is begun as soon as possible. Even after the preparation of standards, it will take time for their implementation. The industry will have to be allowed sufficient time so that the small industrialists may not suffer unjustly.

A few important reasons why we need proper standards and an outline of the plan proposed for the work are given below:

I. The Local Market Demands Quality

In a country like ours the percentage of consumers for processed foods is very small because of the high prices of such foods as compared with the standard of living. With the economic development of the country, this number is likely to rise. Also, consumers are getting more and more quality-conscious. Consequently, the canning industry which saves wastes of seasonal crops and helps to relieve food shortage should pay special attention to the quality of its products.

Adulteration does not help in saving certain of these perishable foods of high nutrient value, but spoils the quality. As a result of this practice among some manufacturers, a fairly large number of consumers of high quality products are prejudiced against Indian-made goods as a whole. Of course, this represents a very narrow outlook, but it is justifiable. For instance, it is fairly well-known today that potato and red pumpkin are used as adulterants in manufacturing cheap tomato ketchup. This may undoubtedly make the product cheap and within the reach of some consumers, but its sale as *tomato ketchup* should not be permitted. Perhaps 'Tomato-Pumpkin sauce' would be a suitable name for such a product. If there were proper standards, it would be possible to make ketchups of various grades bringing the product within the reach of a large number of consumers and yet giving them the quality they desired or could afford. The same would hold good for many other products.

II. Export and Competition Abroad

Dr Mogens Jul, the Technical Director of the Food and Agricultural Organization of the United Nations, has said that countries which are short of staple foods can make up for the cost of foods they import by exporting some of their indigenous luxury foods. The latter are, at present, being wasted in many countries. This is undoubtedly true in our country. We are exporting some of our indigenous foods and some of the firms have met with a great deal of success because of the high quality of the foods. Their high reputation was, however, affected adversely when some of the Indian goods of inferior quality appeared on the foreign markets.

If our Government were to consider the subsidization of some of the products as a means of earning exchange, the export could be very easily increased and the economy of the nation would benefit from it. The subsidy should be given to the extent of making the sugar and cans available at the international price, only for export at present. But, if we are to do this it would be absolutely essential to have proper standards and, if necessary, *special standards for export,* as has been done in the United States for the last few years. We can also compete with some of the non-indigenous products such as canned pineapples, provided that our standards are high enough to stand up against the competition from Singapore and Hawaiian Islands. It is learnt that Indian missions abroad are using Indian products for their social functions. Such outlets can help in popularizing our products abroad, but we must maintain competitive quality.

The Armed Forces of our country are the largest single consumer of canned foods. They are constantly having difficulty in purchasing goods in India. On the other hand, the industry is having difficulty in dealing with them because of the absence of proper standards. The Army has been very considerate but, at times, the industry's complaints are also justifiable. The Army Service Corps had to formulate their own standards, which are vague and not quite satisfactory. Their difficulties would have been solved if there were proper national standards. As a result of the lack of standards, they have specially to invite tenders and get products made every time they need them. They cannot depend upon the quality of goods available on the market, because most of the products are below their standards. If quality products were available readily, they could purchase their requirements as and when required. The Chief Director of Purchase was very cooperative and called a conference for revision of the ASC Specifications and this work is now in progress. We hope that this will be a fore-runner of the development of national food standards. Some of the standards can be revised without much research, because sufficient data are available, but some of the standards will require new research. One such example can be found in the processing time of curried preparations. First of all, there are no standard curried preparations, and secondly, no one has studied the resistance of thermophilic micro-organisms in curry. Therefore, the processing time for such products cannot be specified. The only temporary alternative is to over-process the food!

Preliminary Outline for the Development of Standards

I. Raw Material: Standard raw material is the pre-requisite for the preparation of quality finished goods. It is here that we are first handicapped because our farmer is not yet educated to know the requirements of the canning industry. The experience in Bombay shows that small farmers mix several types of French Beans of varying maturities and then sell them on the market. On the other hand, mangoes are perfectly graded according to size as well as maturity. It is true that some of the raw materials are graded by the Directorate of Agriculture and Marketing, but not well enough to serve the needs of the industry. This system of grading could be improved upon to suit the needs of the Food Processor. A set of proper standards could be developed for raw material grading, based on:

(1) The type of fruit, vegetable, fish or meat; (2) Variety; (3) Maturity, (this could be done by devising objective physical and chemical tests, wherever possible. Standard colour grading systems could be used); and (4) Size.

Methods of handling and distribution will have to be improved upon in order to prevent damage to the raw material. Improvement of the quality of raw materials will be beneficial to the producer, manufacturer and the consumer, because it will reduce spoilage, get higher prices for the producer and give a better manufactured product.

II. Sanitation Standards: If the number of advantages derived from proper sanitation were pointed out to industrialists, they would agree that sanitation is not only an ethical duty they owe to the consumer, but also it is a great help to the industry. A few of the advantages derived from sanitation are:

1. Improved quality due to: (a) less spoilage—resulting in better yield, and (b) lower processing temperature and time, thus saving on fuel and making possible better productive capacity of the plant; no scorching or burning of the product.

2. Better consumer acceptance resulting in more sales, more turn-over and lower over-head.

3. Reduction in loss of time resulting from accidents and equipment breakdown.

4. Greatly improved employee morale resulting in better production.

5. No trouble with hygiene inspectors.

The U.S. Federal Food, Drug and Cosmetic Act should be of help to us in framing our laws on sanitation: 'A food shall be deemed to be adulterated if it consists in whole or in part of any filthy, putrid or decomposed substance or held under insanitary conditions whereby it may have become contaminated with filth.' Some of the States have gone further and created special bodies under the Health Board for inspecting canneries. This part of the standards could be worked out in collaboration with the representatives of the Health Department in our country.

Perhaps, it is known to some of those present here from the industry and the Government that a few canneries having the construction of cow-sheds were given licences to operate.

It is suggested that the hygienic or sanitary standards for food plants should be developed on the following basis:

A. *Location*

Location of the building must be in hygienic surroundings. Proper drainage system must be available and there should be adequate supply of water.

B. *Building Construction*

The building construction should be such as to permit proper cleaning. There should be a drainage available at distances of 15 ft. from every place of operation. A specified slope of about 3 inches for every 15 ft. length or breadth should be maintained to prevent water collection on the floor. Walls must be easily washable up to a height of three feet from the floor. The floor must be made according to specifications most conducive to sanitation.

C. *Lighting*

Adequate lighting, on the basis of square feet of window space per cubic foot of area under operation, or adequate artificial lighting on the basis of foot candles of light per area must be specified.

D. *Rest Room and Toilet Facilities*

Every food processing plant must have one latrine per every 20 workers. This requirement is fairly well carried out in many States.

The number of wash basins should be fixed depending on the number of workers. It is usually advisable to have one wash basin for every 10–15 workers. Provision must be made for wiping hands, otherwise the worker is likely to wipe his hands on his own clothes which are far from clean in most cases.

It is advisable to have a floor mat soaked in a mild germicide at the exit of every latrine so that the bacterial count of the factory floor is kept as low as possible.

Constant inspection of hygienic condition of the toilet facilities must be maintained.

E. *Fly-proofing*

This is absolutely essential in a tropical country like ours. A single fly entering the cannery can undo a large amount of sanitation work. Care must be taken not to reduce light while fly-proofing the factories. Swinging automatic doors with proper screening of windows must be compulsory. In order to have adequate ventilation, exhaust fans should be provided.

F. *Rodent Control*

Rats are responsible for spoiling a large amount of stored raw material. They may be responsible for some of the most dangerous infections also. Therefore, it is advisable to make the raw material store-room rat-proof by proper screening of windows.

G. *Uniforms for the Workers*

Workers concerned with the preparation of raw material must have either white or light coloured uniforms which must be changed at least twice a week. These uniforms must completely cover their own clothes. The women employees must have an adequate head gear to cover all the hair.

H. *Health of the Workers*

The workers must be medically examined at least twice a year for all possible infectious or communicable diseases. No one having any disease must be permitted to work in a food plant, and the medical certificate should be submitted to the health authorities.

Improperly trimmed nails can carry a large number of bacteria. A constant check must be maintained on the cleanliness of the workers' hands. Every time a worker steps out of the cannery, he or she must not return without washing the hands.

I. *Water Supply*

The cannery water supply must be certified by the Health authorities. Techniques for maintaining minimum bacterial count of the water supply must be recommended for the benefit of the industry. The wash water must not be re-used. Water must be chlorinated to 'break-point' where all the organic material is oxidized and there must be at least 50 parts per million of available chlorine at the end.

J. *Equipment*

All equipment must be maintained clean. Wood harbours bacteria in crevices and cannot be properly cleaned; therefore, wooden equipment must not be used. Certain metals, such as copper, affect the nutritive value and keeping quality of foods. Their use must be banned in food plants. Every food processing plant must have steam cleaning equipment, which must be used at regular intervals of four hours each, for complete clean up of the plant.

III. Quality Standards for Canned Fruits and Vegetables: All canned foods must be graded according to their quality. An illustration of this is given in the following sets of specifications for pineapples and French beans.

PRELIMINARY DRAFT SPECIFICATIONS FOR THE QUALITY OF CANNED PINEAPPLES

1. *Types of Canned Pineapples.*
   Queen—Variety.
2. *Styles of Canned Pineapples.*
   A. SLICES
      (1) Large slices between 4″ and 3¼″.
      (2) Small slices between 1–5/8″ and 2″.
   B. TITBITS OR CHUNKS

GRADES OF CANNED PINEAPPLES

GRADE (A). Canned pineapples are units (large or small slices) of pineapples of similar varietal characteristics which possess a normal flavour and which are of such quality with respect to colour, uniformity of size, absence of defects and character of fruit so as to score not less than 75 points when scored in accordance with the scoring system outlined herein.

GRADE (B). Canned pineapples are units of pineapples of similar varietal characteristics which possess a normal flavour and are reasonably good and uniform in colour, are reasonably free from defects, possess a reasonably tender texture and are of such quality with respect to uniformity of size as to score not less than 60 points when scored in accordance with the scoring system outlined herein.

Canned chunks of pineapple shall be classified in Grade (B) and shall meet with the requirements of this grade.

CUT-OUT SYRUP DENSITIES: Fruit packed as *Grade* (*A*) shall not have syrup tests below 19° or above 25° Brix and the fruit packed as *Grade* (*B*) shall not have syrup testing below 17° Brix.

ACIDITY OF CUT-OUT SYRUP: The acidity of the cut-out syrup calculated as citric acid shall be between 0.50 and 0.80 per cent.

FILL OF THE CONTAINER: The container shall have only one style of prepared fruit per batch or lot tendered.

The container shall be filled with pineapple units, as full as practicable, without impairment of the quality. The product and packing medium shall occupy not less than 90 per cent of the total volume capacity of the container. The net weight shall not be below 30 oz.

Drained Weight: Drained weight of canned pineapple is determined by emptying the contents of the can upon a circular sieve containing 8 meshes to an inch (0.097 inch perforations) and allowing to drain for 3 minutes. The minimum drained weight shall be 15 oz. per A-2½ can, an average of all cans, or in case of small number of samples, an average of at least six cans being taken into consideration.

Ascertaining the Quality: The quality of the canned pineapples may be ascertained by considering, in addition to the foregoing requirements, the following factors:

Colour, uniformity of size, absence of defects, and character of fruit. The relative importance of each factor has been expressed numerically on a scale of 100. The maximum number of points that can be given for each factor are:

Colour	...	20
Uniformity	...	15
Absence of defects	...	30
Character of fruit	...	35
		100

ASCERTAINING THE RATING OF EACH FACTOR

I. Colour: Under this factor are considered the uniformity and the intensity of the typical pineapple yellow colour.

A. In order to receive a rating of 15–20 points, the pineapple units must possess a good, practically uniform colour. 'Good, practically uniform colour' means that the colour is bright and typical and the fruit is free from brown colour, resulting from over-ripenness, oxidation, physical damage in handling, improper processing and other causes. Presence of a few white specks due to improper distribution of the natural pigment of the fruit will be allowed.

B. If the colour of the pineapples is *reasonably* good and *reasonably* uniform, a score of 10–14 points may be given. 'Reasonably uniform and reasonably good' means that the colour is reasonably bright but may vary slightly in shades; there shall not be any brown spots due to reasons such as over-ripenness, defective processing or physical damage. Presence of white specks due to natural maldistribution of pigment will be tolerated.

II. Uniformity of Size:

A. In order to receive a rating of 14–15 points, the units must be practically uniform in size. 'Practically Uniform' means that the units are practically uniform in size (diameter in case of slices) and thickness. The size of large slices must not be below 3½" or above 4" and the thickness of the thickest slices must not be 25 per cent more than the thinnest slice. The diameter of the small slices must not be below 1¾ inches.

B. If the pineapple units are reasonably uniform in size, that is, they vary slightly more in size and thickness than as mentioned in (A) a score of 10–13 points may be given. The thickness and diameter being permitted to vary 1/8 inch more than in (A).

If the chunks are fairly uniform they may be scored 8–13 points. 'Fairly uniform' means that the chunks are not less than ¼ inch in size and not less than 3/16 inch thick.

III. Absence of Defects: This factor refers to the degree of freedom from harmless extraneous material (such as pieces of stems, crowns, etc.) peel and damage from mechanical, pathological, insect and other injury.

'Blemished units' are units that are blemished with some material injury such as worm-whole, insect damage, etc. In order to classify a unit as blemished, it must have a blemish area of at least 1/4 inch in diameter.

'Remnants of the eyes' are small black dots which can be seen in some of the slices after the eyes are removed.

'Normal Shape' means that the units must retain their original conformation although there is evidence of trimming for the removal of eyes or other purposes. Units which have gouges or holes other than for the removal of the cores are not of normal shape.

'Crushed or broken units' are units that have been crushed or broken to the extent that they have lost their normal shape. Units that are slightly split from the edge but not broken into two are not considered broken or not classified as 'not of normal shape'.

A. If the pineapples are practically free from defects, a score of 25–30 points may be given. As used in these grades, the term 'practically free from defects' has the following meaning with respect to the various styles of canned pineapples.

SLICES: No units are crushed or broken, no harmless extraneous material is present, no peel is present, not more than 5 per cent by count of the units are blemished, and not more than 5 per cent of the units have remnants of the eyes. No units are trimmed to the extent that normal shape of the unit is destroyed and none of the units possess any defect exceeding the area of 1/4 inch. No eyes are present.

B. If the pineapple units are reasonably free from defects, a score of 19–24 points may be given. As used in this grade, the term 'reasonably free' has the following meaning:

SLICES: No units are crushed or broken, not more than one piece of extraneous material is present per 30 oz.

net content and not more than 10 per cent by count of the units are blemished and not more than 10 per cent of the units have remnants of the eyes. No unit is trimmed to the extent that normal shape of the unit is destroyed. No eyes are present.

CHUNK OR CUBES: Not more than 1 per cent by weight of the units are broken. Not more than one piece of harmless extraneous edible material is present per 30 oz. net content. Not more than 10 pieces containing remnants of the 'eyes' are present and not more than 5 per cent by count of the units are blemished. No eyes are present.

IV. CHARACTER OF THE FRUIT: Under this factor, consideration is given to texture and condition of the pineapple units.

A. If the fruit possesses a tender 'fleshy texture' a score of 28–35 points is given. (A tenderometer test for this should be worked out by the Central Food Technological Research Institute, Mysore, and made applicable later.)

B. If the units are reasonably tender, that is, the fruit is reasonably mature but not at its optimum maturity, a score of 20–27 may be given.

TOLERANCE FOR OFFICIAL INSPECTION: When samples are drawn for inspection, grading will be done on the basis of an average of all the samples drawn provided that the number of samples is larger than six, otherwise, the average of a minimum of six samples will be taken into consideration.

The average of samples taken at not more than 5 per cent of the samples should fail in some respect to meet the requirements. None of the containers may fall 5 points below the requirements for each individual factor. The individual average score for each factor shall not fall below the minimum score required for the factor when the average score of all containers is taken into consideration for certification.

PROPOSED PRELIMINARY STANDARDS FOR CANNED FRENCH BEANS

TYPES OF CANNED FRENCH BEANS:

1. Flat Type, *e.g.*, The Bombay French beans.
2. Round Type, *e.g.*, The Pachmari French beans.

STYLE OF CANNED FRENCH BEANS:

1. Whole—means that the strings are removed by cutting the ends and the beans are not arranged in any definite position in the container.

2. Cut or Cuts—means canned beans consisting of pods that are cut transversely into pieces between about 2½–2¾ inches in length, and may contain shorter end pieces which result from cutting.

GRADES OF CANNED FRENCH BEANS:

1. GRADE A. This is the quality of canned French beans which possess similar varietal characteristics; possess a normal flavour and odour; possess a uniform typical colour; are young and reasonably tender; are reasonably free from defects; and are of such quality with respect to clearness of liquor (brine) as to score not less than 70 points when scored in accordance with the scoring system outlined herein.

2. GRADE B. This is the quality of canned French beans that possess similar varietal characteristics; possess normal flavour and odour; possess a *fairly* uniform typical colour; are *nearly* mature and *fairly* tender; possess a fairly good liquor; are fairly free from defects; and score not less than 60 points when scored in accordance with the scoring system outlined herein.

FILL OF THE CONTAINER:

1. The product and the packing medium must occupy not less than 90 per cent of the total capacity of the container. The net weight of A-2½ cans shall not be below 28 oz.

RECOMMENDED DRAINED WEIGHT:

1. Whole French Beans — 16–3/4 oz. for the A2½ cans.
2. Cut French Beans — 17–1/4 oz. for the A2½ cans.

The drained weight of the French beans is determined by emptying the container upon a circular sieve of proper diameter containing 8 meshes to an inch (0.097 inch square openings) and allowing to drain for 2 minutes.

ASCERTAINING THE GRADE:

The grade of canned French beans may be ascertained by considering, in addition to the requirements of the respective grade, the following factors: clearness of liquor (brine), colour, absence of defects and maturity. The relative importance of each factor is expressed numerically on the scale of 100. The maximum number of points that can be given to each factor are:

1. Clearness of liquor	...	10
2. Colour	...	15
3. Absence of defects	...	35
4. Maturity	...	40
Total	...	100

'Normal flavour and normal odour' means that the canned French beans are free from objectionable flavours and objectionable odours of any kind.

ASCERTAINING THE RATING OF EACH FACTOR:

The essential variations within each factor are so described that the value may be ascertained for each factor and expressed numerically.

I. CLEARNESS OF LIQUOR:

A. If the canned French beans possess reasonably clear liquor, a score of 7–10 points may be given. 'Reasonably clear liquor' means that the liquor may be cloudy or may contain a small quantity of sediment.

B. If the French beans possess a fairly good liquor, a score of 4–6 points may be given. 'Fairly good liquor' means that the liquor may be dull in colour, but not off colour, may be cloudy, or may possess noticeable accumulation of sediment.

II. If the canned French beans possess a reasonably uniform typical colour, a score of 12–15 points may be given. 'Reasonably uniform typical colour' means that the canned beans possess a colour that is typical of young and reasonably tender French beans of similar varietal characteristics with not more than 10 per cent by count, which vary markedly from this colour.

B. Canned French beans that possess a fairly uniform typical colour may be given a score of 8–11 points. 'Fairly uniform typical colour' means that the French beans possess a colour that is typical of nearly mature and fairly tender beans of similar varietal characteristics with not more than 15 per cent, which vary markedly from this colour.

III. Absence of Defects:

The factor of absence of defects refers to the degree of freedom from extraneous *vegetable* matter, loose seeds and pieces of seeds, unstemmed units, ragged cut units (a unit means a cut portion or whole bean as the case may be), split units, small pieces of pods, units damaged by mechanical injury, and units damaged by scars, pathological injury or blemished by other means.

'Blemished unit' means that any unit in which the aggregate affected exceeds the area of a circle 1/8 inch in diameter.

'Seriously blemished' means blemished to such an extent that the appearance or eating quality of the unit is seriously affected.

'Extraneous vegetable matter' means leaves, detached stems, and other similar vegetable matter.

'Ragged cut units' means sections of pods that have very ragged edges or are partially cut.

'Small pieces of pods' means pieces of pods less than ½ inch in length.

'Damaged or mechanical injury' means damaged to such an

extent that the appearance or eating quality of the unit is seriously affected.

A. If the canned French beans are reasonably free from defects, a score of 28–35 may be given. 'Reasonably free from defects' has the following meaning with regard to whole or cut French beans:

The units are practically intact; the weight of all loose seeds and pieces of seeds does not exceed 5 per cent of the drained weight of the units; the combined weight of all the other defects and defective units does not exceed 15 per cent of the drained weight of the units; and that for each pound drained weight may be present:

not more than 3 pieces of extraneous vegetable matter, exclusive of detached stems;

not more than 7 unstemmed units or seven detached stems, or any combination of not more than 7 unstemmed units or detached stems;

not more than 16 ragged cut units or 12 units damaged by mechanical injury; and

not more than 75 pieces of pods in cut style.

B. If canned beans are fairly free from defects a score of 20–28 may be given 'Fairly free from defects' has the following meaning with regard to WHOLE AND CUT BEANS.

The units are practically intact; the weight of all seeds and pieces of the seeds does not exceed 7 per cent of the drained weight of the units; the combined weight of all other defects and defective units does not exceed 20 per cent of the drained weight of the units, and that:

there are not more than 6 pieces of extraneous vegetable matter, exclusive of detached stems;

there are not more than 8 unstemmed units and nine detached stems, or a combination of not more than nine detached stems and unstemmed units;

there are not more than 16 blemished units per pound drained weight, of which not more than 8 are serious blemishes; and,

there are not more than 80 units per pound which are less than ¼ inch long in cut style.

IV. MATURITY:

The factor of maturity refers to the degree of development of pods and seeds and the tenderness of the pods.

'Trimmed pod' means any pod from which there has been trimmed off, as far as the end of the space formerly occupied by seed, any portion of the pod from which seeds have become separated.

'Tough strings' means strings or pieces of strings at least ½ inch in length which will support a ½ pound weight for not less than 5 seconds.

A. If the canned French beans are young and reasonably tender a score of 31–40 points may be given. 'Young and reasonably tender' means that the units may, to some extent, have lost their fleshly structure; the seeds may have passed the early stages of maturity but not the late stage of maturity; are not fibrous; and not more than 7 per cent by count may possess tough strings.

B. If the canned French beans are nearly mature and fairly tender a score of 24–30 may be given. 'Nearly mature and fairly tender' means that the pods may have lost, to a considerable extent, their fleshy structure, and that:

the trimmed pods contain not more than 15 per cent by weight of the seed and the pieces of seed;

that the deseeded pods contain not more than 0–20 per cent, by weight, of the fibrous material; and

that not more than 10 per cent, by count, of the units may possess tough strings.

TOLERANCES OF OFFICIAL INSPECTION

When certifying samples that have been officially drawn and which represent a specific lot of canned French beans, the grade for such lot will be determined by averaging the total score of all containers, if:

more than one-tenth of the containers comprising the sample fail to meet all the requirements of the grade indicated by the average of such total scores, and with respect to such containers which fail to meet the requirements of the indicated grade by reason of a limiting rule, the average score of all containers in the sample for the factor subject to such limiting rule, must be within the range for the grade indicated.

None of the containers comprising the sample fails to score more than 5 points below the minimum score for the grade indicated by the average of the total scores.

V. NUTRITION STANDARDS:

There are fairly large number of canned foods, such as fruit juices, which are not only consumed for their taste but also for their nutritional value. One of the major health problems of our country is malnutrition; therefore we cannot neglect this aspect of foods while setting up standards. If the food is properly processed, it is possible to retain a large amount of nutritional value. In fact, it is fairly well-known that most of the fruits and vegetables are freshly obtained for processing and are richer in certain nutrients than 'fresh' food available in large cities, because the latter may have taken several days to get there and may lie for a long time before being sold.

Some of our seasonal indigenous products are excellent sources of vitamins. Mango is among the richest fruits known to contain vitamin A. It has as much as 4,800 International Units of this vitamin per 100 g., yet people suffer from night blindness. 'Amla' is the richest source of vitamin C. Guava contains about 230 mg. per 100 gms of vitamin C which is about three times as much as in citrus fruits. Yet, scurvy is not an uncommon disease in some areas. Thus, processed food industry can play a very valuable role in solving nation's health problems, provided that proper nutrition standards are developed for the processing industry.

The following U.S. Standard for ascorbic acid content of grape fruit juice ought to be helpful in framing our standards.

U.S. grade A Fancy Concentrated grape fruit juice contains *per degree Brix;*

not less than 0.033 mg. of ascorbic acid;

not less than 0.10 per cent or not more than 0.20 per cent acid, calculated as anhydrous citric acid; and not more than 0.0013 ml. of recoverable oil per 100 gms of the concentrate.

Similarly, grades B and C have been established.

VI. Standards for Processing Time and Temperature:

This seems to be one of the major problems in India. Very little work has been done on the thermal processing of foods taking into account Indian microbial flora and storage temperatures. As in other countries, fruits do not present much of a problem in India, but vegetables do. The Army Service Corps has reported large spoilages on several occasions. Most of them occurred in vegetables.

As a result of several years of experience, some of the countries have established standard vegetable processing times and temperatures. They have been a good success as a result of this. There is no reason why we cannot learn from their experiences and set up our own standards for the thermal processing of vegetables. But this will require a lot of work.

The following is a preliminary outline of processing standards which may be worth considering for discussion. It could be modified and improved upon as and when more data will be available on the subject.

DRAFT SPECIFICATION FOR PROCESSING OF CANNED FOODS

All the canned foods shall be adequately processed. 'Adequately processed' means that:

the contents of cans shall be commercially sterile and show no bulging or swells when cooled to 30°C after an incubation period of 15 days at 55°C, and that

there shall be no over-processing which results in burnt or scorched flavour and loss of valuable thermolabile nutrients. The microbiological tests as given in the latest volume of the A.O.A.C. Book of Analysis shall be negative for all pathogenic micro-organisms.

EQUIPMENT: The approved factories shall have adequate processing equipment. 'Adequate processing equipment' includes:

1. Steam pressure cookers or retorts.
2. Thermometer, reading from 210°F to 250°F, fixed on each retort.
3. Pressure guage, reading from 0 to 30 lb., fixed on each retort.
4. Steam trap for removing condensate from the retorts.
5. The retorts must have one steam inlet on top and preferably one additional inlet at the bottom.
6. The steam pressure in retorts shall be automatically controlled and recorded. (This clause should be brought into force after the end of the year 1955.)
7. Safety valve and bleeders must be provided on the retorts.

RETORT OPERATION: Retort operator shall be a person who has been licensed to operate the retort after an examination by the Deputy Food Development Officer of the area. If necessary, an examining committee consisting of food technologists may be appointed for the purpose of licensing the retort operators.

The retort operator must sign the operation chart as outlined herein at the end of the day. These charts shall be open to inspection by the ASC Officials any time.

INSPECTION AND INCUBATION: The production shall be sampled at the rate of two cans per every two hours when the production does not exceed 8 tons per day. If the production is more, the sampling shall be increased at the rate of two cans per every two-ton increase in production per day. One of the sample cans shall be opened for cut-out and the other shall be kept in an incubation chamber at 55°C for at least two weeks. The incubation chamber and the cut-out reports shall be open to inspection by the ASC Inspectors.

All the cut-out reports shall be on a standard cut-out form as outlined herein.

The following tentative processing times and temperatures are suggested for canned vegetables in A-2½ cans.

Vegetables	Processing Temp. (°F)	Time Recommended (Minutes)
Carrots	240 250	35
French beans ...	240 250	40
Cabbage	240 250	40
Cauliflower	240 250	30
Potatoes	240 250	40
Peas (Green)	240 250	45
Okra (Ladies Fingers)	250	35

SUMMARY AND CONCLUSION

The Indian Food Processing Industry has developed to a stage when it has become imperative to establish proper standards for the raw material, sanitation, nutritional value, thermal processing and quality of the finished products. If this is done, the consumer will be assured of a uniform quality of goods, and a high reputation could be built for the Indian processed foods at home and abroad. Increased consumption of Indian processed foods will save foreign exchange and help alleviate the food problem of the country. Export of luxury foods will go a fairly long way towards making payment for imported staple foods.

CUT-OUT REPORT

Canning date.............................

Product.............................

Cut-out Date.............................

No.	Code	Size	Inches		Weight in oz.				Fl. oz. Liquid	Salt %	°Brix	pH	Acidity %	Appearance		Taste	Remarks
			Vacuum	Head Space	Gross	Can	Nett	Drain						Pro.	Can.		

Lab. Assistant.

TECHNOLOGIST.

DAILY PROCESS REPORT

Bombay..............................195

Batch	Product	Crate No.	Retort No.	Size Cans.	No. Cans.	Code	Time in	Time up	Time out	Cook Min.	Temp.	Pressure

RETORT OPERATOR.

CHEMICAL ENGINEERING IN FOOD INDUSTRIES

By

Y. K. Raghunatha Rao

(Central Food Technological Research Institute, Mysore)

In this article, emphasis is laid on the urgent need for a large number of trained and qualified chemical engineers to man our food and allied industries. Chemical engineering research is essential for securing initiative in industry and to obtain practical benefits of fundamental research by commercial exploitation of discoveries. Only by this means can front-line 'know-how' be obtained. The formation of a Central Laboratory for pilot plant operations and plant design is suggested.

TECHNOLOGY aims at the application of fundamental principles to practical problems and the introduction of new methods and techniques into industrial practice. Chemical engineering is a distinct body of knowledge, which utilizes principles common to such branches of science as engineering, mathematics, chemistry and physics, etc., and extends and combines them in a unique manner. Industries need chemical engineers (i) for process control, operation and maintenance (ii) for construction and installation of plant, and last but not the least, (iii) for the more important function of research, design and development. The chemical engineer, having a background of scientific training and knowledge common to many chemical engineering unit operations, must also have initiative, originality and adaptability of outlook. He is, indeed, a key figure in the urbanized and mechanized society of today.

NEED FOR CHEMICAL ENGINEERING: Chemical engineering has an important bearing on the remarkable and rapid progress of industry in the U.S.A. Sir Harold Hartley in his Presidential Address last year to the British Institution of Chemical Engineers compared the large output of chemical engineers in America to that in the U.K. He quoted Dr Conant, President of the Harward University, who remarked that in spite of 15,000 chemical engineers trained in the last 5 years (1947–51), there was still a great shortage of such personnel in America. The Hankey Report showed an estimated annual output of only 200 chemical engineers in the U.K. during 1950–54. Sir Harold Hartley is of opinion that although British Science and discoveries were excellent, the results did not benefit Britain since the discoveries were exploited outside the U.K. For instance, British discoveries such as those of aniline dyes were developed in Germany, penicillin in America, and more recently, synthetic fibres again in the U.S.A., because British chemical engineering was not adequate. He considers it most urgent, *in order to recover British initiative in industry*, that Britain should expand educational and training courses in chemical engineering. He says that otherwise, they have to buy the 'Know How' from abroad, at a great cost, and even then, not always the latest 'Know How'. The position is worse in India where there are merely a handful of trained chemical engineers. Unless their numbers, ability and standards of training are raised considerably, our design and construction industry will not be established. *There can be no vigorous expansion* in industrial production and in the essential variegated growth of food industries in particular, until the urgent need for trained chemical engineers is met by Government, by establishing Chemical Engineering Courses and creating professional chairs in the universities. Industrialists in India should also become aware of this need and insist on such training being imparted to promising students who will turn out to be the builders of future industries. The urgency is greater in India than in other countries like the U.K., the U.S.A. and Germany where early steps were taken to train chemical engineers in large numbers.

It is of great practical interest to compare the numbers of members of the institutions of chemical engineers, as indicative of the extent of industrial advancement in some of the English-speaking countries. In 1951, there were 11,376 members in the U.S.A., 2,671 in the U.K., 2,572 in Canada, and 179 in India.

CHEMICAL ENGINEERS AND INDUSTRY: Especially in the U.S.A. *science is in active partnership with industry.* Fundamental scientists work along with chemical engineers and great commercial results follow from it. Lord Woolton, Lord President of the Council, addressing British Industrialists said, 'It is of tremendous importance that they should bring scientists into their works, who would improve their business and also safeguard the prosperity of their country'.

The Cremer Report as well as the addresses of several Presidents of the British Institution of Chemical Engineers lay emphasis on two aspects in the development of chemical engineering research: (1) The *Analytical approach* which stresses co-operation with industry and deprecates the isolation of the laboratory. The chemical engineer collects data from existing large-scale operations in factories, analyses them, and makes them available so that his findings serve as basis for plant design, (2) The *Synthetic approach* is by experimental investigations on large-scale pilot plants to obtain data to fill up the gaps in knowledge as revealed by the first, namely, the analytical approach, and to collect, co-ordinate and publish such data.

In India, chemical engineering research has to advance along similar lines. More direct contacts between the Industry and the Research Scientist are essential. The U.K. Committee suggested the establishment of a Central Laboratory for pilot plant operations. A similar policy should be followed in India in the development of scientific discoveries and plant design under the auspices of a central organization which may function as a Research Development Corporation. Increasing stress will have to be laid on chemical engineering research, because this alone can bring about rapid industrial progress and help the establishment of new industries. Large-scale investment on training and research in chemical engineering, and pilot plant operations are the *sine qua non* of industrial progress.

Another instance, reported from abroad, of the application of chemical engineering methods is the utilization of solar energy in the photosynthesis of carbohydrates, proteins and fats in lower plants, particularly in the unicellular alga: *Chlorella* which utilizes

30 per cent of incident solar light as contrasted with other vegetation, which can use only 1 per cent. Chlorella produces proteins in the first stage and fats in later stages. Industrial scale experiments for increasing food production in this way are reported to be in progress in U.K. It is called bio-chemical engineering in partnership with nature.

It is essential that Indian developmental plans, like those concerning the proposed National Research Development Corporation, should take urgent notice of advances and methods in other parts of the world and include tours to study the comparative progress of chemical engineering researches in other countries in order to build up a *prosperous India.*

AID TO INDUSTRY THROUGH PROPER STORAGE OF FOODSTUFFS

By

S. V. Pingale

(Central Food Technological Research Institute, Mysore)

In the storage and preservation of raw and processed foods, the interests of man clash with those of insects which not only consume the foodstuff they infest, but also contaminate it with their excreta and dead bodies. Occurrence of these in the case of processed foods damages the reputation of the manufacturer, thus bringing a bad name to the product. The Indian Food Industry in order to establish itself on a sound footing has to do its utmost to tackle this problem of insect damage. It is in this respect the various food industries require the cooperation of scientists.

In the storage of food, the interests of man clash with those of insects, rats and other vermin.

The insect damage to stored materials is not easy to show in figures. Loss in weight may be thought to give a true picture, but rarely does it bear relation to the extent of actual damage to foodstuffs. Thus, a cockroach leg in a biscuit or a few insect larvae in pickles will not reduce the weight of the product, but will make it unacceptable for consumption, affecting at the same time the reputation of the industry.

Whatever the nature and magnitude of these losses, they cannot be allowed to occur in these days of food shortage.

Foodstuffs are generally stored before they are sent to local or foreign markets. Insect appearance in stored foodstuffs is sometimes very sudden. The infestation in such cases starts either in the field or through the producers' methods of mixing old stock with the new. The infestation, when premature, may be invisible to the unaided eye. The industry, in spite of strict vigilance, is therefore liable to purchase foodstuffs which are insect-infested. The infestation multiplies further in storage on the factory premises and may extend to parts of the machinery, godowns etc., and thus become a permanent source of trouble.

To avoid this, it is necessary to detect and eliminate infestation even when it is yet apparently invisible at the time of the purchase. It is possible to detect even very early stages of insect infestation by means of staining methods which have been developed in recent years.

For elimination of the infestation, mechanical or chemical methods are used. The mechanical methods consist in subjecting the food material to a very high centrifugal force in an apparatus known as the 'entoleter'. Though this appliance is very effective in destroying insects, quantities that could be treated by it are comparatively small, and therefore, it is not suitable for large-scale work. Further, treatment with this appliance has no residual action and the treated foodstuffs require other methods of protection during storage. At present, there are hardly any installations of this kind in the country, though it is learnt that some industries are shortly going to install this equipment.

The chemical methods are either preventive or curative and can be employed for any quantities. However, care should be taken that any chemical that makes the food hazardous or unpalatable for consumption should be avoided. The chlorinated hydrocarbons which recently appeared on the market are powerful in their action, but are harmful in goods. Therefore, their use is to be necessarily restricted. For the elimination of infestation, the curative methods to be employed involve the use of gaseous chemicals, the effective operation of which requires air-tight conditions. Ordinarily, such conditions are not available very easily. Investigations carried out at this Institute and also elsewhere indicate that the gaseous chemicals can now be used on any premises. Advice and further information regarding the selection of proper chemicals, methods of application, their after-effects etc., will be supplied by this Institute.

After the elimination of any existing infestation, food materials require to be protected during storage in transport. Here, the container plays an important role. Jute bags which are commonly used for storing grains and flour not only fail to offer adequate protection, but actually serve as a source of infestation. A method of making them insect-free and insect-proof by impregnations with certain chemicals has recently been developed at this Institute.

The processed food industry, besides having to eliminate infestation in stored raw materials, has to face the problem of endemic infestations in the machinery and packaging materials. In preventing infestation of the machinery, sanitation has to play a great part. Once the infestation of the production-rooms takes place, it could be removed only with the help of gaseous chemicals. Air-tight conditions not being possible in this case, the group of chemicals known as 'spot fumigants' which give out heavier gases at a very slow rate have to be employed. The use of some nitriles, which belong to this group, is recommended for the disinfestation of plant and machinery.

It is usually believed that an air-tight package is insect-proof as well. This is not so. Not only can insects survive for years without food, but they can also live under air-tight conditions. If the raw materials and the machinery are cleared of all infestation, there is little possibility of living insects being inside packed food and the problem is then reduced to protecting the food product during its shelf life. In order to ensure a long shelf life, smooth surface of the packaging material and air-tight sealing are necessary, though they may not, in many cases, be adequate to afford protection against insects. This is particularly so when the packaging material used is paper. Instances are on record that even tin packages have been penetrated at joints by insects. Exhaustive tests on the impregnation of packaging materials with different insecticides are in progress at this Institute.

Rats are also a great menace to stored foodstuffs. But, their control is by no means easy, since whatever is dangerous to rats is also dangerous to man. A group of anti-coagulants has opened up a new line of attack which is being followed at this Institute and it is hoped that effective methods of rat control will be suggested in the near future.

THE NEED FOR STATISTICAL QUALITY CONTROL IN FOOD INDUSTRIES

By

S. K. Ekambaram

(*Maharaja's College, Mysore*)

In this paper, written deliberately in a popular way, an attempt is made to bring home to the industrialists engaged in food industries, the need for statistical quality control. Progress of statistical quality control in industries in various countries is briefly mentioned. The need and possibilities of S.Q.C. in the food industry are considered with reference to raw materials, stages of manufacture, final inspection, standardization of products, and with reference to canning, bottling and other means of packing. An organizational help is also indicated in a practical way.

In a recent Editorial of the Bulletin of the Central Food Technological Research Institute,[1] a hope was expressed that Indian food industries may utilize statistical quality control techniques to improve and modernize their methods of manufacture. This is an indication of the progressive outlook of the Indian industries in general; and certainly, the modern advances in science and technology are there to be harnessed in the service of the Industry.

Amongst the most spectacular techniques evolved and successfully used in the mass-scale manufacturing programmes during the last three decades, the statistical quality control takes a preeminent place; the progress has been rapid and substantial in the U.S.A., U.K., and other western countries. In India, statistical quality control has received much attention of late, especially after the World War II. The Indian Standards Institute has been paying attention to the statistical quality control methods in evolving standards of quality and testing. At Ahmedabad, the textile industries have demonstrated the use of and benefited immensely from the statistical quality control techniques. The Indian Society for Quality Control and the Indian Statistical Institute have been interested in the statistical quality control, especially in the training of technicians and other personnel engaged in industries. At Bangalore, the Quality Control Association has been conducting periodic courses on statistical quality control and many applications in diverse industries have been made. Recently, a team of U.N.T.A.A. experts toured the country under the auspices of the Government of India and conducted courses on statistical quality control at four centres: Delhi, Calcutta, Madras and Bombay. The experts found some time to visit Bangalore and they were full of praise for the work done by the Statistical Quality Control Association at Bangalore for various industries.

But no food industry has come yet within this statistical quality control influence at Bangalore. Perhaps, in some other cities in India, statistical quality control methods are tried even in the food industry. From the nature of the food industry and the necessity of manufacture spread over a period, either on a mass scale or on a cottage industry-scale, the need for statistical quality control methods can be felt.

The need for the use of statistical aids in market analysis, consumer research, cost and production problems and time and motion studies has been indicated in a clear manner in a paper[1] that, I see, was read at the Symposium 'On Development of Food Industries in India' held at Mysore in May 1951; the need for quality control is also emphasized. In many other papers,[3, 4] read at the Symposium, the need for quality standards is explicitly mentioned and insisted on.

Let us see how we can set about this job. Like all industries, the food factories depend on raw materials; these may be fruits, vegetables and many other ingredients that go into the making of any food product. It is understood that the highest quality standards possible should be maintained in the raw material. To ensure this, a system of raw material check, and a system of grading, if necessary, has to be evolved. We have to draw up regular specification clauses and inspection procedures for the acceptance of the raw material. This subject of accepting or rejecting the raw material submitted can best be faced by the particular type of statistical sampling, which has been developed to suit the industrial conditions and is technically known as 'Acceptance Sampling'. Especially if the acceptance has to be after tasting, it is obvious we cannot test, even if we could, the entire lot of the raw material. We have to test a sample; and that should be arranged in the most economical manner. Even where other means of testing are available, sampling often becomes a necessity. For testing consignments of fruits or vegetables, that can be counted in units, the many schemes in the Columbia Research Groups 'Sampling Inspection'[5] may be readily adopted. Where the product is in bulk (solid or liquid), sampling techniques evolved in the chemical industries may be helpful. What is needed at the raw material stage is rigorous formulation of specifications and proper methods of inspection procedures. Here the 'Acceptance Sampling' has to come in, especially in larger factories where mass-scale manufacture is practised.

Next, at every stage in the manufacture, inspection procedures should ensure standard quality. This implies that the methods of statistical quality control demonstrated in some engineering processes and chemical industries have to come in, with suitable modifications. Especially from the experience of chemical industries,[6] we may be able to draw much inspiration and guidance. Wherever test data become available during normal inspection of products, the analysis by control charts would ensure the standard product at which we are aiming. The methods of 'Analysis of Variance' may be used in suitable cases. The main theme to be noted is that, at every stage in the manufacture, standard product should be ensured by proper control with the aid of statistical quality control charts and analysis. I am told that, by such methods, the quality of Swiss Chocolates was improved and standardized a few years ago.

Besides proper stage inspection and statistical quality control programmes in production processes, the final testing of the finished product before it is bottled, or canned, or otherwise marketed, is a necessity to ensure uniform standard of the product. In food, where sometimes tastes have to be cultivated, the uniformity of the finished product with respect to taste, appearance and other characteristics cannot be overemphasized. This uniformity is vital to the trade. But, as every manufacturer knows, uniformity does not mean that all products will be '*exactly alike*'. It is a well-known saying in industry that 'no two products can be *exactly alike*'. Certain inherent variability is inevitable in any manufacturing process. But, this inherent variability should be kept at a minimum, economically possible. Also, it must be ensured that the average level of quality is steady. In fact, we should be able to indicate by means of proper statistical quality control programmes that the product marketed has a certain level of quality and a known inherent variability. In other words, we should be able to specify the quality of our product and guarantee a standard with known tolerances. Then only, customer confidence can develop and the product accepted as a 'standard' one.

After this has been done, the product can be considered ready for canning, bottling or packing or otherwise marketing as the case may be. Assuming that we always have a standard finished product which we want to pack properly, we have many problems in packing which will need statistical quality control methods for efficient working. Examples are given, in many books[7] and papers, of the applications of statistical quality control in controlling the weight and other qualities, in packing the product. For example, if biscuits are sold in 1 lb. packets, the customer would expect to have 1 lb. or slightly more than 1 lb. of biscuits in the particular packet he buys. This can be ensured, with the minimum necessary excess in the average of the 1 lb. packets. Similarly, in bottling processes statistical quality control techniques can be of great use.

Further, in air-tight packings and especially in canning, there are many stages where statistical quality control methods have got to be used for economic mass-scale manufacturing. Errors in canning or packing can be disastrous to the industry and utmost care and most modern and reliable methods must always be sought and used. Where the storage period is likely to be long prior to the use of the product, proper follow up tests on samples chosen from manufactured lots should be continued at the factory.

The above account on the need for statistical quality control in food industries might have convinced you that the technique is there and ought to be heeded. But, some of you may wonder how to initiate these quality control methods with reference to the nature, structure and organization of a particular factory. The Quality Control Association at Bangalore may be able to offer its co-operation, wherever needed and wherever possible. But, it is for the factories themselves to think on these improvements. Perhaps all the practical men of business know that nobody else can do the hard thinking and hard work that are necessary to build up our food industries. We have to do that ourselves. Something has got to be done to obtain aid from the statistical quality control methods. The need is there.

BIBLIOGRAPHY

1. *Bulletin of the Central Food Technological Research Institute*, 1952, **2** (2), 37.

2. Bhatnagar, H. C., Fruit and Vegetable preservation Industry in India, *Food and Population and Development of Food Industries in India*, C.F.T.R.I., Mysore, 1952, (pp. 182–188) pp. 357.

3. Bhatia, D. S., Future of Food Processing in India, *Food and Population and Development of Food Industries in India*, C.F.T.R.I., Mysore, 1952, (pp. 265–272) pp. 357.

4. Rajagopalan, R. and De, S.S., Quality Control in Food Manufacture, *Food and Population and Development of Food Industries in India*, C.F.T.R.I., Mysore, 1952, (pp. 280-286) pp. 357.

5 Columbia Research Group, *Sampling Inspection*, McGraw Hill, 1948, 1st ed., pp. 221.

6. Danies, O. L. (Ed.), *Statistical Methods in Research and Production with special reference to the Chemical Industries*, (1949). 2nd ed , revised.

7. Grant, E. L., *Statistical Quality Control*, McGraw Hill, 1946 edition (pp. 48–52).

REQUIREMENTS OF INDIAN FOOD INDUSTRIES: RAW MATERIALS, PLANT AND PERSONNEL

By

(Major) N. V. R. Iyengar and Y. K. Raghunatha Rao

(Central Food Technological Research Institute, Mysore)

In this paper the authors have reviewed and assessed the requirements of Indian food industries in regard to various raw materials, packaging materials, plants and machinery and technical personnel if the factories have to work to full capacity and produce high grade products at economic prices.

In common with other industries, food industries need adequate supply of raw materials, chiefly agricultural produce at economic prices in relation to the market value of the finished products. The manufacture of processed foods requires, besides machinery and equipment, several accessories such as chemicals, steam, water, power and packaging materials for converting agricultural crops into more valuable foods in the desired form. Further, skilled labour and technical personnel are required for the manufacture of quality goods. Marketing and distribution of processed foods are also very important and require an honest merchant class and a satisfactory transport system.

Indian food industries are today comparatively in an underdeveloped state except for some major industries like sugar and oil. It is to be emphasized that several agricultural food materials need very little processing and in some cases no processing at all. Any mistake made in processing of food materials by needless treatment would result in health hazards to the consuming public by the removal of valuable nutrients, minerals, vitamins, etc. This is the case in the manufacture of wheat flour, hulling of paddy, preservation of fruits, vegetables and other food commodities. Foods in their natural form are astonishingly well-balanced. The knowledge of nutrition is still advancing so that food practices should be changed with caution and the processing should aim at preserving all the nutrients in original materials. The object of processing food is to make 'ready to serve' products as well as products which are more nutritious or richer in certain food components. For all this, adequate supply of proper raw material, the appropriate techniques of manufacture, necessary equipment and, above all, trained personnel are essential.

Raw Material

Availability of adequate quantities of raw material forms the very life blood of an industry. It is necessary that every concern should stock enough of raw materials for its satisfactory working. Usually, raw materials which can withstand long storage are stocked enough to last for about a year while those which do not bear storage are brought from time to time.

Raw material requirements of any food industry can be classed in three broad categories, viz: (1) basic raw materials which form the bulk of the manufactured product, (ii) auxiliary ingredients such as fats, colouring agents, flavours, acids, and other chemicals, and (iii) packaging materials like cellophane, paper boards, glass bottles, corks and wooden crates.

There are at present about 30 types of food industries in India. A consolidated estimate of the requirements of the more important raw materials for these industries is given in Table I.

Table I

Annual requirements of raw materials for Indian Food Industries

Indigenous	Tons	Imported	Tons
Cereals			
Wheat Flour ...	22,800	Edible Gelatin ...	150
Maize	2,200	Starch	2,620
Oats	4,600	Liquid Glucose ...	5,000
Barley	9,000	Malt	175
Cholam	450	Condensed Milk ...	600
Sugar	34,340	Yeast...	60
Vanaspati (Hydrogenated Oil)	3,400	Bicarbonates	200
Milk	1,06,000	Citric and Tartaric acids	230
Cocoa Beans ...	600	Essential Oils	50
Molasses	6,000	Colours and Essences ...	90

These estimates have been arrived at by taking into account the full capacity of the existing units. At present, a majority of the industries such as biscuit, chocolate, confectionery, malt extract etc. are not working to full capacity owing to inadequate supply of raw materials like wheat flour, sugar, cocoa beans, etc.

It is seen from the table that the food industries are dependent for some of the essential raw materials on imports. A good proportion of wheat flour (*maida*) is imported, although indigenously manufactured wheat flour is also used. In respect of commodities like flavouring essences, colours, edible gelatins, organic acids, liquid glucose, condensed milk and cocoa beans, the Indian industry is entirely dependent on imports. It seems obvious that attempts should be made to manufacture in India as many of these items as possible in required quantities.

The requirements of existing Indian food industries in respect of packaging materials are given in Table. II.

TABLE II

Packaging Materials

Tin Plate	...	23,000	Tons
Wrapping Paper	...	2,400	,,
Bottles and Jars	...	20,00,000	Gross
Crown Corks	...	20,00,000	,,

It is seen that for packing foodstuffs, tin plate to an extent of 23,000 tons is required, a large proportion of which is at present imported. It is therefore important that alternative packing materials, like synthetic resin, laminated paper boards and fibre packs, wherever they can be substituted, should be developed in India. The glass containers made in India have to be improved in quality and made cheaper. Further, suitable varieties of cork-trees should be grown to meet the requirements of the indigenous cork industry. Cellophane wrapping papers, attractive synthetic foils, aluminium foils and several other varieties of packing papers should be produced from the abundant forest and mineral wealth in India. Much information is available from the publications of research laboratories and industries in foreign countries about the manufacture of suitable wrapping materials, but an intensive effort is needed to obtain practical results in this direction.

For attractive packaging, colour printing is very essential. Indian synthetic dye industry has simultaneously to develop itself to meet this important requirement. In addition, colour printing technique should also be developed. Plastic adhesive tapes, transparent synthetic packing materials, light-weight paper boxes are among other requirements for the food industry.

Food Machinery and Equipment

For manufacturing processed foods from agricultural products, various implements, machines and equipment are needed. Machines and equipment like vacuum pumps, dehydration and freezing machines are to be employed in food industries. At present it is necessary to import the equipment from abroad. The imports of food machinery during the period 1946-1950 are given in Table III.

Table III

Imports of Machinery into India

(Value in *lakhs* of rupees)

Food Machinery	*1945–46*	*1946–47*	*1947–48*	*1948–49*	*1949–50*
Aerated Waters	0·08	0·30	1·60	4·99	3·96
Oil Crushing and Refining	6·18	49·56	71·36	54·41	42·24
Refrigerating ...	14·39	49·61	149·82	131·83	139·09
Flour Mill	4·01	16·93	14·06	19·41	27·70
Rice Mill	1·89	4·28	11·82	11·45	10·72
Sugar	30·43	55·44	94·66	151·78	172·24
Tea	47·85	48·51	56·28	56·93	70·47
Total ...	104.83	224.63	399.60	430.80	466.42

In addition, other types of food machinery are imported to meet the needs of the other food industries in India, but figures for these are not easily available.

It is not advisable to continue to import all this machinery for long. Therefore, plant and machinery for food industries have to be designed and made locally. This has an additional point in its favour. The design of new equipment follows development of new processes. Such a step would encourage new inventions and discoveries besides increased employment, training and experience in machinery manufacture. The production and use of various instruments of control will ensure standard quality of the foods produced. There is considerable demand at present for such instruments and equipment, but they cannot be used by all the small- and medium-sized units in India. Imported plants are prohibitively costly and the capacities and sizes of the plants are unsuited to Indian needs. It is time therefore for Indian engineers, technologists and industrialists to make an all-out effort in this regard to fill the lacunae which threatens to keep India on the permanent list of importers in the world.

Personnel

For producing the finished goods from the natural raw material, skilled labour and supervision are most essential. In India very few concerns have given sufficient thought to this important problem. Many factories often go without any technical control of the processes and the qualified technical personnel employed is thoroughly inadequate. The number of food processing establishments in India being over 5,000, at least 10,000 qualified technicians are required to man them. For this purpose, suitable training facilities should be provided in technical institutions and colleges, and national proficiency certificates awarded to the persons who will then take up positions in industrial concerns. In this connection the course adopted in U.K. of awarding the British Higher National Certificates may be suggested as an example. As the training of 10,000 men needed for the industry requires time and training facilities, suitable planning in this regard for imparting the necessary training in the shortest possible time requires to be made by the authorities concerned. Regular education in the basic knowledge of the sciences including agriculture, a specialised instruction in chemical engineering and training in the food industries should be provided. This system of planned building up of technical and supervisory personnel has yielded excellent results in Europe, U.K. and the U.S.A. There is a dearth of qualified technical leaders which must be quickly filled up if the country is to progress industrially.

THE BISCUIT INDUSTRY IN INDIA

By

Sunder Dass H. Kuckereja

(*Messrs M. S. Jaipur Biscuit Factory, Jaipur*)

In this paper, various causes for the low production and present quality of biscuits in India are mentioned. Measures to improve the grading and marketing of products, supply of raw materials and technical know-how have been indicated.

THE Indian Biscuit Industry has not yet established a firm reputation for itself. Before the Independence, the Industry was represented by some factories which were financed partly by Indian and partly by foreign capital. Even now, the number of factories and their production are hardly commensurate with the size of the population of the country or its demands. There are several reasons for the absence of a co-ordinated development of this industry in this country. Some of the most important ones are discussed in this brief note.

It is well known that, save a few notable exceptions, the biscuit manufacture in India is still on the whole in its incipient stage; most of the manufacturers do not seem to possess the so-called industrial potentiality, *i.e.*, the stamina and the sense to develop the industry to its full stature. This is due not only to the lack of finances, but also to the lack of co-operation between the investors and producers. Those who have started manufacture do not aspire for full-fledged developments for lack of the necessary 'know-how', finances and other facilities. The net result is that today the country has a large number of small-scale manufacturing units which do not possess hygienic arrangements or equipment for the production of biscuits on scientific lines. Some of the even moderately large-scale factories do not have laboratories attached to them. This has led inevitably to the production of low quality goods in many cases resulting ultimately in fall in demand.

Need for State Aid

Another major difficulty facing the Industry is the lack of Government help in matters where help is necessary. The State Government has not recognized this industry, although the Government of India have accorded their recognition and help to a small number of mechanized factories on the recommendations of the various Directors of Industries. The present conditions with regard to this industry in certain States, and especially in the Rajasthan State, are therefore far from satisfactory. As far as is known, there is no legislation in this State governing a biscuit factory, and no definite aid is rendered by the State for the development of this industry in a scientific manner. The State does not take any responsibility with regard to the procurement of raw materials for any factory, however important they may be for the production of quality biscuits. For instance, besides a number of bakeries, the two large-scale factories in Rajasthan have not yet been able to obtain the hydrogenated oil for their *bona fide* use in the production of biscuits. Such an attitude of the State is a great handicap for the proper working of a factory. There is no technical aid provided by the Government for improving the quality of biscuits, nor have any standards been prescribed for the purpose.

Grading and Marketing

The industry is faced with a still greater difficulty which retards its progress. There is no efficient system of grading, sampling and packing, and as such, the possibilities of developing a wide market in India and overseas are greatly hampered. The biscuit manufacturers in India stand in dire need of proper grading of their products. There should be some method of helping the industry to obtain this assistance easily.

Six Point Programme of Help to the Industry

In order to assist the industry in its improvements, the six points mentioned below, are suggested for consideration:

1. This Symposium should resolve that the whole biscuit industry (whether large-scale or small-scale) in the country should

be brought under the jurisdiction and control of the Central Government.

2. The Central Government should provide timely technical help to the biscuit industry by maintaining a large-scale laboratory where different formulae should be worked out and made available to all biscuit factories.

3. The Government of India should take the responsibility of supplying the best type of raw materials needed for the manufacture of biscuits and allied products in India, and take steps for their easy procurement, and if necessary, undertake suitable measures for their manufacture, wherever possible.

4. The Government should pass legislation to discourage unfair competition between manufacturers by the fixation of prices of products of different qualities produced by various firms.

5. The Government as well as the local bodies should organize marketing organizations in big towns in India and abroad in order to provide a wide market for Indian biscuits.

6. All the State Governments should be requested to give their full co-operation to support the biscuit industry in their respective States.

It is hoped that this Symposium will be able to convince the producers and the Government of the needs of the industry, and obtain a large-scale acceptance of the principles involved. A food industry like the biscuit industry, is as essential for the national development as a heavy chemical industry, since the former affects the life of the nation and the latter its industrial development.

THE NECESSITY OF STANDARDIZATION OF RAW MATERIALS FOR THE BISCUIT INDUSTRY

By

N. M. Chauhan

(Messrs Parle Products Mfg. Co., Ltd., Bombay)

In this paper, the author who is one of the leading biscuit manufacturers traces the development of the biscuit industry in India, and sets forth the practical handicaps encountered with respect to the raw materials available to the industry. Some of the factories have at present excellent modern equipment and well-qualified technical staff. All concerned with the biscuit industry should come together and evolve a practical scheme of standardization of raw materials. Quality biscuits can be produced only when quality raw materials are available.

In pre-war days, the Biscuit Industry in India was run on a very small scale. Hardly one or two factories were manufacturing quality goods, which could compare favourably with foreign biscuits flooding the Indian markets. So far as raw materials required for the biscuit industry were concerned, abundant supplies were available from local as well as foreign markets. But, our technical knowledge was limited, with the result that every individual baker followed his own standards for raw materials. In the majority of cases, he used to rely entirely on the information given by suppliers of the raw materials.

During the war-time, military demands and stoppage of foreign imports gave a sudden impetus to our industry. No doubt, we produced big quantities of biscuits, but we had to use raw materials of any quality, that were made available by the controlling machinery of the Government. Since 1950, these conditions underwent a gradual change. During the past few months, sugar and wheat flour were more freely available; this is therefore the opportune time for the biscuit industry to standardize its raw materials, if it wants to produce quality goods that would stand competition with foreign goods, both in Indian and foreign markets.

At the outset, it will be asked whether our problem of manufacturing quality biscuits will be solved only by getting standard raw materials. Yes, almost all the leading biscuit factories are installing or have installed the most modern machinery and there is no dearth of technical talent with them, but there is paucity of standard raw materials to manufacture really good biscuits. The following short survey of raw materials will show where exactly we stand so far as availability of standard raw materials is concerned.

1. WHEAT FLOUR: It is common experience that we have to accept whatever wheat flour the Government will give us. The consignments are invariably from at least a dozen millers and the quality of wheat flour varies from bag to bag. When we require hard wheat flour for our cracker sponges, we are supplied with soft wheat flour, and when soft wheat flour is required, we are sure to get hard wheat flour. The same condition exists with the wheat flour milled by local millers. It is not the miller's fault, as he has to take whatever type of wheat is released to him by the Government. It is neither the fault of the Government nor of the purchasing missions, as they do not know what are our standards for wheat flour.

2. SHORTENINGS: (a) *Hydrogenated oil*: Only a few manufacturers are producing hydrogenated shortenings which are suitable for use in biscuit manufacture under our climatic conditions. None of them care to improve the keeping quality of their shortenings. And so far as stabilization of the shortening with an antioxidant and emulsifier is concerned, they are more than orthodox. Some of them are agitating for a high melting point fat. We would like to caution our friends in the biscuit industry here, that the use of such a fat without an emulsifier will spoil the appearance of their biscuits.

(b) *Oils*. There are only a few manufacturers who can supply pure oils. In the majority of cases, we get mixed oil, and these oils are often rancid at the outset.

3. SUGARS: This is the only material where it is possible to obtain a good quality, since we have a choice of the sugar factory to buy our requirements from.

4. MILK PRODUCTS: Our experience in this respect is that whenever we go in for milk products (powder or condensed) from the local market, the majority of suppliers offer spoiled stocks. This is due to the storage of products in an unscientific way.

5. LEAVENING AGENTS: *Dried Yeast and Live Yeast*: Live yeast available from imported stock always gets infested with black mold under our climatic conditions. A consumer always gets his stocks from this infested consignment. Only a few suppliers and consumers have proper storage and transport facilities to keep the live yeast free from infestation. Further, the dried yeast, available from local sources, is more often than not inactivated dried yeast, and it is of no use for manufacturing Cracker type of biscuits.

6. FLAVOURS: *Citrus Oils*: Usually due to improper storage, we always get citrus oils which are terpene at the outset, or which will turn terpene after use in biscuits.

Vanilla Extract: There are only a few concerns which can supply natural vanilla extracts, others dissolve synthetic vanilline in organic solvents and supply the same as natural extract.

Vanilline: There are several concerns which offer synthetic vanilline. This is hardly stable in biscuits after baking.

7. PACKAGING MATERIALS: The cardboard used for carton making is never of a quality which will not impart bad odour to the biscuits.

A number of suppliers offer synthetic wrapping materials, without regard to whether the product is suitable for use under our climatic and working conditions; consequently, we often use the wrong material.

These problems can only be solved if we standardize our materials taking into account the following factors: (1) that the biscuits are to be manufactured, stored and consumed in a tropical country like ours; (2) that the raw materials are shipped, transported and stored before supply under most favourable conditions, and (3) that we shall discontinue imports of raw materials in a short time, *e.g.*, within a few years, we may no more be obliged to import wheat flour.

The standardization can only be achieved if we in the Industry, officials of the C.F.T.R.I. and other Scientific Institutes, officials of the Food Departments of the Centre and the States and suppliers of raw materials come together, discuss the problems, solve the difficulties and evolve a practical scheme of standardization of raw materials. If the standardization so evolved is brought into force, we feel that it would not be long before all of us get the best type of raw materials to produce the best biscuits.

TECHNICAL AID TO BAKING INDUSTRIES

By

R. B. Rao

(*Chief Chemist, The Britannia Biscuit Co., Ltd., Calcutta*)

The baking industry is classified into three categories according to the three basic mixtures of flour and water, from which the products are manufactured. Biscuit and bread making involve highly scientific and engineering principles. A survey of the present conditions and problems of the Industry is made and the lines on which improvements are possible are indicated. The Indian factories face a number of technical problems and an acute lack of technical personnel and to deal with this situation satisfactorily, the establishment of a Baking Research Institute is suggested.

ALL bakery products come under the category of flour confectionery. As the name implies, the major constituent of these goods is pure white flour except in products like meringues, etc. To get a general picture of the various baking industries, it is logical to look at the composition of the products they make.

Generally speaking, all baked goods can be regarded as derived from three basic flour and water mixtures. Various changes are made by way of incorporating different amounts of fats, sugar products, egg products, milk and milk products, and different aerators so that a variety of finished products are marketed. The first category uses mixtures of flour and water in equal proportions usually called 'Batters' which give rise to finished goods like wafers, waffles, picklets, pancakes and sponge rolls. The second category makes use of mixtures of flour with half its amount of water, usually called 'Doughs' containing different aerators like yeast, baking powder, varying amounts of fat, sugar and eggs resulting in a number of products like bread, tea cakes, butter buns, scones, cakes, butter sponges, sponge cakes, etc. The third category uses flour with a minimum amount of water, using a high fat content usually giving rise to 'Plastic Pastes' giving products like plain biscuits, short pastry, puff pastry, sweet pastry, sweet biscuits, etc.

From the above broad classification and a general survey of the existing baking industries in India, it can be seen that progress has been made mainly in the third category, namely Biscuit Manufacture. The next important product that is being made in quantity is bread, belonging to the second category. I think that it is fair to say that the rest of the products have not made any progress on the manufacturing side except that pastries, buns, cakes, etc., are being made in a few restaurants and big hotels in cities like Calcutta, Bombay, Delhi and Madras where it is practised more as a craft than technology.

Hence, I want to devote the rest of the paper to discussing the various technical problems facing the bread and biscuit manufacture in India, leaving others for a future occasion.

Bread making or biscuit making is no longer considered as either an art or a craft or a combination of these two, but a new technology based on scientific and engineering principles. With this hypothesis, I shall first take up the problem of bread manufacture by giving (*a*) a general survey of the present conditions of the Industry in India, (*b*) the lines on which improvements can be made to get an attractive loaf and thereby popularize bread consumption, and (*c*) sketch out some of the fundamental problems on which investigation has to be carried out in order that bakers may improve their products.

Bread Making

Although as much as a quarter of the white flour consumed in the country goes for bread making, the Industry is still run on a cottage industry scale, except a few big bakers in cities like Calcutta and Bombay. These are mainly owned by large hotels and restaurants. It is estimated that, in Bombay, there are at least 400–500 bakeries and that, in Calcutta, about 200 bakeries each making 500–1,000 lbs. of bread a day. The usual sizes of loaves are ¼ lb., ½ lb., and 1 lb. and occasionally sandwiched loaves are also manufactured.

The two main ingredients of paramount importance are: (1) strong white flour and (2) good quality Baker's Yeast.

Flour. Strong flour is derived from strong high protein wheats and can be defined as a flour which on processing gives a bold, large-volumed loaf, with a silky texture. Hence, it is essential that the trade gets the right type of flour in order to make the bread more palatable and attractive.

Flour is not a simple powder, but a mixture of complex chemicals like starch, proteins, fats, minerals, vitamins, etc., coupled with powerful enzymes of the diastatic and proteolytic types. Hence, the nature of the enzymes present in flour will have a tremendous influence on the final loaf, *e.g.*, if the maltose figure is lower than 1.5 there is the danger of insufficient gassing powder and if it is over 2.3 there is the danger of stickiness in the crumb of the loaf. Hence, it is important that bakers get a flour with a maltose figure between 1.5 and 2.3. The flour with low maltose content can be improved by adding malt extracts, powders, etc. Also proteolytic enzymes play an important part in what is called 'Ripening' of the dough and these can be controlled by chemicals known as 'Improvers' which will be dealt with separately.

Yeast. Even today most bakers use varying concoctions, apart from barms made by the help of wild yeasts present in the atmosphere. It is not uncommon to find in some bakeries that use is made of fermented toddy, occasionally sour milk, or butter milk incorporated with soda to get aeration. All these methods are extremely unsatisfactory and, moreover, require considerable attention and skill in their preparation. Hence, there is a definite need for a good fermenting agent like Bakers' Yeast which belongs to the strain of *Saccharomyces cerevisiae*. This is usually manufactured by two methods, one being the mollasses method, the second the grain method. The first method is quite economic in India as huge quantities of mollasses are going to waste every year. A rough estimate for the potential demand of Bakers' Yeast is about 5 tons per day.

The quantity of Yeast used per sack of 280 lb. of flour varies with the type of flour, bake house conditions and method employed, but it can be safely calculated at 3 lb. per sack when the straight dough method is used. The sponge and dough method which is rather cumbersome gives an attractive flour to the finished product, and use of yeast can be reduced in this to as little as 1 lb. per sack.

In this connection, it may be added that a firm in South India is manufacturing yeast on a small scale and I hope that they will explore more fully the possibilities of making 'Dried Yeast' in large quantities. The problem of transporting yeast, by air and providing cold storage facilities on trains etc., can be easily overcome. It is generally appreciated that Dried Yeast can be stored longer under proper conditions and in this form it is more compact. Dried Yeast is about twice as strong as fresh yeast which in effecting delivery, a considerable saving can be made in freight charges of yeast in powdered form. It may be mentioned that yeast is required in the manufacture of Cracker type of biscuits apart from bread making.

Most bakers are not familiar with the use of Bakers' Yeast and the principles of panary fermentation. This is a job which can be tackled by the Central Food Technological Research Institute, Mysore, by way of supplying samples of yeast, providing methods of use and establishing the advantages to be gained by using a clean fermenting agent as opposed to the various mixtures in vogue today. The Government whilst restricting the import of this essential bakery raw material is not taking any steps to popularize the indigenous product. If need be the Government should spend money on propaganda popularizing this item so that the yeast industry can be built up on a sound basis. Most of the bread marketed today is not manufactured under hygienic conditions and not properly wrapped. The volume is poor and the bread is devoid of any real flavour. To improve the exising conditions in the trade, the idea of a 'National Food Loaf' has to be evolved and the Institute can take the lead in this direction. Specifications of flour, samples of good quality yeast and processing details have to be given in a popular language to the numerous small bakeries in order to improve their products. This will in turn create a healthy competition among the bakers and will thus lead to a general improvement in the standards of the finished loaf. Various improvements can be effected by adding 4–5 lb. of vegetable fat per sack which will enhance the crumb texture and eating quality of the present-day bread and will in turn promote better sales.

Also, it is difficult to make an attractive bread unless salt is used in good quantity, say, 4–5 lb. per sack of flour. Salt boosts up the flavour and toughens the gluten. Due to the retarding effect of salt on yeast, the amount of yeast will have to be increased.

After reviewing the bread trade and possible ways of organizing the trade on a sound technical basis, there are various fundamental problems which have to be tackled in the science of bread making by institutions like Central Food Technological Research Institute, Mysore.

(1) *Evaluating the different kinds of Indian wheat for their baking quality*

It is interesting to note that Plate wheats are being graded now according to baking quality of the flour they yield. The evaluation of the strength of different wheats is essential in order that the miller may know something of their quality so that the wheats can be blended to give a flour suitable for different purposes—bread making, biscuit making, etc. In this connection, modern dough testing machines like Brabender Farinograph, Dr Halton's Extensograph (Research Association of British Flour Millers) and the more recent instruments like Chopin Alveograph are useful in assessing the baking quality by eliminating the margin of human error.

(2) *Effect of Milling and Baking Quality*

It has been established that, during milling, some of the starch cells are ruptured and damaged to such an extent that the final product exhibits different gassing powers, although milled from the same wheat. Starch granules which have sustained mechanical damage show a different appearance under microscope than sound granules. The former exhibit a peculiar flat appearance and can be detected by different staining.

(3) *Bread Improvers*

It is a common observation that freshly milled flour does not have the same ability to produce a pleasing bold loaf as a flour which has 'aged'. This improvement of the flour is done almost immediately by adding 'Improvers' like potassium bromate, ammonium per-sulphate, chlorine and nitrogen trichloride, in minute quantities. The use and manufacture of these chemicals has to be popularized among bakers and in the chemical industry respectively.

(4) *Distribution Methods and Bread Staling*

Generally, people do not like stale bread and this is one of the factors that has to be tackled so that consumption can be stepped up.

The usual way of distribution of bread, for instance in Calcutta, is in the evening and by the time it reaches the consumer it will be about 12 hours old. On the other hand, if the bakers are able to distribute fresh loaves early in the morning, the problem of supplying oven-fresh loaves is solved. All bread becomes stale, but bread made from under-ripe doughs, over-ripe doughs, too slack or too tight doughs stales more quickly. There have been various theories for the cause of staling but the most accepted view is relating to the conditions of the partially gelatinized starch in the loaf. In fresh bread gelatinized starch is in the *alpha* form which is unstable and hence changes to *beta* form, which is unable to hold as much water as the *alpha* form. This explains the general impression that stale bread is drier than the fresh one. Many anti-staling agents have been claimed to be effective, *e.g.*, acetaldehyde, pyridine, polyoxyethylene stearate. This problem has yet to be overcome and is one which can be tackled by the Central Food Technological Research Institute, Mysore and will provide invaluable help to the bread industry.

(5) *Improvements in Hygiene and Nutrition*

The modern tendency is to well wrap the bread so that there is no foreign contamination during distribution. With new machinery that has recently been designed, manual handling is almost eliminated from the time the ingredients come into the store till the loaf leaves the factory.

More attention has to be paid to preserve the natural vitamins in the flour which can be achieved by improving the technique of milling so as to retain most of the vitamin B, which occurs in the scutellum, the outer covering of the germ of the wheat grain. This is where the millers can come to our assistance by improving their methods of milling. Different varieties of bread have to be marketed like wholemeal loaves, gluten enriched bread, etc.

(6) *Bread* versus *'Chapaties'*

Nutritional studies have to be initiated to find out the best way of consuming wheat and wheat products. It is suggested that the biological value of the wheat proteins is much higher in bread apart from being a 'Ready to Serve' food than in *chapaties*.

Biscuit Manufacture

The largest consumers of white flour are the biscuit manufacturers who use as much as 1/3rd of the total flour consumed in India. The value of the goods produced annually is in the region of 30 million rupees. This quantity relates only to the consumption reported by members of the Federation of Biscuit Manufacturers of India. It is estimated that at least another one-fourth of the total flour is consumed by other small biscuit makers scattered all over the country.

At the outset I want to deal with these small biscuit makers since they are establishing themselves in a position where they may well be a serious threat to public health and are also making unhealthy cut-throat competition in the market. Recently, I had occasion to test some of their samples and these cannot be considered in the category of any acceptable standard of biscuits but a mixture of flour and some fat dried out in the oven, which is unsuitable and almost unfit for human consumption.

These products have practically none of the flavour and aroma normally associated with a good quality product; they are, in fact, doing more harm than good to the industry by unpopularizing biscuit-eating among the public. Some of these small bakers even use old newspapers to wrap their biscuits and consequently the biscuits become soft in a matter of hours, and the goods turn rancid during the course of a few days, under the prevailing climatic conditions. It is well known that rancid fats cause poisoning apart from the destruction of other nutrients like vitamin 'A' etc. We hope that this menace to the genuine biscuit industry will receive Government attention since it amounts to wasting good white flour and endangering public health by causing food poisoning, etc.

It is really essential at this stage that the growth of these mushroom producers be stemmed by enforcing strictly the existing provisions in Municipal Health Acts and also by enacting at an early date uniform laws throughout the country by the Central Government as regards hygiene, purity, labelling, marketing, etc.

In large well-organized manufacturers, hygienic and scientific methods of production are practised; indeed, we recruit labour force only after they are qualified by the Company's Medical Officer and they have satisfactorily passed the necessary tests. The large units of production can institute a rigorous programme of chemical and micro-biological control over their products, which a small producer cannot afford to. Moreover, without the help of specially experienced food technologists, no new advancements can be made either in processing or quality control programmes in the industry. Due to extremes of climatic conditions it is all the more important that the Industry enforces strict sanitary conditions in the factory and pays more attention to the purity of ingredients, correct methods of manufacture and packing in order that the public are assured of oven-fresh goods. This is the fundamental principle of the Federation and unless its member factories satisfy the above conditions they cannot become members of the Federation.

With these introductory remarks concerning conditions in the trade, I shall now comment on the technical problems facing the Biscuit Industry in general.

The problems are quite different from that of bread manufacture inasmuch as the making of biscuits is a much more specialized job and, on account of the nature of the product and methods of distribution, demands a longer storage life. Moreover, the Industry has installed modern up-to-date automatic plants to the tune of many lakhs of rupees, which, of course, are designed mainly to work with particular kinds of doughs made from standard ingredients.

It is a well-established fact that the biscuit manufacturer cannot produce quality goods unless he starts with the right type of ingredients coupled with purity. I can cite the example of flour which is also a major constituent in biscuits. We are forced to take up strong Canadian wheat on several occasions which is suitable for bread manufacture but quite unsuitable for biscuit making, especially certain varieties. It may be added that biscuits are much more sensitive to the quality of flour. In our opinion Australian weak wheat is the best that can be obtained for our purposes. Even here, we have to take into account the recent developments in wheat-growing in New South Wales. Some of the varieties grown now-a-days like 'GABO' 'YALTA' yield good-strength flour suitable for bread making. Hence, it can be seen that the problem of selection is very tricky and we would ask the milling industry with the help of the Government of India to mill suitable flours for different industries. In this connection we have to add that milling must be improved to give a higher degree of smoothness to the flour than that we get at present and the extraction rate will have to be fixed at 70 per cent. In this connection, flour testing machines like Chopin Amilograph, Viscosimeters, etc., are also made use of in assessing the flour suitability for biscuit making. Flours having glutens with a high extensibility and a low elasticity are found suitable for making biscuits.

Baking Fats. As I have already mentioned, fats play an important role in biscuit manufacture. The industry requires various types of baking fats, *e.g.,* butter, margarine, pastry margarine vegetable shortenings and deep frying fats, etc. Although the Vanaspati industry has been in existence for over two decades, no systematic plan has been evolved to market such special fats on a large scale.

Today the Vanaspati available in the market is far from satisfactory for biscuit making. The bazaar quality Vanaspati has a granular texture, along with some free oil, having an iodine value nearabout 70.

The Biscuit Industry requires a smooth plastic fat without any grains, having a good body at normal working temperatures in the Bake House. The fat should have also a higher stability than at present so that the shelf life of the biscuits is enhanced.

Recently, the Government has given permission to the Vanaspati industry to increase the melting point of the fats from 37°C to 41°C for biscuit manufacture. Undoubtedly, this measure gives the Vanaspati manufacturers a chance to develop special baking fats, but I should caution that the higher melting fats tend to spoil the eating quality. Already, much criticism has been levelled at Indian biscuits that they cling to the teeth on eating and that they do not melt in mouth as the famous English biscuits. This is what naturally happens if the fat used has a higher M.P. than the body temperature. Hence, the problem has to be solved in close association with the biscuit and Vanaspati industries on one hand and the Government on the other. I suggest that the Federation of Biscuit Manufacturers of India be given representation on the Vanaspati Committee for developing these special fats according to specifications since the Baking Industry is one of the largest users of vegetable ghee.

Yeast and Yeast Foods. The problem of yeast has already been dealt with under bread and the problem is gaining more importance in the biscuit industry since the Cracker type of biscuits are becoming very popular in India, *e.g.*, cream crackers, salt crackers and other fermented dough biscuits.

Special Ingredients: (Malt Extracts, Dessicated Cocoanut.) Malt extracts are used for several purposes in the Industry namely as a yeast food, as a colouring agent, and also as a flavouring agent. These products have to be marketed separately for these purposes. This is achieved by alterations in the kilning and processing of the germinated grain. The indigenous product made in Central India has to be improved on the above lines so that this ingredient is made available to the industry freely. The biscuit industry is one of the largest users of dessicated cocoanut in conjunction with the pastry and confectionery trades. The indigenous product has a higher moisture content and is not shredded uniformly. The drying has to be improved so that it does not go rancid quickly and the dessicated cocoanut has to be graded in three separate classifications—coarse, medium and fine. This industry can be built up and put on a firm basis in India provided the products are marketed according to the requirements of the confectionery trades.

Essences and Essential Oils: This industry is in its infancy and recently two internationally well-known firms have begun compounding some essences from imported raw materials. There are various other small unqualified concerns putting on the market a number of essences which are unsatisfactory. Moreover, the essential oil industry is a very specialized one and even some of the American oils are not comparable to the Mediterranean oils. The two main qualities that an essence must have for baking are, first, stability to the usual baking temperatures, and secondly, a good fixative property so that the flavour is retained during storage. In this connection, it is worth investigating the possibilities of manufacturing aromatic chemicals like vanilline which are used in substantial quantities. Vanilline is made from the natural oil of cloves, which are grown in good quantities in India. Synthetically, possibilities of utilizing the lignin material from the liquor obtained from paper mills, have to be investigated.

The Industry is quite willing to support the indigenous products provided they reach a fair degree of perfection. The best manufacturers cannot go in for second-rate products, nor those different in quality they have been using for years. It is interesting to note that the Indian consumer is very sensitive as compared with his counterpart in the West with regard to flavour, eating quality, etc. The Government of India have to take into account these factors if they intend to restrict the import of these or similar products on the ground that the products are being made locally.

Packing Materials: The availability of good quality packaging materials like grease-proof papers, grease-proof corrugated

7

papers, wax papers, etc., is vital to the biscuit industry. It gives no satisfaction to the diligent manufacturer when he turns out quality products in his factory unless they reach the consumer over this sub-continent in oven-fresh condition. When we take into consideration that the goods have to be conveyed over thousands of miles, often under the worst conditions of temperature and humidity coupled with rough handling and the unorthodox ways of the dealers in marketing, the packaging problems with which we are faced call for very close attention. Examples can be cited to illustrate this. It is not uncommon that consumers purchase cartons after a long period, sometimes 2 or 3 years, from the date of manufacture and complain that the contents have gone bad which is, of course, natural in our climatic conditions. It is suggested that some of the paper mills may take up the manufacture of grease-proof paper which is in constant demand by the food industries. We persuaded a local paper mill to manufacture grease-proof paper, but the results are unfortunately not very satisfactory. The mill has to contend with factors like the supply of the right kind of pulp, the right type of agitators, etc. When once grease-proof paper is made it is a simple matter to manufacture corrugated grease-proof paper. There is a mill at present in Bombay making corrugated straw board, and the experiment conducted in our laboratory showed that on packing biscuits with straw-board paper, infestation took place in the paper and then spread to the biscuits. Hence, it is essential that the manufacturers should conduct micro-biological tests before they market these for food packaging. The Government of India has to take into consideration these practical problems when regulating the imports in conjunction with the developing of indigenous industries.

The Wax Paper Industry is not very popular and most of the manufacturers at present dip the packets in molten wax. This has many disadvantages and very often the wax reaches as far as the biscuit surface. This also involves heavy wastage of wax. The main advantage of wax paper is that wax is filled on all the pores of the base paper uniformly and that the wax content can be controlled to the desired degree. The wax used should be of good setting quality, without any odour. The paper and paper board industry has to pay attention to these requirements and make an effort to produce this kind of paper.

After reviewing the technical problems in connection with the industry, there are various fundamental problems on which research has to be conducted. These can be broadly divided into three categories.

(1) *Substitute or Alternate Raw Materials and New Materials*

Under this category come materials like soyabean flour, peanut flour, tapioca starch, different kinds of fats with higher shortening values, utilization of some of the indigenous spices as flavouring agents, various sweetening agents and their effects. The use of these materials in biscuits requires a lot of experimental and research work which must be carried out by the Industry or by a Food Institute like the Central Food Technological Research Institute, Mysore.

(2) *Chemicals used in Baking Industry*

The manufacturers use chemicals to improve the nutritional value, enhance the consumer acceptability and preserve foods so that they are readily available to the public. As long as these chemicals are not used at the cost of a good sanitary practice in the factory, these preservatives are useful. The chemicals can be divided into those which are added intentionally for a specific reason and those which find their way in small quantities during manufacture and distribution. Under the first group come all the artificial colouring matters, synthetic flavours, sweetening agents, vitamins, anti-oxidants, fat extenders, mould inhibitors and bactericides. Under the second group, come pesticides like D.D.T., gammexane, etc. The best way of incorporating these useful chemicals into the products, their advantages and their pharmacological properties have to be studied in greater detail.

(3) *Development of New Machinery and New Packaging Materials*

The automatic filling of biscuits and their wrapping is one of the biggest problems facing the industry. There have been many machines developed for filling free running products like tea, but the problem with biscuits is made more difficult due to the fragile nature. Similarly, special kinds of creaming machines have to be fabricated to suit the Indian conditions for Cream Sandwiched Biscuits.

There are various new packing materials like alkathene, fibre seal wrappers, pliofilm whose properties have to be studied with a view to putting them into use in the packing industry.

Technical Aid from the Central Government

In addition to what has been said with regard to technical and research problems in the industry, there is a lack of trained technical personnel in both the industries for executive posts and key positions like foremen, supervisors, etc. Moreover, there have been no real statistics collected with regard to bread-makers, small scale biscuit makers, pastry cooks, etc. Hence, there is a real need for a survey so that planning is done systematically.

These problems can be solved, I believe, by the establishment of a Baking Institute, the main concern of which will be to impart instruction in baking materials and methods and also to conduct industrial research with a view to solving the day-to-day problems of the industry. Examples can be cited in most of the Western countries where the State Governments give substantial grants to the Trade Associations to start such projects. The Master Bakers' Association in England conducts such courses in Baking Technology and awards Diplomas in conjunction with the Ministry of Education. They have recently established to their credit spacious research laboratories at Chorleywood, England. The American Institute of Baking is also run on both State-aid and private enterprise to the advantage of the consumer.

These proposals merit the attention of the Central Government and Trade Associations like the Federation of Biscuit Manufacturers' Association of India, which will be only too willing to play its part for the successful running of this new venture.

Technical Collaboration Between the Industry and Semi-Government Organizations

It has been felt that organizations like the Council of Scientific and Industrial Research should come into closer contact with the industry.

Although the majority of the bread or biscuit factories are not having well-equipped laboratories, the bigger units with scientific managements have established up-to-date laboratories to solve their technical problems.

The main functions of these laboratories are (i) to solve their day-to-day problems arising out of manufacture coupled with development work, (ii) to conduct quality control programme by scientific methods, (iii) to make sure that the products are made under hygienic conditions with a view to supplying the public with wholesome foods, and (iv) to conduct research on fundamental problems which have a direct bearing on the industry.

Much as the managements would like to spend more money on industrial research, they are confronted with many economic problems over which they have no control; some of the problems of national importance facing the industry could not be undertaken. Two of such problems are: (i) investigations on the evaluation of Indian wheat for bread-making, biscuit-making, and *chapati-making,* and (ii) improvement of the standards of Service Biscuits for Army as well as Navy so as to make them popular among our fighting forces.

These problems can best be tackled by the industry itself, since ultimately the industry has to process the Indian wheat or supply Service Biscuits to the Army. Moreover, the large units have at their command many years of practical experience coupled with highly specialized techniques. Hence, it is in the fitness of things that organizations like the Council of Scientific & Industrial Research and the Indian Council of Agricultural Research should initiate research projects on the study of Indian wheats. Similarly, the Ministry of Food and Agriculture in collaboration with Defence Science Organization can start a scheme to improve the palatability and storage life of Service Biscuits in order to make them more popular with our fighting forces. It may be mentioned in this connection that the American Biscuit Industry is largely responsible for the technical development of Cracker type of biscuits for the Army, which are very popular among the U.S. Forces.

By close collaboration between the Industry and the Research Organisations, therefore, special problems of technical nature can be solved, which will generally give a fillip to the development of industrial research in India.

Technical Aid under Colombo Plan

India has been obtaining wheat from several wheat-producing countries like Australia, Canada, the U.S.A. and Argentina. Since they are also the major wheat-growing countries of the world over a long period, they have made simultaneously tremendous progress in the processing of wheat and wheat products.

In order to use the wheat products in India to the maximum advantage, arrangements have to be made to send representatives from the private baking industry as well as Government officers, who are directly connected with this industry, on study tours. These visits can be arranged under the Colombo Plan with the active support of the Wheat Boards of the above-mentioned countries so that the industry can be posted with up-to-date information.

In this connection, it is interesting to note that, under the Colombo Plan, the Ceylon Government has already taken active steps in this direction by sending three of their representatives selected from the private industry and Government cadres to Australia. From the reports so far reached, it appears that this plan is yielding excellent results.

It may be added here that the study of improved methods and techniques need not necessarily mean extra expense to the industry, resulting in high prices to the consumer. On the contrary, these studies will be helpful in effecting economy in production costs along with improvement in quality, which is most desired.

This proposal merits the attention of the Planning Commission and the Government of India, in order that the public may get better bakery products than at present.

Finally, I like to point out some novel ways adopted now-a-days to keep the small baker in touch with modern advances in science and technology.

(1) Trade films can be made describing vividly the various processes, connected with the industry and exhibiting them at various centres.

(2) Arranging demonstrations by experts where quality goods are turned out from available ingredients in the presence of bakers.

(3) Arranging trade competitions and exhibitions of products made by individuals and firms, and awarding prizes for the best products.

(4) Publication of a Trade Journal which will act as a mouth-piece of the industry and consumer.

Some of these suggestions must be tackled by the Central Food Technological Research Institute, Mysore, by way of disseminating knowledge, through regular bulletins and abstracts to the industry, which will involve little cost and unlimited benefit to production and consumer.

In conclusion, I have to thank the Board of Directors of the Britannia Biscuit Co., Ltd., for giving me permission to put forward these views at this Symposium, for taking a lively interest in the preparation of this paper, and making the above suggestions.

TECHNICAL CONTROL IN CEREAL PROCESSING AND BAKING INDUSTRY

By

G. S. Bains and D. S. Bhatia

(*Central Food Technological Research Institute, Mysore*)

Technical control in cereal processing industries entails scientific selection of raw materials, standardization of processing and packaging techniques, effecting improvements in the quality and shelf-life of products, and strict sanitary control in factories and godowns. Various aspects of technical control in the manufacture of cereal products with particular reference to some of the outstanding problems of the industry are dealt with.

The cereals, when processed into one form or other, constitute the main bulk of the dietary of millions of human beings. This basic fact has a great significance for the cereal processor who has to produce economically, palatable, stable and nutritive products. To attain these objectives, research and technical control in the running of our cereal processing and baking industries is a vital necessity.

It is well known that the cereal grain is a highly complex entity. It continues to be the subject of vigorous scientific and technological studies in various countries. A recent survey (1945) of the private industrial research laboratories in the United States revealed that as many as 61 laboratories, involving an aggregate investment of 25 million dollars, were devoted to research on processing of cereals and soyabean. The scientific staff of these laboratories consisted predominantly of chemists and engineers, and numbered 669 and 125 respectively. Besides, the industry liberally sponsored fellowships for fundamental research on cereals in the various Universities, Research Foundations and technical institutions. Recipients of Fellowships, at the end of their terms, often find employment at the sponsoring industry. All this bears testimony to the scientific outlook of the cereal processing and baking industries of the United States. We might think that the United States is a surplus country in food grains, and so, the country can afford to invest money in this direction, but it is not so. The industry itself is well-organized. Let us for a while consider the state of the industry in a heavily deficit country like Britain which normally imports wheat to an extent of 80% of her total requirements. The cereal processors in U.K. are well-organized and have their own Cereal Research Station located at St. de Albans. Recently, the British Baking Industries Research Association has also started its own research laboratories at Chroleywood. In addition to these facilities, services of private consulting and cereal testing laboratories are extensively available to the industry in that country.

We have deliberately referred to the co-operation between scientific organizations and cereal processing and baking industries in Great Britain and the U.S.A., so that our industry may emulate their example and harness science to its aid. *The productive potential and capital investment of the cereal processing and baking industries of our country is large enough to warrant such a measure. The capital investment of the milling industry alone is of the order of rupees 20 crores.* Our biscuit industry is rapidly expanding in spite of various hurdles. The number of registered factories has increased from 33 in 1946 to 79 in 1950. The breakfast food industry is in an infant stage and there is scope for vast expansion. It is amazing to find grocery stores laden with imported breakfast foods selling at higher rates in preference to the indigenous products. The future of flour roller mills which number 81 having a total grinding capacity of 1.8 million tons depends primarily upon the progress of our baking industry. Scientific and technical control in cereal processing and baking industries can be classified under the following 5 heads:

1. Selection of suitable raw materials, by applying scientific tests.
2. Rigorous control and standardization of the processing conditions and mode of packaging.
3. Effecting improvements in the quality and shelf-life of the manufactured products.
4. Use of the latest findings in the fields of milling, baking and technology of breakfast food.
5. Maintenance of strict sanitary conditions in the factories and warehouses.

In order to implement the above suggestions, technical control in our industry, availability of trained scientific personnel and recognition on the part of industry of such a necessity are essential.

Technical enquiries received from the breakfast food and biscuit industries reveal multifarious problems demanding solution. It may not, therefore, be possible to divorce research altogether from technical control. An organized effort on the part of the industry and the establishment of liaison with technical institutions would go a long way in solving various technological problems facing the industry.

Further, the basic quality of our cereal food grains has also to be improved to suit various purposes. Varieties of wheat suited for bread are not equally suited for biscuits. In fact, the success of the British biscuit industry is attributed to the quality of the flour yielded by the soft varieties of English wheats. Biscuit factories in India have to be satisfied with imported wheat flour, whatever its quality. Good varieties of oats required by the breakfast food industry are not grown in India. It seems clear that collaboration between cereal breeders and cereal technologists which is at the moment non-existent in our country should be brought about as early as possible. The first Cereal Technology Laboratory in India was established jointly by the I.C.A.R. and the Punjab Government at the Punjab Agricultural College and Research Institute, Lyallpur, in the year 1939–40, to assist the cereal breeders in the evolution of better quality wheats. This laboratory was equipped with modern cereal testing, milling and baking appliances. But, as a result of the partition, this laboratory is no longer in India. It is to be hoped that similar facilities will soon be available in the Central Food Technological Research Institute, Mysore, for the benefit of the cereal processing industry in the country.

Technical Aid to the Industry

Adverting to some outstanding problems of the industry, referred to this institute, the following information may be of interest.

Breakfast Foods

Packaging and shelf-life of wheat and corn flakes:

The moisture content of flakes is of paramount importance in influencing the shelf-life of the product. At low moisture levels, the product turns rancid, and at high moisture levels, it loses crispness and develops mustiness. We have determined the uptake and equilibrium moisture content of flakes under varying conditions of humidity. A comparative study of the efficiency of the different types of package used by the Indian Breakfast Food Industry has confirmed that the present package is unsatisfactory. Data on water-vapour permeability have shown that the outer carton of the Indian package was not inferior to its foreign counterpart, but the moisture-proof quality of the waxed paper used by the Indian manufacturer was very poor. The Indian flakes cannot, therefore, stand storage in the humid regions, particularly in the coastal towns like Bombay, Madras and Calcutta. The success of foreign varieties of Corn Flakes in distant places of the world, even in humid climates, is attributed to the superior protection which the package affords against the ingress of moisture. Investigations are under way to design a suitable package for the flakes. Co-operation of the Indian Paper Industry in this direction will be of great value.

Insect infestation in packaged Indian breakfast foods:

We had an opportunity to examine a number of packaged Indian breakfast food samples for insect infestation. The results show that the insect infestation occurs mostly in the factories, although the possibility of subsequent infestation, particularly in damp warehouses, cannot be precluded. Living insects were found in closed tins in quite a few cases. Wheat products showed greater degree of infestation than corn flakes did. Thus, this problem is mainly associated with the sanitary conditions prevailing in the factories. A number of chemical and physical methods of disinfestation were tried, and it was found that heat treatment of the products prior to packing was very essential. The product should be packed at about 130°F. The tin cans should also be heat-treated to eliminate any possible contamination. The paper package should be carefully sealed from the top as well as from the bottom. Beetles (*Tribolium spp.*), Indian meal moth (*Plodia interpunctella*) and *Pscocids* were the predominent infecting insects.

Quality of Indian processed oats and causes of spoilage:

In respect of palatability, the Indian processed oats do not approach the imported brands. The results of an organoleptic test on freshly made Indian oats showed that considerable improvement in the flavour of the product was needed. The indigenous product is devoid of the characteristic aroma found in foreign brands. A very common complaint is that our products turn bitter soon after they are made. We have studied the causative factors of bitterness. It is associated with the high free-fatty acid content of Indian products as a result of the survival of the lipolytic enzymes during processing. Adequate steaming of the groats as soon as they are made or of the oats before hulling is an effective remedy. Before the groats are pressed and the products packaged, it is necessary to see that there is no residual lipase activity in the product. The use of insect-infested oats and groats for processing affects adversely the flavour of the finished product.

Shelf-Life of Biscuits

Effects of packaging and antioxidants on the development of rancidity in biscuits:

The biscuits were made with a shortening of m.p. 37°C with and without the incorporation of proprietary brand of the antioxidant (B.H.A.). The results of an extended storage test for about a year show that the inner packaging paper is the main seat of rancidity development as a result of the oxidation of the thin film of absorbed fat from the biscuits. The extracted fat from the biscuit did not show any perceptible change in the peroxide value, whereas the peroxide value of the absorbed fat in the paper was very high. However, organoleptic evaluation tests revealed that the biscuits wrapped in such a paper were rancid. This showed that the biscuits tended to absorb the rancid off-flavour from the wrapping paper. In the case of superior grease-proof paper, very little fat was absorbed and the taste of the biscuits was better. Samples containing the antioxidant and wrapped in superior grease-proof paper were adjudged superior as they retained the characteristic oven-fresh flavour of the product. Storage under accelerated conditions in accordance with the Schaal's test at 60°C very conclusively brought out the carry-through properties of the antioxidant. The control sample developed rancidity in 5 weeks, whereas the sample containing the antioxidant stood well for 12 weeks.

It is felt that the problem of rancidity in biscuits should be tackled in a combined way. Information regarding the stability characteristics of the shortenings made in India is lacking. Melting point of the shortening is not a true index of its suitability for biscuits. Seepage of fat is governed, besides the melting point, by such factors as the moisture content and proportion of non-fat solids to the fat in the biscuit and the quality of grease-proof paper, etc. Extraction rate of the flour and degree of metallic contamination particularly with copper and iron of the various ingredients entering the composition of biscuits and of the inner grease-proof wrapping paper accelerate rancidity. Use of grease-proof paper impregnated with antioxidants has been observed to check rancidity development in various baked products.

MODIFICATION IN SHORTENING FOR BISCUITS

By

M. R. Sahasrabudhe

(*Central Food Technological Research Institute, Mysore*)

The short shelf-life of biscuits made by Indian factories has been found mainly due to quality of the shortening used. The author has found that, by the use of hydrogenated oils of higher melting point (about 42° C) and suitable combinations of antioxidants, the keeping quality of biscuits could be considerably increased.

In spite of the fact that India has a well-developed Vanaspati Industry, no suitable shortenings which can meet all the requirements of the baking industry are manufactured in our country.

The term shortening applies to all fats and oils, like butter, vanaspati, margarine, liquid vegetable oils and animal fats. Shortenings are generally classified into (i) animal fats, lard, (ii) blended shortenings, and (iii) hydrogenated vegetable oils. In India, vegetable oils are used for frying, while hydrogenated groundnut oil is used mostly for baking. There are about 49 vanaspati factories in the country with a total capacity of 3,21,000 million tons, but very few of them manufacture the appropriate shortening for baked goods.

Shortenings used in frying should have the following characteristics: (*a*) they should allow the proper structural development to occur, (*b*) they should be absorbed in relatively constant quantities, and (*c*) they should have the physical characteristics which would prevent their setting too rapidly during cooling.

The shortenings for cake- and biscuit-making should have, in addition to the colour and flavour, the proper consistency, creaming quality, emulsifying capacity and good stability. For biscuits, in particular, the main function of the shortening is to control the development of the gluten giving the product the desired crispness.

In India, the hydrogenated groundnut oil is the main source for bakery shortenings, on account of its availability in large quantities, its ease in processing, and its non-reverting nature. Two or three specific products from hydrogenated groundnut oil have been prepared for biscuit manufacture.

Biscuits should be capable of being stored over long periods without their eating quality being affected. Based on a fairly exhaustive study carried out in the Division of Food Processing, Central Food Technological Research Institute, Mysore, on the storage behaviour of biscuits manufactured by some factories in India, it could be concluded that one of the main factors responsible for the development of rancid and other off-odours in biscuits on storage over short periods is the nature of the shortening used. In our study, indigenous brands of biscuits were compared with similar ones from abroad. Biscuits made in India contained more 'free oil' than the foreign brands.

Moreover, in a tropical country like India, in the absence of air-conditioning facilities, the storage of biscuits becomes a serious problem. One of the important factors influencing the shelf-life of biscuits is the 'free oil' content, *i.e.*, the content of available free oil which oozes out of the biscuits on to the wrappings. It is found that the melting point of the shortening used influences the free oil content. A comparative study of this factor was carried out with biscuits baked with 2 shortenings having different melting points. The 'free oil' contents as determined by the method of Landrock and Proctor[4] are given in Table I. The biscuits containing concentrations of 8%, 10%, 15%, 20% and 30% of two shortenings, I and II, melting at 37°C and 42°C respectively were baked under comparable conditions in the laboratory. Refined oil was used as a control.

TABLE I

Free oil content...48 hour test at 37°C (98.6°F) and 90% R.H.

Shortening	Per cent of fat in biscuits 8	12	15	20	30
Refined oil	1.02	3.2	5.90	6.8	10.2
Shortening I (M.P, 37°C.) ...	0.52	1.06	2.16	4.1	5.0
Shortening II (M.P. 42°C.) ...	0.12	0.48	1.05	1.1	3.1

Observations made on biscuits indicate that the development of rancidity makes its beginning in the 'free oil' which oozes out of the product to the surface of the inner wrapping paper. The major oxidative deterioration takes place on the film of fat formed on the wrapper. It appears therefore that this 'oiling off' can be controlled by the use of a modified shortening.

The above result has further been confirmed by semi-large-scale trials with a shortening which was hydrogenated groundnut oil emulsified with lecithin and monoglyceride and tempered (1, 2). The modification consists in proper emulsification and plasticizing of the shortening in order to make it pliable in the doughts. A further stabilization was achieved by incorporating a mixture of antioxidants and synergists (2), based on a previous study on the comparative evaluation of different antioxidants in groundnut oil and its hydrogenated products (3). The combination consisted of butylated hydroxyanisole, propyl gallate and citric acid.

Biscuits were prepared from wheat flour, sugar, honey, liquid glucose and the modified shortening. A proprietary brand of shortening was used for comparison in control samples. The products were stored under different storage conditions at R.T. 37°C and 60°C (Schaal's accelerated test). Regular periodical observations on the eating quality and organoleptic rancidity development, as well as chemical analysis for peroxide, Kries and acid values were carried out.

The products made with the modified shortenings were found to be generally acceptable over a storage period of 52 weeks as compared with 20 weeks in the case of biscuits made with shortening commonly used. The results clearly indicate the beneficial effects of the modified shortening which increased 2–3 times the shelf-life of biscuits. (Table II). The full experimental details of the study have been reported elsewhere (2).

TABLE II

Organoleptic observations on biscuits stored at 26–27°C

Experimental Batch No.	Shortening	Shelf-life in weeks (Period at which the product was given an average rating below 6)
1	Shortening I	12 weeks
2	Shortening I + BHA ...	16 weeks
3	Shortening BHA + PG + CA	20 weeks
4	Shortening II	26 weeks
5	Shortening II BHA ...	36 weeks
6	Shortening II BHA + PG + CA	52 weeks

BHA = butylated hydroxyanisole: PG = Propyl gallate;
CA = Citric acid.

The use of this shortening does not in any way impair the eating quality or the appearance of the product.

Further investigations on shortenings, packing materials and antioxidants will be carried out to determine the performance of different fats and their blends.

References

1. Sahasrabudhe, M. R. and Bhatia, D. S.—A note on shortening consistency and the shelf-life of biscuits. J. sci. industr. Res. (India), 1953, **12B,** 35.

2. Sahasrabudhe, M. R., Bhatia, D. S. and Subrahmanyan, V.—Effect of shortening consistency and added antioxidants on the keeping quality of biscuits, J. sci. industr. Res. (in press).

3. Sahasrabudhe, M. R.—Comparative evaluation of several antioxidants for groundnut oil and its hydrogenated products, J. sci. industr. Res. (India), 1953, **12B,** 63.

4. Landrock, A. H. and Proctor, B. E.—Modern Packaging, 1951, **24,** 107.

RAW MATERIAL STANDARDS FOR THE INDIAN BARLEY INDUSTRY

By

M. N. Reid

(*Reckitt and Colman of India Ltd., Calcutta*)

The main problem facing this industry is the unavailability of barley of graded and standard specifications, necessary for producing quality products. The author has suggested the formation of a Central Body representing both the Government and the Industry, which should take steps to increase the production and advise on proper sowing, harvesting, cleaning, grading and packing of barley.

From the time of Hippocrates, barley in the form of the decoction popularly known as Barley Water, and in India as *Kunjee,* has afforded a mucilaginous drink, used in convalescence and for infant feeding. In its last use it is known to prevent the formation of large milk curds by its protective colloidal character, and in consequence to aid digestion.

The Barley Milling Industry in India was established by about 1924, with its main centre in Calcutta, to meet these important demands. In spite of the indigenous industry being about 30 years old, there have been a number of problems which have prevented complete fulfilment of the large demands of the country to develop this infant food industry.

The efforts of manufacturers have been hampered largely because of the inadequacy of local grain supplies and also because of the specifications or standards. The methods of dealing in and acquiring grain also require improvement. These facilities to aid the industry are primarily technical and require assistance from the Government and support from the Milling interests.

The opportunity for the Barley products industry to expand has been evident with the cutting off of imports of finished products. In the past, raw materials were easily available from Australia and parts of the Pataudi (India), but they are not so at present.

It may be stated that this industry is one which produces products comparable to imported articles and it is well equipped having modern plant and machinery. But, with the reduction of areas under this particular grain and lack of import of raw materials, the mills are under an ever-present threat of finding themselves idle.

The accent of this Symposium is to see where technical aid to the food industry could be afforded so that they would be in a good position to help themselves.

On this point the first answer which comes to our minds is that the pattern of sampling, storing and buying, as arranged by the Australian Barley Marketing Board, which is Government-sponsored, is perhaps a suitable method for helping to standardize on grain specifications required for the industry.

At the moment, when buying grain, it is quite impossible to buy on a sample because when the bulk supply arrives there is a great deal of variation between the consignment and the representative sample.

It is an important factor to the industry, whether they are Millers, Decorticators or Maltsters, that crops be graded by an independent, partly Government-assisted Central Body who will also help marketing, and ensuring that samples and bulk are similar.

Now that the barley industry would appear to be more and more dependent upon local supplies of grain, it is increasingly important that steps are taken to organize the growers under a mutual scheme supported by the industry and the Government in order to maintain the standards and specifications necessary for producing quality barley products.

Such an authority is most essential to assist and advise on proper harvesting methods. The users of barley grain from local resources find that apart from mixed grain, which is to say grains of different maturity, there is a large percentage of foreign seeds, and grain and dust present in bulk supplies of Indian Barley.

The reason for the grain being mixed is because the barley is grown in small holdings and the acreage sown by individual farmers is small as compared with the areas under barley in other producing countries such as Australia.

A central authority could very easily assist with the problems of storage, movement and also prices. At the moment the ravages of weevils and other grain-destroying insects cause a great loss to the grower, to the quality of products and, last but not the least, to the national exchequer.

In conclusion, the aid required by this industry would be mainly on its raw material side. Such aid should be vested in a State and privately sponsored technical body.

This body would help to overcome the problems of:

1. Inadequacy of local supplies of barley grain due to the fact that the demands of the industry are not clearly known to the farmers.
2. Sowing of grain of suitable quality for the industry.
3. Correct harvesting of grain, its storage and help to rationalize marketing methods.
4. Grading and standards of packing.
5. Refraction and cleaning of the grain which could be organized according to the best standards of the specific user industry.

It is realized that the achievement of these aims and the development of such aid will take time, but nevertheless a strong plea is made that an important indigenous industry continues to suffer because of lack of technical assistance in respect of raw materials which ultimately affect the consumer.

THE BASIC NEED OF THE CHOCOLATE INDUSTRY

By

G. T. Kale

(*Central Food Technological Research Institute, Mysore*)

In this paper the author has put forth a plea for the cultivation of the cocoa plant in this country in order to meet the demands of the Cocoa and Chocolate Industry in India. This industry, unlike most other food industries, suffers from the handicap of lack of the basic raw material, viz., cocoa beans, in the country. This state of affairs should be changed and efforts made to find suitable areas for the cultivation of disease-free cocoa plants on a plantation-scale.

THE *Cacao* plant (*Theobroma cacao*, L.) from which the *cacoa* of commerce is derived belongs to the Natural Order *Sterculiaceae* and has its home in the Amazon and Orinoco valleys in eastern Venezuela. From these areas, where the plant was said to be in cultivation even before the discovery of America, economic types slowly spread to other parts of the continent and to Africa, West Indies, Asia and Oceania. By 1850, the world production of cocoa beans was of the order of 16,500 tons; by 1900, it reached 100,000 tons and in 1950 it was 768,000 tons (1). This spectacular increase in output was accompanied by a shift in production from America to Africa, though these two continents, with 9–10 producing countries in each, accounted, in 1950–51, for about 93% of the world production of raw cocoa. Africa alone produced 514,000 tons which exceeded the aggregate production of the rest of the world. In Africa, the country with the highest production is the Gold Coast with a production of about 262,000 tons; in America, Brazil with about 131,000 tons and in the West Indies, the Dominican Republic with 27,000 tons. In Asia and Oceania, Ceylon and Western Samoa stand almost on a par with an annual production of 2,000 tons each. India is not on the map of cocoa-producing countries.

Demand

During pre-war years, India was importing cocoa and chocolate at a steady rate of 229–254 tons per year. It is said that half of these imports were of cocoa powder and half of covering chocolate. During war-time, imports were restricted, and in 1944 they were about 134 tons.

The restriction on imports also gave an impetus to the establishment of a cocoa and chocolate industry in India. The import figures during the latter part of the war and the post-war periods, which are shown under 'Cocoa and Chocolate' in the *Accounts of Sea-borne Trade of India* may therefore be assumed to include those of cocoa beans required by the cocoa and chocolate industry in India. Under the plan of allocations of cocoa beans by the Combined Food Board and the Ministry of Food, London, India received her quota from Ceylon. It is stated that the beans from Ceylon were not of the same quality as those from West Africa or Brazil. The Indian Tariff Board recommended that facilities should be granted to the industry for imports of cocoa beans from any part of the world and that the 30 per cent *ad valorem* duty on cocoa beans should be abolished (2). These facilities tended to increase the imports of cocoa beans in subsequent years. The average annual demand during the years 1935–37 was about 237 tons and that during 1942–44 was 276 tons. The imports increased to 581 tons valued at Rs. 20 lakhs in 1948. The demand for cocoa and chocolate is increasing and it is estimated that it would soon exceed 1,000 tons a year.

Need for Cocoa-growing in India.

Thus, it will be seen that the cocoa and chocolate industry in India has to depend entirely on foreign sources both for the quantity and quality of the supplies of the cocoa bean. Unlike most other food industries, this industry suffers therefore from the basic handicap of the lack of its main raw material in the country. This is perhaps the greatest single factor which stands in the way of the full development of this industry. On account of this, the working season, which could be extended to 12 months in factories with air conditioning installations to meet the requirements of temperature, has now to be cut down to 5–6 months in a year. Further, the quality of imported beans is not always uniform. It is important that, concomitantly with the grant of facilities for imports, attempts should be made to grow disease-resistant, high yielding and good quality cocoa in the country in order to make the industry self-sufficient with respect to its raw material. India is fortunate in having a wide range of soil and climatic conditions and it should not be difficult to find suitable areas for cocoa cultivation. Cocoa-nut, rubber, bananas, etc., which are interplanted as shade plants for cocoa in other countries can grow and are already grown on a large scale in India.

It is well known that the economic cultivation of cocoa is limited to the belt between the latitude 20°N and 20°S. Within this belt lies a good part of India, south of Nasik in the West and Puri in the east. Like the cashew, the cacao tree thrives in a warm, moist climate and attains a height of even 40 ft. For reasons of yield, quality etc., the height of the tree is maintained at 20 ft. in plantations. The highest and lowest ranges of temperature required for the plant are 65°–95°F and 65°–70°F. Experience in Kallar and Burliar Fruit Stations (near Mettupalyam) shows that cocoa plants in these localities do well even in the temperature ranges of 80°–100°F and 45°–60°F (3). Low altitudes (500′–2000′) with higher night temperatures and a well-distributed rainfall of 60″–100″ and a retentive but well-drained soil mainly of pumice origin are some of the essential pre-requisites for the growth of this plant. It is considered that areas like Wynad, Lower Palnis, the Agency Tracts, West Coast, Nilgiris (lower slopes), Kolli hills, Yercaud and Javadi hills may be potential cocoa lands.

Well-known varieties of cocoa

The two varieties of cocoa which have found favour with planters and manufacturers are Criollo and Forastero. They can be likened to the two species of coffee: *C. Arabica* and *C. robusta* respectively, grown in South India. Criollo is valued for its quality and flavour, whereas Forastero, like *Coffea robusta,* is popular on account of its robust growth and high yields. The Criollo pods are characterized by a comparatively soft wall with prominent warty ridges and furrows, and contain plump or rounded seeds, white to pale violet or purple in colour. The Forastero pods have a hard and smoother wall and contain more or less flattened seeds of a deep purple colour. In common with coffee, the cocoa beans have to be fermented, roasted and cured in order to bring out their typical flavour. After fermentation, the colour of Criollo kernels changes from white to pale brown, and that of Forastero to violet, purple, purple brown or brown. It is the last strain of Forastero which is considered most desirable for cultivation.

Search for Planting Material

If cocoa plantations are to be firmly established in India, it is necessary to undertake this task in a systematic manner, on the same lines as has been done with wheats and potatoes in other countries with very beneficial results. In the case of these crop plants, as many varieties as possible were collected from different countries, and especially from their home lands, for testing and breeding work. This is particularly necessary when the soil and climatic conditions where a plant is to be introduced are new to it. The work and findings of the Kallar and Burliar Fruit Stations will be of great value so far as the Criollo type of cocoa is concerned. It may be mentioned, however, that Criollo contributes to about 5% of the world production of cocoa. In view of this, ways and means will have to be considered to grow the more sturdy high-yielding, disease-resistant and early types of Forastero. The home of Forastero is Venezuela where is was originally known as Trinitario or Carupano. The crop itself is an assemblage of types and forms which, in plantation parlance, are known as Amelonado, Angoleta, Cundeamor, Calabacillo, etc. The Angoleta sub-variety is reported to possess characters which approach those of Criollo. Amelonado, on account of its high yields, supplies the best part of the world production of cocoa. Botanists, plant pathologists, representatives of the departments of agriculture, food institutions and of the industry should be sent on study tours and expeditions to collect the necessary planting materials: buds, budwood, seeds, seedlings, and rooted cuttings of these and other varieties for trials and breeding in suitable areas in India. Special care will have to be exercised in selecting plants which are resistant to diseases, particularly virus diseases of the type of 'Swollen shoot' which has been a threat to cocoa plantations in the Gold Coast and elsewhere.

Encouragement for Cocoa-growing

It may be mentioned that, by and large, the world's cocoa plantation industry has been a development of the past fifty years. Countries which did not grow cocoa 30–40 years ago are now producing substantial quantities of this commodity. There is a keen trend of expansion of cocoa cultivation in several countries in the eastern hemisphere. The methods generally adopted comprise (*a*) prospecting for potential cocoa lands, (*b*) introduction of right types of cocoa, and (*c*) encouraging the cocoa cultivation in all possible ways. Cocoa plants were introduced in India about 30 years ago, but their development on plantations scale has not yet materialized. Some preliminary work has already been done as regards the potential cocoa areas in South India. Early action should be taken to procure the necessary planting material. Various incentives including subsidies should be given to small growers and planters, and commercial firms with capital resources should be invited to start cocoa plantations. At the average production level of 700 lb. an acre, an acreage of 10,000 under cocoa will make a significant difference to the indigenous cocoa and chocolate industry. It is of urgent necessity that, in India, cocoa-growing should be started as a matter of policy and steps taken to implement it along these lines. It will then be reasonable to expect that, in the course of the next few years, the industry will develop to its full stature and it will be in a position to supply its nutritious products such as cocoa, chocolate etc., at economic prices to the common man in India and abroad.

References

1. Byles, L. A., *Trends in the production and consumption of raw cocoa*, Cocoa Conference, London, 1951, p. 3.

2. Director of Agriculture, Madras, *Cocoa—its importance to South India and cultural possibilities*, The Madras Agr. J., 1951, **38**, 8, 377.

3. Indian Tariff Board, *Report of the Indian Tariff Board on the cocoa powder and chocolate industry*. Bombay, 1946, 21 pp.

TECHNICAL AID TO CONFECTIONERY INDUSTRY

By

K. Lakkappa

(*Chemist-in-charge, Confectionery, The Mysore Sugar Co., Ltd., Mandya*)

The author has drawn attention to the need for utilization of high-grade raw materials and sanitary controls in the production of high class confectionery products. In order to produce confectionary economically, ways and means have to be devised for the production of essential auxiliary raw materials such as essences, flavours, colours and packaging materials in India. This necessitates intensive research and close co-operation between the Industry and various Research Institutes in the country.

CONFECTIONERY products are in increasing demand in this country. It should be indeed all the more so because of the fact that the *per capita* consumption of sugar in India is far below that in Western Countries. This industry in India has therefore a bright future and great care should be bestowed on the manufacture of high grade confectionery and its sales.

Right from the stage of the cooking pan till the confectionery reaches the consumer, the modern factories handle the product with skill and according to specific hygienic standards. But, if the dealers handle the material carelessly, the very object of the maintenance of quality and keeping the product free from contamination is defeated. To illustrate this point, let me take the example of street vendors of various food commodities. They carry the material in dirty containers, expose it to attacks of micro-organisms, allow dust to settle on it, and handle it throughout with unclean hands. Innocent children who buy the materials will naturally be victims to diseases. Such things should be stopped at any cost in the larger interests of the country.

In order to discharge this difficult duty, Research Institutes will have to play their part. They will have to help setting up standards on the quality of food materials sold in the market so that they contain the requiste quantities of nutritious materials. In this connection, the Department of Health and others concerned should co-operate and see that only healthy food materials are sold in the market in the hygienic way. They should visit food industries, big and small, and find out whether the location of the factory, the water and other raw materials are satisfactory, whether the workmen are healthy, whether the processing is up to the mark and then certify the quality of the finished products. This means that the research institutions must have direct contacts with food industries and assist them to maintain high standards. The Research Laboratories have to work like a team to standardize routine tests etc., and to impart the results of their work to the industry to enable it to solve its problems.

It should be borne in mind that with low quality raw materials, it is not possible to manufacture high quality products. Hence, the quality of raw materials has to be rigidly controlled. Economical processing is another important factor which is beneficial both to the manufacturer and the country. Sugar is the most important raw material for the Confectionery Industry. Even in the highest grade refined sugar, there are differences in the minute contents of impurities in the mother liquor sourrounding the crystals, thus resulting in wide variations of the final product. Hence, the selection of a suitable grade of sugar for confectionery manufacture is an important factor. It is well known that confectionery manufacturers require large quantities of liquid glucose. The research institutions should suggest ways of manufacturing this material in India, which will result in saving considerable dollar-exchange. Glucose is the most satisfactory medium for controlling degree of granulaton in Sugar Confectionery.

High-class, boiled sweets are also made without corn syrup (liquid glucose) by the addition of cream of tartar during final stages of boiling. Since the solubility of invert sugar is greater than that of sucrose, this results in the increase of osmotic pressure which prevents fermentation as a result of rupture of the yeast cells. Invert sugar is manufactured from sugar by the use of either invertase or acids or acid salts.

Large quantities of citric acid are used in confectionery production and this material, instead of being imported, may be manufactured in our country either from molasses or tamarind by the well known fermentation process, using the micro-organism, *Aspergillus niger*. Both these raw materials are plentifully available in India.

Various essences and essential oils are also used in this industry on a large scale. How far can indigenous products replace the imported materials is a matter which should be carefully investigated by research organizations. Also, if the essences made from indigenous products lack in certain characteristics, the method of fortifying the same with synthetic essences to bring them to the standard of imported ones is another interesting problem for study and research. This will involve the production of synthetic flavours and extraction of essential oils from available indigenous products. Let us take the example of citrus fruits. By throwing away orange and lemon peels as waste, valuable materials like pectin, orange oil, lemon oil etc., are lost. While supplying fruit juices in cans or bottles, we have to think of utilizing the peels for extraction of the valuable flavouring materials present in them. In the same way, we have to take into consideration the exploitation of other indigenous fruits and spices grown in the country. When the processes are perfected, the imports of foreign materials can be stopped, which will result in enormous savings of foreign exchange.

Production of food colours is another problem to be tackled in India. The colouring is done with the object of making the goods attractive. For many years, colouring was done with products of vegetable origin, but now it consists mostly of synthetic dye-stuffs. Colouring matters are subject to fading and hence it is necessary to produce fast colours suitable for use in the confectionery.

We have to plan not only to be self-sufficient regarding these materials, but also to be able to export the materials to neighbouring countries. Then alone we may hope to enrich our country. This will be possible if the results of research are transferred from the laboratory-scale to large-scale production. Also, research workers have to be on the alert to find out suitable substitutes either for imported products or for indigenous ones which are likely to be exhausted or are insufficient for our requirements. Regarding the machinery required, there is vast scope for production of most of it, though not all, in our country.

Before concluding, a word about packaging will not be out of place. It is not enough that a smaller manufacturer equals or excels the quality of products of established brands. He has to ensure that his package is more attractive than that presented by his competitors. A pictorial description of contents enables the customer to make a quick selection of the material he intends to buy. Now-a-days, the sale trend is towards packaged merchandize and this is due to the rapid development of high-speed wrapping and packaging machinery.

Confectionery of hygroscopic nature requires protection against the ingress of moisture and, as far as possible, against exposure to high temperatures. While packing, the goods should be held in an atmosphere of low humidity, not exceeding 60%, to obtain the best results. In the protection of the confectionery against exposure to high temperatures, the control lies in the process of its manufacture. Attempts are worth making to produce suitable wrapping papers in our country and also to find out suitable substitutes for tin containers which are used abundantly in the confectionery industry.

I, for one, feel certain that the Central Food Technological Research Institute, Mysore, will be a source of great inspiration and assistance to existing food industries, and also for starting new food industries in the country.

I wish to thank Dr V. Subrahmanyan, Director of the Institute, and the authorities of the Mysore Sugar Co. Ltd., Mandya for giving me this opportunity to present my views on this important subject.

SOME TECHNICAL PROBLEMS OF THE CONFECTIONERY INDUSTRY IN INDIA

By

S. N. Gundu Rao and H. R. S. Iyengar

(*Ravalgaon Sugar Farm Ltd., Ravalgaon*)

The authors have detailed, in this paper, some of the technical problems that face the confectionery industry in India. These problems relate to the quality of raw materials, processing equipment, technical know-how, packaging and storage of confectionery. The means of enhancing the nutritive value and fortifying confectionery by vitamins and minerals for combating nutritional deficiencies are also dealt with.

THE Sugar Confectionery in India recorded a very rapid progress during the period 1940–1950. This was mostly due to the cessation of imports and an increased internal demand for confectionery products. The significant feature of this development was that the sugar factories, the producers of the chief raw material, *i.e.*, sugar, themselves put up new confectionery manufacturing plants or expanded their already existing units. Such an expansion by sugar factories also received encouragement and support from Government who appreciated the special advantages that the sugar factories had for developing the industry on effcient and sound economic lines, the absence of which was the feature of this industry during the pre-war years. Apart from the availability of the chief raw material, sugar, at ex-factory prices, steam and power are available at nominal costs as also technical supervision, workshop, laboratory and research facilities. One can even foresee the necessary packing materials forthcoming from the waste products of the sugar industry such as bagasse, trash etc., and the acids and flavours from the fermentation of molasses and sugar. The dairy products required for these industries can come out of the dairy farm, for developing which, the sugarcane farm with its extensive farming and green cane tops provides special advantages. Such a dairy farm would also serve to maintain a favourable cycle of soil fertility of the farm.

Technical Problems

In common with many other food industries, the technical problems relate not only to the quality of production, but also to its shelf life, *i.e.*, its keeping quality till it is consumed. Both these aspects are considerably inter-related and depend on the consumption of the materials entering into the product, processing conditions, equipment and storage. The need for a thorough study of these aspects and achievement of a very high standard of quality becomes necessary, particularly when we think of exporting Indian confectionery in competition with manufacturers in foreign countries.

During the last few years, the confectionery industry has faced great vicissitudes due to the changing control policy of the Government and unhealthy competition from spurious small-scale producers. With a view to ensuring improvement in the quality of the confectionery produced by its members, the Confectionery Manufacturers' Association set up a committee to lay down minimum quality standards. Further studies should be made to examine if these standards laid down by the Association's Technical Committee could be improved to achieve the objective. Such a study for laying down specifications and analytical limits for quality confections would require considerable analytical work. Another problem before the Association is the laying down of minimum standards of hygiene and sanitation as also permissible limits of harmful substances in confections. The industry would welcome the study and guidance in evolving the above standards. The practical aspects of efficient enforcement will have to be considered by the Government.

Raw Materials

Sugar, the chief raw material, has to be of the best quality corresponding to the refined sugar used by foreign confectioners. Sugar produced by carbonation is superior to that produced by sulphitation. The major production of sugar in India is by the latter method. In using sulphitation sugars, every care should be taken to see that it is very pure and contains as low a proportion of sulphur dioxide as possible. Another important ingredient that enters into confectionery is the confectioners' glucose or corn syrup. This is an important product obtained mostly from America and to some extent from Holland. Medium conversion glucose with a dextrose equivalent of about 42 is what is generally used and recommended. The price of this ingredient has been subject to very great fluctuations and it is high time that this material is produced in India. A few firms have been manufacturing liquid glucose in India, but the quality is far from satisfactory, the dextrose equivalent of this syrup is often high, pH is too low, and it is not free from colour. The price is also very high. The manufacturers of this product would obviously need encouragment and technical aid for manufacturing the product of quality and at cheap cost. Citric acid and tartaric acid, particularly the former, is required in considerable quantities by the confectionery industry. Every effort should be made to produce these commercially in India. It is understood, that some efforts in this direction are being made at the National Chemical Laboratory. Some manufacturers in India have been offering flavours and essences suitable for the confectionery industry. These firms will have to be encouraged and it should be seen that these are not merely firms who blend imported chemicals, but that the entire requirements are made from raw materials available in India. The Dyestuff Industry is making considerable headway in India and these manufacturers should now direct their attention to the manufacture of edible colours for use in the confectionery and beverage industries. The manufacture of toffee would require the products of the dairy industry. Obviously, therefore, development of the dairy industry would be very important, if toffee manufacture is not to depend on imported condensed milk and milk powder.

The above are only a few of the raw materials that enter into the manufacture of the numerous types of confections. With the availability of various types of nuts, fruits and other products in India, there is no doubt that sooner or later these will enter into the composition of our confections and, as such, they require a thorough study and examination.

Processing Equipment

Equipment used in sweets manufacture is from the simplest machines to the most complicated ones. Modern automatic food processing and packing equipment represents the typical modern chemical engineering development and skill. There are some firms in India which have successfully designed and produced certain equipment. It is high time that a beginning is made in the direction of producing equipment for the confectionery and other food industries in India.

Moisture Absorption, Stickiness and Creaming

With hard-boiled confections, the greatest problem is moisture absorption, stickiness and creaming. Hard-boiled goods are the most popular confections, but at the same time, the most difficult to produce. These confections, which are glassy and transparent, are of the nature of super-cooled colloids, the granulation tendencies of the sugar being controlled by invert sugar or the dextrose and dextrins of corn syrup or in some confections by gum and gelatin. Invert sugar, and particularly fructose, has the tendency to absorb moisture. The moisture absorption depends on the invert sugar content, on the decomposition products during processing and the residual moisture in the final product. These tendencies for moisture absorption are very much reduced if the invert sugar content is controlled between 10% and 12% and the residual moisture below 1% (vapour pressure of the product at less than 20). For controlling invert sugar content in the product care should be taken in using good quality sugar, good water with pH near 7.0 (distilled water or steam condensates being preferable) and standard neutral invert sugar. If the invert sugar content is too low, there is a tendency for creaming either during processing or in a short time after storages. Such a creaming spoils the appearance of these confections. Where a cutting agent or 'doctor' is used, its quantity in relation to the temperature and time of boiling requires rigorous control. Confectioners' glucose or corn syrup of medium conversion is a much safer material to use. For controlling the time and temperature of boiling very good equipment is now available. The Baker Perkins Microfilm Cooker has reduced the time of boiling to 8 seconds. The V. H. R. Cooker of Baker Perkins enables the final stages of boiling at high temperatures to be eliminated, the last stages of moisture removal being done under vacuum. The Ureka Continuous Vacuum Cooker reduces both the temperature of boiling as well as the time of boiling and represents the ideal machine for boiled sweets production. Absolutely clear boilings without colour formation and with moisture contents below 1% can be obtained with this machine. The shelf life of boiled goods made with this machine is the longest. The problem with this machine, however, is that it is not easily possible to carry out sugar invert boilings with the minimum invert sugar contents. Some suitable procedure or solution to the problem of making of boiled sweets with the vacuum type of cooker without the need of glucose would be very helpful. Suitable edible and highly protective colloids will have to be found which, when added to the normal sugar invert mixture, will prevent granulation at the high turbulance obtaining in the vacuum cooker.

Certain parts of the processing and packing sections have to be air-conditioned. The material should actually leave the air conditioned section in hermetically sealed containers into air conditioned stores. The best conditions for the hard candy processing and packing sections as well as for storage room are 70°–75°F, with a relative humidity of 40–45%. Conditions of transport and shop sales in India are very unfavourable for the shelf life of the confections. These are, however, beyond the control of the manufacturer, but even so every organizational effort will have to be made to ensure that these conform to the requirements of longer shelf life so that consumers will get as fresh a product as possible.

Colour and Polish Fading

The edible colours used in confectionery are mostly synthetic. The rapid fading of these colours by which the sweets lose their attractive appearance is a very important problem to the manufacturer. Sometimes it is due to the excessive sulphur dioxide contained in the sugar and in other cases fading may be due to exposure to light, to high temperatures etc. Investigations into the ways and means of maintaining the bright colours for long periods in the finished confections particularly the goods of the coated type, COMFITS, which fade on keeping are very necessary. These confections are generally glazed by using some waxes like bees' wax, paraffin wax, carnauba wax, shellac etc. It would be interesting to investigate into the causes responsible for this fading and to evolve suitable procedures to ensure permanent glaze on these types of confections.

Utilization of Confectionery Wastes

In spite of care in handling and re-use of confectionery waste considerable proportions of various types of confectionery scrap accumulate in the factory. All these being of complex compositions which have undergone changes in processing, present problems. This is particularly so with boiled goods containing sugar, glucose, acids, colours and flavours of all types. It would greatly benefit the industry if proper methods of utilization could be found for these wastes. At present the best procedure appears to be to recover the sugar and glucose without further inversion and re-use in the hard-boil mix in regulated quantities. The process involves neutralizing the acid with milk of lime at high temperatures adjusting the final reaction to 6.5–6.8 pH, filtering, treating the filtrate with activated carbon, and concentrating. The wastes either as such or after treatment in the above manner can also be used in the manufacture of some varieties of jams, jellies, edible syrups, etc.

Rancidity and Anti-Oxidants

Another important and difficult problem met with in some types of confectionery like toffee etc., which contain fats, is the development of rancidity. Rancidity that occurs in the fats entering into the confectionery are of two types (1) Oxidative and (2) Hydrolytic. The former is caused by atmospheric oxygen acting on the active unsaturated compounds in the fats. To some extent this is reduced by using hydrogenated vegetable fats which are more stable or also by choosing fats which have a low iodine value. The hydrolytic rancidity is due to the presence of water and is promoted by amounts of enzymes, acids and alkalies. Certain metals such as copper, iron and nickel as also certain pigments have been found to increase the oxidative changes resulting in rancidity. There are many types of anti-oxidants which have been offered for preventing rancidity in confectionery. Many naturally occurring substances such as the tocopherols of the wheat germ oil or carrot oil and lecithin of soya bean or corn oil have anti-oxidant properties. Substances like citric, tartaric and phosphoric acids have the properties of increasing the life of the anti-oxidants in the confections and are termed 'Synergists'. Of these may be mentioned the Octyl and Dodesylgallate and the N.D.G.A. (Nordihydroguaiaretic acid) and the bivalent phenols. Though these anti-oxidants are required in much smaller quantities, they are specific in their action and their cost is very high. Further, there are differences of opinion as to the effects on the human constitution by constant use of these compounds. Certain articles very familiar to us such as tea extract, garlic and some species are considered very effective either as anti-oxidants or in masking the rancid taste. Intensive investigations are, therefore, very necessary to find out cheap indigenous anti-oxidants which are safe to human health even on continued use. The economic importance of this investigation can be realized when one finds large numbers of tins of toffee which have become rancid and are unfit for consumption.

Increasing the Nutritional Value of Confectionery

Considerable criticism has been levelled against pure sugar confectionery, that it supplies only calories and that it has no nutritional value. Dental caries has also been ascribed to the excessive consumption of highly refined carbohydrates. There is no doubt that the use of sugars and starches will lessen the ingestion of food needed for the maintenance of normal nutrition. Enrichment of candy with vitamins, minerals and other nutrients is helpful in overcoming the above criticism. Toffee, however, is a very rich food in so far as it contains, in addition to the sugar and glucose, considerable quantities of fat and milk solids. With new developments in the technique of making confectionery, such as soft-centre fillings, it is possible to incorporate into the various hard-boiled goods, delicious and nutritious pasters and liquids made of fruits, nuts and other ingredients suitably reinforced with vitamins and minerals. There is no doubt that confectionery presents the most suitable medium in making up the vitamin and mineral deficiencies in the diets of children.

The technique of vitaminizing the confections will have to be perfected. Vitamins, A, B, and C being heat-labile require 20 to 25% more addition as a safety factor against manufacturing and storage losses. Vitamins A and D, which are fat-soluble will have to be incorporated suitably dissolved in the fatty material entering manufacture. The water-soluble vitamins, viz., B complex and vitamin C are added to the sugar either in the dry or liquid state. All these are first prepared into a small pre-mix and then thoroughly incorporated into the main mass to ensure uniform composition. The additions are to be based on the estimate of daily consumption of the sweets by the average child or individual. This estimate becomes very incorrect when we consider the wide variations in the sweets consumption in India. One safety factor, however, is that within limits a little excess of vitamins may not be harmful. This being an entirely new field to the confectionery manufacturers in India, considerable investigation is called for.

Cocoa and Chocolate Industry

The technical problems of the Cocoa and Chocolate Industry in India primarily relate to the very adverse climatic conditions of high temperature. Air-conditioning of the factory as well as of the vehicles of transport would be necessary if this industry is to work throughout the year. Cocoa and chocolate being very highly nutritious and most popular are increasing in demand. It is understood that some experiments have been attempted to use the higher melting point fractions of the cocoa fat for the tropical conditions. Much should not be expected from this, as the beauty of the chocolate melting in the mouth would cease to exist if such a high melting fat comes to be used. There are other problems in processing like fat bloom and sugar bloom which have been sufficiently studied and the causes found out.

Packaging of Confectionery

The packaging of confectionery varies from bulk packings and small packings to the wrapping of the smallest individual sweet. The materials used for packing are numerous and consist of materials like cellophane, glassine, alkathene films, waxed and ordinary paper, paper and box boards, tin sheets and wooden crates and packing boxes. A number of these materials are at present being imported.

Some of the indigenous Rayon factories are making cellophane. This, however, is not suitable for confectionery packing, since packing materials for wrapping sugar products should have the special properties of being moisture-proof and heat-sealable. It is suggested that firms in India start making the special types of cellophane required for packing confectionery. Even the printing on cellophane is not satisfactorily done in India. Some firms have made a start in this direction. In the absence of sufficient quantity of tin plates, the development of other types of moisture-proof and air-tight packagings for confectionery is urgent. Indigenous woods used for packing cases are not satisfactory. They do not have the required lightness combined with strength. The attention of various forest departments is requested to the increasing need for packing wood in India, suitable types of which should be cultivated in our forests.

It is said that 'nothing sells candy like candy itself'. While this is true with displayed candies, it is more often the package with the 'BUY ME' appeal that sells the best. The packing has to be strong, attractive and air-tight. It is desirable to examine if certain types of confectionery, such as toffee, which are liable to oxidative changes, can be packed with advantage in vacuum gas packings in metal containers.

Very closely related to packing, advertisement and sales of confectionery is the industrial art. It is high time that industrial art and the creative genius associated with display, planning and advertisement are developed in India.

New Lines

Confectionery of the types at present being made in India are mere imitations of foreign confections and in most cases indigenous products are very poor imitations of the corresponding foreign brands. The drawback in the Indian Sweets Industry is that it has been confined to the small producer without the backing of modern scientific and technical developments. Some of the Indian confections are very good. It is suggested that a thorough study should be made of some of the selected types of Indian sweets which can lend themselves to large-scale production using modern methods and equipment. Where necessary, the composition of the confection or the design of the equipment could be altered. Even the processing details could be modified whereever possible to retain the maximum food value in the sweet. If with Indian raw materials new lines are evolved, there is no doubt that they could be exported to foreign countries.

Training and Research

There is a very great need for an extensive course of training covering the fields of confectionery-chemistry, engineering and food technology. Food industry itself being new to India, there is no doubt that the Institute of Food Technology can be looked forward to, to be of the greatest service to the development of the Indian Food Industry by becoming the centre for training and research in the diverse fields of food technology.

PROBLEMS CONNECTED WITH THE DEVELOPMENT OF INDIAN SWEETS INDUSTRY

By

W. B. Date

(Central Food Technological Research Institute, Mysore)

In this paper, the author has stated that Indian sweets form quite a sizable portion of the Indian diet. The industry is now run on a cottage-scale and no attempt has been made so far to standardize the preparation of Indian sweets. The keeping quality of Indian sweets is also very poor. The author has drawn attention to the need for research on problems of packaging, canning and storage of Indian sweets. Preliminary work done at the C.F.T.R.I. has shown that, by the addition of suitable antioxidants, the shelf-life of commodities like 'Besan wadi' and 'Shrikhand wadi' could be considerably extended.

SWEETS comprise quite a sizeable part of our dietary. In Indian homes, preparation of sweets is usually associated with religious or social functions. The methods of preparation of sweets in India differ greatly from those in Western countries. Moreover, there are a number of types of sweet-meat prepared in India, each being characteristic of the place of production. Besides, the method of preparation and the ingredients that go into the sweets differ widely, depending upon the ingenuity of the manufacturer.

Some cheap varieties of Indian sweets are 'Battasa', 'Gurpapadi' and 'Chirongi', while some typical expensive varieties are 'Rasagoolas', 'Pedhas', 'Burfee', 'Sonpapadi', 'Halwas', etc. The most essential ingredients of these sweets are sugar, milk, ghee and some kinds of cereal or non-cereal flours. On the other hand, the so-called European *bon-bons* are made from sugar, flavouring materials, milk, butter, cocoa butter and various kinds of nuts.

A Small-scale Industry:

The preparation of the highly delicious sweets in India is a delicate art handed down from generation to generation and it is mostly done by a set of people known as *Halwais* in every town. The turn-over by any outfit is limited and is never more than what could be sold within a fortnight or so. The gross turn-over of Indian sweets is difficult to estimate. However, the enormous quantity of Indian sweets made in the country is revealed by the fact that about 100,000 tons of sugar are consumed for the preparation of a variety of Indian sweetmeats every year.

Composition and nutritive value:

From an examination of the formulae of different Indian sweets, it is found that they contain a high proportion of fat, in the form of either vanaspati or ghee. They are also rich in sugar. Bengali sweets contain a high proportion of moisture, whereas those made in North India and West India are mostly of a dry nature. Some preparations like 'Jilebi' have a certain amount of sugar syrup inside the product.

No data are available so far on the chemical composition of Indian sweets with respect to sugar, fat, protein, vitamins etc. An examination of a typical sample of *Besan wadi* has shown the following composition: proteins 10%, sugar 34% and fat 30%. Such information in respect of other sweets will be useful.

Since the main constituents are fat, sugar and some cereal or legume Indian sweets are very nutritious. They are in most cases, compact in nature and hence are convenient for use on special as well as emergency occasions. Their caloric value per lb. ranges from 1,500 to 2,000 which will certainly meet the sustenance requirements of an individual. Such sweets can, therefore, be used as an emergency ration-pack for the defence services. The food values of different sweets, however, have not been reported so far. The well-known D-Ration or the Survival Ration of the U.S. Defence Services comprises of confectionery products only. The R.A.F. Emergency Ration is made of milk toffee, hard-boiled candy, etc. Sweets like *Besan wadi* or *Shrikhand wadi,* besides having the same calorific value for a unit weight, have better nutritive value than that of sweets of the Western type.

Preservation Problems:

Sweets are perishable commodities. If suitable precautions are not taken to protect them against long exposures, they are liable to become inedible. A food processor has, therefore, to take the utmost precautions to protect them against contamination, infection, and rancidity. The role of some of the antioxidants in checking the development of rancidity in foods is now well known. The mode of packing also plays a very important role in checking rancidity. Research is, therefore, needed to find out the best and, at the same time, the most economical methods of processing and packaging Indian sweets.

Work in Progress:

Investigations on the keeping quality of products like *Besan wadi* and *Shrikhand wadi* carried out at the Central Food Technological Research Institute, Mysore, have shown that the shelf-life of these sweets is not very satisfactory. The work was planned to study the following aspects: (*a*) improvements in the usual formulae: reduction of the amount of fat and use of blended fats to reduce seepage and rancidity, (*b*) incorporation of a suitable antioxidant in the product, (*c*) increasing the nutritive value by using cheaper foods and by increasing the mineral and vitamin contents, and (*d*) canning of sweets and devising methods of packaging in suitable packaging materials. Results so far obtained have shown that Indian sweets undergo spoilage within a couple of months after their preparation. Products like *Besan wadi, Burfee,* when treated with antioxidants, have kept well for as long as 8 months. It has also been observed that the reduction of fat in any recipe to the lowest level possible is helpful in prolonging the keeping quality of the product. The use of blended fats, mixture of low- and high-melting point fats, have given still more satisfactory results. This investigation is being extended to other varieties of Indian sweets.

Prospects:

Indian sweets have the potentiality of building up a foreign trade, particularly in the Middle East and Far East countries. It is therefore necessary to develop this industry on systematic lines.

NAME OF SWEETS	REGION WHERE POPULAR	PRINCIPAL COMPONENTS OF THE SWEET
1. *Anarse*	Bombay, M.P.	Rice, Sugar, Fat
2. *Balushai*	Gujerath	Gram flour, Sugar, Fat
3. *Bundi*	All over India	Gram or Pea flour Sugar, Fat.
4. *Burfi*	,,	Khoa, Sugar and dry fruits.
5. *Darbesh*	North India	Gram flour, Rice flour Sugar, Khoa, Fat, Ary fruits.
6. *Gathe*	Gujerath	Gram flour, Maida, Sugar, Fat.
7. *Golabjam*	Bengal, Bihar, Orissa	Khoa, arrowroot, Sugar, Fat.
8. *Halwa*	All over India	Sarustina (Wheat), Sugar, Fat.
9. *Jehangir*	North India	Sarustina, Rice flour, Sugar, Fat.
10. *Jilebi*	,,	Gram flour, Sugar, Fat.
11. *Kalascand*	,,	Khoa, Sugar
12. *Ladoos & Wadis* of diff. kinds	All over India	Cereal or pulse flour, Sugar, Fat and Gums.
13. *Lady canning*	Bengal	Channa, Khoa flour, Sugar, Fat.
14. *Mysore pak*	South India	Gram flour, Sugar, Fat.
15. *Motichur*	North India	Gram flour, Sugar, Fat
16. *Pedhas*	All over India	Khoa, Sugar.
17. *Petha*	North India	Sugar, Ash gourd.
18. *Rabdi*	,,	Milk, Sugar.
19. *Rasagolla*	Bengal, Bihar, Orissa	Channa, Starch, Sugar;
20. *Raskara* or *Kobrimithai*	All over South India	Cocoanut, Sugar
21. *Rewadi*	North India	*Til* or Sesamum, Sugar
22. *Roshmalai*	Bengal, Bihar	Channa, Starch, Sugar
23. *Sajappa*	South India	Jaggery, Fat, Cocoanut, Wheat flour.
24. *Tandesh*	Bengal	Channa, Sugar
25. *Shrikhand wadi*	Maharashtra	Milk curd, Sugar
26. *Sitabhog*	Bengal	Flour, Channa, Sugar, Fat
27. *Son Halwa*	North India	Wheat, Sugar, Fat, dried fruit.
28. *Sohanpapadi*	,,	Gram flour, Sugar, Fat.

TECHNICAL AID TO COLD STORAGE INDUSTRY IN INDIA

By

P. B. Mathur and K. Kirpal Singh,

(*Central Food Technological Research Institute, Mysore*)

The need for a greater development of the cold storage industry in India is emphasized with special reference to (1) research on biological problems (2) development of refrigerated transport (3) full utilization of the existing cold storage space and (4) establishment of an All-India Cold Storage Owners' Organization. A summary of the research work done at the Central Food Technological Research Institute, Mysore, and a brief account of the technical aid rendered to the industry are given in this paper.

THE cold storage industry in India is comparatively of recent origin. Although a few units, especially at port towns, had been installed a long time ago, most of the present installations were established during the past decade. The difficulties in the import of seed potatoes during the World War II led to the establishment of cold storage installations in the major potato-growing areas, especially in Northern India. We have now about 115 cold storages, the main commodity stored being potato. However, the refrigerated space *per capita* is still very small in India as compared with that in other advanced countries of the world. Lack of proper storage and transportation facilities naturally result in substantial losses of perishable foods. There is thus a distinct need for further development of this industry in India.

For this purpose, it is essential that attention should be paid to the following points:

(1) *Collection of more data concerning the optimum conditions of cold storage for Indian-grown fruits and vegetables and other commodities like eggs, meat, fish and dairy products.* Although considerable work has been done on these problems in Europe, the U.S.A. and other

countries, research work done in India is not sufficient to give confidence to cold storage owners to handle all types of produce. It is well known that, in the case of fruits and vegetables, factors such as variety, soil conditions, climate, etc., have considerable bearing on their cold storage behaviour. Although, in certain cases, the optimum cold storage conditions for Indian-grown varieties of fruits and vegetables have been found to be the same as those determined by European or American workers for the varieties grown in their own countries, yet there are a number of cases in which the effects of soil and climatic conditions have been so pronounced as to change materially the optimum conditions for cold storage. Tomato, banana and mango are the outstanding examples of the latter type. It may be mentioned that research work on the cold storage behaviour of fruits and vegetables was done in the past at Banaras, Lyallpur and notably at Poona. With the opening of the Central Food Technological Research Institute at Mysore, this type of work received a further stimulus and a number of biological problems of immediate interest to the cold storage industry are now being systematically investigated at this Institute.

(2) *Development of refrigerated transport:* It is well known that the post-storage lives of cold-stored perishable foods in many cases are short and, in consequence, one of the important requirements for the proper distribution of such foods is the availability of refrigerated or insulated transport. Although the Indian Railways have provided a small number of refrigerated wagons for particular industries, the bulk of the perishable foods is still transported in wagons originally designed for the transport of ordinary goods. Thus, there is a great need for research in the design of refrigerated wagons suited for the transport of such commodities as fruits, vegetables, meat, fish, etc.

(3) *Full utilization of the existing cold storage space.* There is need not only for increasing the total refrigerated space in the country, but also for devising means to

utilize the existing space all the year round. The existing potato cold storages are mainly in operation for a maximum period of 8 months in a year. For the rest of the time they are idle for want of adequate data concerning the optimum conditions of cold storage for other perishable commodities.

(4) *Establishment of an All-India Cold Storage Owners' Organization.* The cold storage industry has now developed to a stage when cold storage owners should take more initiative in furthering the interest of this industry. We, therefore, take this opportunity to suggest that a Cold Storage Owners' Organization should be established as soon as possible. This will bridge the gap between the Central Food Technological Research Institute, Mysore, and the commercial cold storage units. Generally speaking, the functions of this Organization should be, among others, to (i) finance the visits of C.S.I.R. scientists to cold storage units to study problems on the spot and give necessary advice (ii) cover the expenditure on such items of research as are not included in the C.S.I.R. research programmes, (iii) popularize the advantages of cold storage of perishable foods, and (iv) carry out commercial trials with important commodities in member cold storage units under the technical supervision of the C.S.I.R., India.

Technical aid rendered by the Central Food Technological Research Institute, Mysore, to the Cold Storage Industry.

This can be dealt with under two heads, namely, (i) research work carried out at the Institute in anticipation of the requirements of the industry and (ii) technical advice rendered to the industry.

With regard to the research work done at the Institute, it may be mentioned that the optimum cold storage conditions have been determined for a number of perishable foods. The results are summarized in Table I. Among other significant contributions from this Institute, mention may be made of the following: (1) Heat treatment of potatoes at 100°–104°F for 16 hours prior to cold storage, by means of which it was found possible to cut physiological losses in weight of potatoes in cold storage by approximately 50%. (2) Ripening of mangoes at controlled temperatures. Hitherto, it was believed that mangoes could be ripened satisfactorily at room temperatures. It is now found that the optimum temperature range for mango ripening is 67°–70°F. (3) Hastening the process of colour change (ripening) in oranges. The rainy season oranges are usually green in colour and fetch low prices. It has been found that the green oranges can be made to develop the characteristic orange colour if stored at 52°–55°F for about 4 weeks. This method can prove of real commercial value in the case of 'Satgudi' oranges in South India.

With regard to the technical advice to the Industry, it may be mentioned that besides paying visits to the commercial cold storages for personal advisory work by members of the staff of the Institute, technical advice on 70 problems has been given to the industry during the last 2 years. These enquiries were received from all the States in the Indian Union which have commercial cold storage units and were mainly concerned with the optimum conditions for the cold storage of various perishable foods or related problems.

In view of a general food deficit throughout India, it is all the more essential that the industry should co-operate with the Government authorities for its development on scientific lines. Our country suffers from food shortage and malnutrition. Greater facilities in connection with refrigerated storage and transport of perishable foods will have a profound effect on both these problems.

TABLE I

Optimum cold storage conditions and approximate storage lives concerning certain perishable foods

Perishable Food	Temperature °F	Relative humidity %	Approximate Storage life
1. Bananas (Cavendish) ...	52–55	85–90	22 days
2. Beet roots	32–35	85–90	1½–2 months
3. Brinjals	47–50	85–90	4 weeks
4. Cabbages	32–35	85–90	2½–3 months
5. Cashew apples	32–35	85–90	5 weeks
6. Cauliflowers	32–35	85–90	6–8 weeks
7. Eggs (shell)	32–35	85–90	9 months
8. Guavas	47–50	85–90	4 weeks
9. Jack Fruits	52–55	85–90	42 days
10. Knol Kohls	32–35	85–90	3 months
11. Limes	47–50	85–90	6–8 weeks
12. Mangoes			
(*a*) Seedling	42–45	85–90	42 days
(*b*) Badami (Alphonso) ...	47–50	85–90	28 days
(*c*) Raspuri (Peter) ...	42–45	85–90	42 days
(*d*) Totapuri (Bangalora)	42–45	85–90	49 days
13. Oranges			
(*a*) Satgudi	42–45	85–90	4–5 months
(*b*) Coorg (Mandarin) ...			
(i) Main Crop ...	42–45	85–90	2½–3 months
(ii) Rainy Season Crop	42–45	85–90	6–8 weeks
14. Potatoes	35–38	85–90	8–9 months
15. Sapotas	35–38*	85–90	8 weeks
16. Tapioca (tubers) ...	32–35	80–90	6½ months

* Temperatures below 35°F have not been tried yet.

QUICK FREEZING OF PERISHABLE FOODS

By

Man Mohan Singh

(*Factory Representative, Messrs Frick Company, U.S.A.*)

The author has pointed out that cold storage applications had already proved their utility both to growers and consumers of fruits and vegetables. Now, the quick freezing of perishable foods like fish, meat, etc., needs to be popularized. He has described in detail the mechanism of the process from both the physiological and engineering points of view. A plea is made for the establishment of Quick Freezing plants in India so that quick frozen mango pulp and papaya could be exported to foreign markets.

THE desire of man to enjoy perishable foods over off-season periods and also to solve the problems of marketing such foods has given an impetus to the food industry to devise ways and means to achieve these objects.

In India, the scarcity of food has thrown a challenge both to the Government and scientists of the country. Grow More Food Campaign seems to be the remedy, but preservation of food is the road to recovery.

Cold storage applications are no longer a novelty in India and their utility has already been widely known to the growers and consumers of potatoes. The farmer has gained immensely from the seed potato storages mainly in Uttar Pradesh and the Punjab. Short-term storage of fruits and vegetables has also been a success.

Fish has been known to be a nutritious food. Long-term storage of this perishable commodity was the target of both the scientist and the engineer. At one time, slow or sharp freezing of fish at as low temperatures as 10°–20°F seemed to be the answer. The perishable foods frozen in this fashion did not, however, hold up well, unless they were packed in sugar syrups or were glacéd. The flavour and appearance of fresh foods could not be maintained after thawing the frozen products.

All animal matter, whether fish, meat or poultry, is composed of minute cells which are filled with a jelly-like fluid containing various chemical salts such as those of sodium and calcium in solution. When the water in these jelly-like cells is refrigerated, crystals of ice of different sizes start forming as soon as the temperature is lower than 32°F. If the temperature is lowered further, the formation of crystals is increasingly rapid.

It is well known that the slower the formation of crystals, the bigger their size, *i.e.*, the freezing time determines the size of the crystals. Large-size crystals tend to break up the tissue of the meat, thus damaging not only its appearance, but also affecting its food value.

Drying Effect

The standard curve showing the moisture-carrying capacity of air at very low temperatures clearly indicates why the product should be frozen at such a low temperature. Slowly frozen products lose considerable weight and shrink in size. They become also discoloured ('freezer burn' as it is technically known), first, due to loss of moisture and secondly, due to oxidation.

If we take air leaving the cooling coils of a freezer at 35°F, its temperature rises 5°F in passing over the foods, its moisture-carrying capacity is increased less than 3/10th of one grain in over 10½ cubic feet. If the initial temperature is 60°F, the ability to pick up moisture when warmed by 5°F as before, is only 1/20th of one grain per lb. of air. When we know that there are 437.5 grains in a single ounce, we see why a blast of very cold air has a negligible drying effect.

In a test run made at a freezing plant in the United States, 15,000 lb. of poultry, each loosely wrapped in a single sheet of wax paper tied with one loop of string, were exposed in uncovered fibre boxes for 9 hours to an air blast at a temperature of 30°–36°F. The air warmed to 6°F while passing over the birds. The total loss in weight of the material averaged only 0.334%.

The quick frozen product when thawed and prepared for eating has the same flavour and appearance as that of fresh food.

Quick Freezing of Vegetables

The application of quick freezing to vegetable is not as advantageous as to meats. The cell walls of vegetables are very inelastic and get ruptured easily during any kind of refrigeration. It is claimed, however, that the cell rupture is, in most cases, beneficial to the vegetable from the point of view of its cooking quality. To prevent large ruptures and also to maintain the flavour, quick freezing systems are adopted. Further, the growth of moulds and similar organisms is greatly inhibited.

Quick Freezers

Cold air freezers do not require any complicated machinery. The equipment is simple and durable. Air at 35°F is obtained by using a 2-Stage Frick Booster System with an auxiliary equipment. The refrigerant used is ammonia.

The freezers are built in many different designs; they can be either hand-operated or automatically controlled. Besides, most quick freezing plants are designed to handle different products with the changing seasons. The cold air method adapts itself to changing requirements better than any other known method.

There are three systems in operation: (1) Blizzard freezers, (2) Tunnel freezers, and (3) Special freezers. The principle underlying all these methods is the same and any of these systems could be applied depending upon the requirements at a particular place.

The Blizzard freezers were developed to meet the need for equipment to effect fast freezing most economically. A typical unit is contained in an insulated box (12'x 10'x 10'). The air is cooled to 30°F or more, below zero, by a bank of coils and is drawn over the food at a high velocity by means of a fan.

Frozen Products Storage

Proper storage of frozen products and their efficient distribution are very important. Excessive loss of flavour, oxidation, and fermentation are the factors which have to be avoided, the former in particular being one of the most serious problems in storing the frozen products. Of course, all the deteriorating changes mentioned take place as the temperature is reduced. The temperature of the storge should be at least 10° below 0° for retaining the quality for long periods.

Transportation

Transportation of frozen products always appears to have been the bottle-neck in the programme of marketing the frozen foods. This problem is not as difficult as it poses itself. It is essential, of course, that no thawing of foods should take place during transportation. If quick frozen food products are allowed to thaw for even a very short time and are subsequently refrozen, the quality of the food depreciates to a large extent.

The only safe way to transport quick frozen perishable foods is to make sure that they remain frozen until they reach the consumer. Such foods have a large amount of refrigeration stored in them and, if placed in small well-insulated boxes in a compact fashion, they can remain frozen for more than 48 hours in insulated wagons. For this purpose, corrugated fibre board containers may be used. A solidly filled container will have less thawing than a similar package less compactly filled.

Freezing Mangoes and Papayas

Some ambitious food concerns in foreign countries have been exploring the possibility of importing frozen mangoes from India.

Both mangoes and papayas are surplus commodities in this country and a good portion of these crops can be prevented from going to waste if quick freezing facilities are provided either by private enterprise or by the Government. Mango pulp can be frozen successfully either in cans or in cellophane paper packages. Some preliminary work has been done, but more is needed to ensure successful freezing of these fruits. The establishment of a Quick Freezing pilot plant will go a long way in giving a lead to the development of this industry in India.

The dollar-earning potentialities of such a venture is very important, and active attention should be given to a mango freezing project in the near future.

REFRIGERATION APPLICATIONS IN FRUIT AND VEGETABLE INDUSTRY

By

N. S. Chadha

(Messrs C. R. Ice and Cold-storage, Agra)

The author reviewing the early development and applications of refrigeration for the preservation of fruits and vegetables has put forward a plea for refrigerated transport facilities from the farm to the market.

AMONG the many useful applications of refrigeration in the fruit and vegetable industry, the most important is refrigerated transport from the farm to the market. Cold storage comes next. The difference between refrigerated transport and cold storage of fruits and vegetables at the distribution centre is that when the products are in cold storage the period of holding is much longer. Besides, the cold storage management which is responsible for the safe keeping of perishable commodities can easily inspect and examine them periodically which is not possible when the produce is on wheels. Quick freezing, a recent application of the principle of refrigeration, has proved to be quite valuable to the fruit and vegetable industry by increasing the commercial life of the surplus products which have a short harvesting season.

Early development: The development of refrigeration of fruits and vegetables in transit from the farm to the market made good progress from simple experiments of early days. Fairly good success was achieved by placing a box filled with ice in the wagon carrying fruits and vegetables. This system was followed by the provision of wagons with insulation; now, a perfect system of insulated refrigerated cars with suitable ice bunkers has been introduced.

Living plants have *vital heat* which results from the life processes going on in the tissues. All living plants respire, consuming oxygen and liberating carbon dioxide and energy in the form of heat. Very little information is available on the quantity of vital heat produced by various fruits and vegetables under standard conditions. The heat of respiration or vital heat can be calculated from the respiration rate, assuming that the source of heat is the oxidation of sugar.

In many fruits and vegetables, oxidation is so rapid that it causes a pronounced lowering of palatability or loss of flavour which occurs more rapidly than in wilting or other changes in the external appearance. From all indications, this defect is due to the non-removal of 'field heat' immediately after harvesting. For many years, a *Standard Refrigeration System* was used for the transportation of most fruits and vegetables. *Standard Refrigeration* is defined as the filling of ice bunkers, generally prior to loading, and refilling them at all icing stations. Transportation tests showed that the *Standard Refrigeration System* was not quite effective for removing the *vital heat* from the load, or for retarding the generation of *vital heat* in less than 4–5 days in many cases. The reason for this is that air circulation by gravity is not sufficient to transfer heat through thermal convection from the loaded part of the car to the ice bunkers during the period of transit. The use of body ice for shipment of cabbage and other leafy vegetables which are not injured by being shipped in wet condition has become a common practice in vegetable shipping. *Body Icing* is defined as placing the ice in the body of the car with the load. *Body Icing* maintains a uniform temperature in the load as long as a reasonable quantity of ice remains on the top of the load.

Progress in pre-cooling: The practice of pre-cooling fruit prior to shipment has practically eliminated the use of *Standard Refrigeration* in much the same way and for the same reasons as *Body Icing* replaced *Standard Refrigeration* in the transportation of vegetables.

Pre-cooling effects quick reduction in temperature of a commodity before shipment so that its temperature remains below that which it might attain during transit under conventional refrigeration practice. By this method, the temperature of the commodity during transit could be maintained at the desired level by removing the *vital heat* generated. The higher the temperature, the faster the ripening and softening of the fruit, and greater its susceptibility to disease. The more quickly the commodities are cooled after harvesting, the longer is their commercial life.

Modern pre-cooling equipment in cars consists of a propeller-type fan mounted on a metal plate which completely covers the upper bulk-head opening of the car. One such unit installed at the end of each car can effect the circulation of cold air from the ice bunker by forcing it out over the top of the load, the air returning to the ice in the bunker through the bottom bulk-head opening. Truck mounted with mechanical refrigerating units have also been used quite extensively in foreign countries. The most rapid and effective method of pre-cooling is accomplished with stationary pre-cooling plants. The latest type is the *Brine Spray System.*

From the foregoing, it is clear that effective and proper pre-cooling of fruits and vegetables as soon as they are harvested, and the provision of adequate refrigerated transport to the market would go a long way in prolonging the life of these perishable commodities.

STORAGE AND PRESERVATION OF SEED POTATOES

By

(Messrs Volkart Brothers, Bombay)

This article refers to the need for the efficient conservation of seed potatoes by cold storage. The equipment required for the purpose has been described.

India produces about 600 lakh maunds of potatoes annually, of which about 100 lakh maunds, valued at about Rs. 2 crores, are lost through damage due to high temperature conditions and lack of adequate storage and transport facilities.

Freshly harvested potatoes cannot be used as seed, as they require a natural rest-period during which they will not sprout even if kept under conditions most favourable for growth. Lack of appropriate storage facilities in certain areas and adverse climatic conditions make it most difficult to preserve potatoes for seed purposes during this rest-period between harvesting and sowing. Statistics show that the major part of the potatoes kept in storage for seed purposes are damaged and lost. Consequently, while it is practically impossible for cultivators to get their own seed, they have to depend on foreign imported seeds or seeds from other potato-growing centres in India.

In order to relieve this situation, Volkart Brothers, at the request of the Ministry of Agriculture, Government of India, in 1944 made a thorough investigation of the problem of suitable cold storage of seed potatoes from the time of harvesting (in February/March) to the time of sowing (in September/October). It was found that a good cold storage plant for seed potatoes should meet the following requirements:

1. It should maintain the most favourable conditions for the preservation of seed potatoes over long periods.
2. It should be an economical proposition to the owner.
3. It should provide for the automatic control of temperature, humidity and ventilation so that, in case of need, the

cold storage plant can also be utilized for storage of articles other than potatoes.

4. It should be so designed that future extensions of the plant are possible.

Based on the above requirements, the following four alternative plants were suggested,

1. A cold storage plant for storing 300, tons of potatoes.
2. A cold storage plant for storing 600 tons of potatoes.
3. A combination plant for the cold-storing of 600 tons of potatoes and for the production of 10 tons of commercial ice per day.
4. A cold storage plant for storing 1,000 tons of potatoes.

These plants were approved by the Ministry of Agriculture, Government of India, and in the course of some years, over a hundred cold storage plants were installed in all the potato-growing districts of India. According to available information, these cold storage plants have been working with excellent results and have helped to solve the acute problem of preserving seed potatoes.

Seed potatoes are living organisms. In order to keep them alive during the 6 long months of storage, three essential factors have to be considered: (1) the right temperature, (2) the right humidity, and, the most important of all, (3) the correct rate of ventilation to replace carbon dioxide by fresh oxygen. An ordinary cold storage plant does not meet these conditions and the plant has to be designed as a *low temperature air conditioning installation.*

Optimum Storage Conditions

Experience has shown that a temperature of 36°F is sufficiently low for the effective storage and preservation of all varieties of potato grown in India; at this storage temperature a relative humidity of 87% has been found to be essential. To maintain such high humidity even during dry and hot summers, auxiliary humidification has to be provided. Experience has shown that approximately 5–6 air-changes are required every 24 hours to keep the concentration of carbon dioxide to a minimum.

With such temperature, humidity and ventilation conditions, sprouting and shrinkage of potatoes is retarded and their appearance remains perfect. The seed value or germination quality is not impaired; on the contrary, refrigeration promotes the formation of starch and usable sugars in seed potatoes. These reserves are not used up during the storage period and result in a larger number of shoots after planting, thus causing considerable increases in yield. The loss in weight due to evaporation or respiration is negligible, *i.e.*, 2–3%. The extent of wastage is dependent on the freshness and quality of the seed potatoes selected for storage, and partly also, on the height and method of piling up potatoes in the cold storage. If proper attention is given to these two factors, the spoilage during storage will be negligible.

Equipment:

In potato cold storage plants, both the direct and indirect forms of refrigeration can be used. The standard design proposed by Volkart Brothers recommends indirect refrigeration by means of brine circulation, although a number of plants using direct expansion, Freon System, have also been installed. The reasons for the recommendation of the Ammonia-*cum*-Brine System in preference to the direct Ammonia System are the following:

1. Brine cooling provides closer control of room conditions than the direct refrigerant and usually results in better plant balance and smoother operation, and hence is most suitable for large plants for the preservation of seed potatoes.
2. It does not require an absolutely tight-fitting pipework to prevent leaks, and *in case a brine-leak does occur it will not damage the product.*
3. Because a large number of ice plants are in existence, sufficient trained personnel is available to look after ammonia-*cum*-brine plants.

As against this, the disadvantages are higher initial costs and slightly higher running costs because of the additional temperature split between the brine and the refrigerant handled by the high side.

Some of the more exclusive features of the plants designed by Messrs Volkart Brothers are:

1. *Two-speed Motors for Cold Diffusers:*

   The cold diffusers are driven by two-speed motors. During the 'Loading' season, when the sensible load is high, the higher speed is used for circulating more air, and helps to cool the product more rapidly. During the 'holding' season, only the heat of respiration and infiltration is to be removed (the product having already been cooled), and hence the lower speed of the fan is used. This ensures lower running costs during the greater part of the storage season.

2. *Temperature regulators:*

   Each cold diffuser is provided with a Fulton-Sylphon Temperature Regulator, which automatically controls the flow of the medium (in this case calcium chloride brine) passing through its valve, by responding to temperature changes affecting the bulb. Action of the valve is both throttling and modulating.

3. *Compressors:*

   Flexibility of operation and safeguard against machine trouble have been ensured by installing more than one compressor. During the 'loading' season (lasting about a month), all the compressors are in operation; after loading has been completed and the room temperature cooled down to 36°F., one compressor is cut out as the remaining compressor or compressors are sufficient to cope with the decreased load. In other words, *the cut-out compressor will remain as a stand-by*. All the compressors are inter-connected so that any one machine can be cut out of service, when desired.

4. *Auxiliary Humidification:*

   Because of the high dry bulb temperature and the comparatively low relative humidity prevailing during the summer months, it is necessary to provide for additional humidification in the rooms, as otherwise the product will shrink, lose weight and be unfit for the commercial use. The additional humidity is provided by installing special turbo-humidifiers, which spray the requisite quantity of water in a fine atomised form into the rooms, working in conjunction with a suitable air compressor. The operation of the auxiliary humidification equipment is automatic.

Reference

Leaflet No. 1 of 1947, issued by the Department of Agriculture, Bombay Province, on Cold and Gas Storage for Food and Vegetables.

COLD STORAGE FACILITIES FOR THE FISHING INDUSTRY

By

(Messrs Volkart Brothers, Bombay)

In this article, Messrs Volkart Brothers, Bombay, have dealt with refrigerating plant and machinery required for the efficient storage of fish in India.

Soon after the termination of the War in 1945, we were approached by the Department of Agriculture of the Government of India to work out and submit a design for refrigeration plants suitable for freezing and storing fish. The design of this refrigerating plant was to be such as to allow for the present state of development of the Fishing Industry in India and also take into account the expected modernization and increased efficiency of this industry due to the special impetus given by the Departments of Fisheries of the Central and State Governments.

Detailed proposals for 3 Standardized Refrigerating Plants for fish storing and fish freezing were therefore submitted after a very careful investigation and thorough study of the particular problems of the numerous fishing centres along the coast of India. The plants as proposed were a combination of: (*a*) ice making, ice crushing and ice storage plants, (*b*) cold storage plant for short-period storage of fresh fish, (*c*) quick-freezing plant working on the most up-to-date methods, and (*d*) cold storage for storing quick-frozen fish for long duration.

The problem of transport of chilled and quick-frozen fish did not form part of these specific projects.

The capacity of the three different plants proposed and the arrangement of the plants were intended to meet

(Scheme 1) requirements of large fishing centres like Bombay,

(Scheme 2) requirements of medium centres like Mangalore, Calicut, etc., and

(Scheme 3) requirements of small fishing centres.

Subsequently, the following installations were added:

Scheme 1. A Pilot Fishery Plant installed in Bombay for the Central Government (which is in operation since one year) and another plant (to be installed) for a private party in Cochin.

The Plants under Scheme 1 have provision for the following:

1. Production of 20 tons of ice for being crushed and mixed with fresh fish.
2. Storage of 30 tons of block ice.
3. Arrangements for cooling a cold storage room (capacity approximately 55 tons) for keeping fish (unfrozen) for short periods not exceeding 7 days, held at a temperature just above freezing point (32°F).
4. Facilities for freezing 5 tons (per 8 hour shift) of thin whole fish, fillets, or slices.
5. Arrangements for cooling a cold storage room (capacity approximately 200 tons) for keeping frozen fish for long periods (some months), held at 0°F.

Scheme 2. Two fish storage, freezing, etc., plants for the Government of Madras for installation at Mangalore and Calicut. These plants are under erection.

The Plants under Scheme 2 have provision for:

1. Ice making	4 tons per day
2. Ice store	12 tons
3. Iced fresh fish store	25/30 tons
4. Quick-freezing	1½ tons in 8 hours
5. Frozen fish store	40 tons

Scheme 3: One plant for a private party in Cochin which has been in operation for 2 years, and is mainly used as a Pilot Shrimp Freezing Plant, has provision for:

1. Quick-freezing	1½ tons per day
2. Frozen store	30 tons
3. Fresh fish store	4 tons

In the design of these standardized plants, due consideration has been given to the possibility of future extension of any part.

These plants are standard and easily worked and attempts have been made by the designers to combine in them a variety of purposes. The selection of refrigerating compressors and lay-out of the refrigerant piping are so made as to give maximum flexibility with the minimum stand-by machinery. Quick freezing of fish is done by the 'Blast-Freezing' method. As the word 'Blast' implies, freezing is done by means of rapid circulation of low temperature air. This method of freezing fish has proved to be most acceptable from the standpoint of results, *i.e.*, quality of the product and low operating costs. The cleanliness of the method and the rapid rate of freezing, as well as the minimum loss of weight are some of the main features which make this method most acceptable. Quick freezing in these plants is done in a very heavily insulated tunnel through which are pushed wheeled trucks containing the fish to be frozen. Standard 'Carrier' cold-diffusers, blowing chilled air (temperature 30°F–40°F) at great velocity over the fish, are installed on opposite sides in the freezing tunnel. The fish-laden trucks are moved, one in and one out, once in 36–45 minutes. When freezing is completed, glazing is done by water spray in a glazing room adjoining the freezing tunnel. Due to this glazing, the quick-frozen fish is hermetically sealed in a thin mantle of ice. In this condition, the fish is held in a low temperature frozen fish store for periods up to one year.

Government are faced with difficulties in the organization of equitable distribution of fresh, wholesome fish, at reasonable prices, to people living far away from the sea, in inland areas. Only refrigerated transport facilities, planned and equipped to meet these requirements, will make it possible to utilize the vast but still insufficiently exploited resources of fish and increase the food supply of the country.

PROTEIN HYDROLYSATE FROM WASTE SHARK FLESH AND OTHER UNECONOMICAL VARIETIES OF FISH

By

G. B. Mohanty and A. B. Roy

(*Department of Fisheries, Orissa, Cuttack*)

The authors have prepared a highly nutritive protein hydrolysate with shark flesh, for use by convalescent patients, nursing mothers and others needing protein food in an easily assimilable form. Satisfactory results were obtained with this food in hospital trials with patients. The authors suggest that large-scale production of this commodity should be undertaken to meet the protein deficiency in the country.

With the increasing prevalence of malnutrition and wasting diseases like tuberculosis in India, the demand for protein hydrolysates which are easily assimilable is also growing. Many products containing hydrolysed protein are being imported from foreign countries under several trade names such as Ledinac, Casydrol, etc., and sold at prohibitively high prices. Some of the indigenous firms are also producing similar products from casein which is also very expensive.

Fish flesh was therefore tried as a cheap source of good quality protein.

During the war-time when there was great malnutrition in Germany, the Germans produced 'Wiking Eiweiss' (Fish albumen), as a substitute for egg albumen. They were using Cod fish and Shrimps for the purpose.

When this problem was taken up in our laboratories, the foremost point was to find out the variety of fish available in Indian waters which would be suitable for the purpose. Shark fish and other varieties of fish were taken up for investigation. Usually, in the coastal areas sharks are caught for their liver oil only, and huge amounts of flesh are thrown away without proper utilization of the same. In the State of Orissa alone, several tons of shark flesh are being wasted as people have a prejudice against eating the same in its fresh condition. Shark flesh has comparatively a higher protein content than that of most other varieties of fish, as can be seen from Table I.

TABLE I

Analytical values of different fish meals

	Mackerel (Gutted)	Mackerel (Ungutted)	Sole fish meal	Anchovies fish meal	Oil Sardine meal	Shark fish meal	Skate fish meal	Dolphin fish meal
H_2O% ...	8·73	8·70	6·08	8·51	9·68	9·87	6·54	4·25
Protein% ...	68·06	60·10	61·42	62·66	65·27	77·84	77·93	69·71
Fat% ...	5·79	6·11	9·01	4·00	9·54	5·31	2·19	6·91
Ash% ...	16·2	20·71	18·05	20·43	14·77	7·46	10·42	14·53
Unidentified% ...	1·22	2·38	5·44	4·49	0·75	...	2·92	4·61
P_2O_5 ...	6·69	6·88	2·75	4·92	5·79	3·00	3·93	5·96
CaO% ...	7·92	9·0	6·22	7·37	6·01	2·79	0·04	4·89
Sodium chloride% ...	0·34	0·10	0·23	0·41	0·32	0·49	0·62	...
Insoluble% ...	0·52	2·87	2·77	2·53	1·78	0·25	0·13	0·88

Experiments were therefore taken up in our laboratory on the utilization of shark flesh as well as other economical varieties of fish obtained from the Chilka Lake.

EXPERIMENTAL

(*a*) *Preparation of raw materials:*

The fish is minced by means of a chopper and washed several times. The optimum period of cooking and the percentage of acetic acid were determined by varying the proportion of acetic acid and time of cooking. The results are shown in Tables II and III.

TABLE II

Showing acetic acid required for cooking

S. No. of observation	Acetic acid used (%)	Inference	Remarks
1	0·3	Muscle fibres not well separated during the cooking period	·5% Acetic acid is suitable for cooking as the muscle fibres get completely separated and some fat comes out of the muscle.
2	0·4	do	
3	0·5	Muscle fibres well separated within the cooking period	
4	0·6	Muscle fibres get digested and thereby the product is wasted	
5	0·7	do	

TABLE III

Showing time-limit for cooking

No. of observation	Cooking period	Inference	Remarks
1	½ hour	Not properly cooked	One hour is the time limit for proper cooking. To test that the product is properly cooked, it is pressed by thumb and forefinger till it feels fibrous.
2	1 hour	Properly cooked	
3	1½ hour	Over-cooked	

It is then cooked at 80°C with 0.5% acetic acid solution for about one hour when the muscle becomes fibrous as observed by pressing it between fingers. The cooked material is washed under the tap until the collagen and acid (separated from the fish muscle by cooking with acid) are completely removed. The contents are then pressed to get rid of water as much as possible. The fat in the product is then extracted with petroleum ether (b.p. 60–80°C) a number of times and fat-free protein is obtained. As the product is to be used by anaemic patients and expectant mothers, it is necessary that it is free from fat.

(*b*) *Hydrolyzation:*

Since proteins are complex substances and are difficult to be assimilated by the human system they need to be broken down into easily assimilable end-products, *viz.*, the amino acids. For invalids with poor digestion it is necessary to hydrolyze the insoluble defatted protein. In the laboratory this was done by alkali (NaOH) hydrolysis which was considered suitable. Acid hydrolysis, specially if the protein contains carbohydrate, usually results in the complete destruction of certain amino acids and partial decomposition of certain other amino acids. The protein prepared as above is weighed and sufficient water is added and stirred. Then, caustic soda (12%) is added. Stirring is continued for 10–20 minutes and the mass allowed to gel for 20–30 minutes. At the end of this period the substance is heated at 80°C for 4–5 hours during which period complete hydrolysis of the protein takes place. Then, it is filtered to remove the bones and other undigested materials. The liquid is neutralized with 85% acetic acid, dried at 80°C and powdered to a flour-like product.

Attempts were also made in the laboratory to hydrolyze the product by the action of enzymes such as pepsin. But the hydrolysis was not quite successful as enzymatic hydrolysis was very time-consuming and was not quite complete.

The final product had a cream colour and its natural flavour. It was found that the yield of the finished product was about 5% of the whole fish and about 10% of the fish muscle. But, with better technical equipment and recovery of the solvent used for fat extraction, the yield of the final product may be 15–25% of the raw materials.

TABLE IV

Total protein content of hydrolyzed protein of different fishes

Types of fish used	No. of Expt.	Amount of fish taken	Total Protein N content %	Mean Protein N content %	Remarks
Mugil corsula (Khoyanga)	1	4lb.	13·12		
do	2	4lb.	12·80	12·96	This fish contains 12·96 % of total N or 12·96 × 6·25 = 81 % of total protein
do	3	4lb.	12·96		
Polynemus Indicus (Sahala)	1	4lb.	13. 0		
do	2	4lb.	12· 5	12·73	This fish contains 12·73 % of total N or 12·73 × 6·25 = 79·5 % of total protein.
do	3	4lb.	12· 7		
Shark	1	4lb.	13·60		
do	2	4lb.	13·44	13· 60	This fish contains 13·6 % of total N or 13·6 × 6·25 = 85 % of total protein.
do	3	4lb.	13·76		

The above Table shows that shark flesh used for the experiment was found to give more total protein in the hydrolyzed finished product than the other two varieties of fish taken, namely Mugil *corsula* (Khoyanga), and *Polynemus Indicus* (Sahala) which are also some of the economical varieties.

ESTIMATION OF TOTAL AMINO ACID NITROGEN

Apart from the determination of total protein nitrogen, that of the total amino acid nitrogen of the product was also carried out. Results are shown in Table V.

TABLE V

Estimation of total amino acid nitrogen

No. of observation	Amino acid Nitrogen per 100 gm.	Mean	Remarks
1	0.82 g.		
2	0.84 g.	0.84 g.	0.84 g. amino acid nitrogen in 100 g. is present in hydrolyzed protein prepared from shark flesh.
3	0.86 g.		

It may be observed that the total amino acid nitrogen in the finished product is more than sufficient for normal medicinal purposes.

COMPARATIVE CHART OF THE NUTRITIONAL VALUE OF THE PRODUCT

A comparative statement of the protein content of this product and some other common foods is given in Table VI.

TABLE VI

Percentages of total protein content in different products

Sl. No.	Different Products	Total protein % (Nx6.25)	Remarks
1	Protein hydrolysate from shark flesh	85	Protein hydrolysate from shark flesh has the maximum amount of total protein amongst the common foods.
2	Eggs (Raw or boiled) ...	11·9	
3	Milk, fresh, whole ...	3·3	
4	Milk, fresh, skimmed ...	3·4	
5	Cheese, Gruyère ...	36·8	
6	Eggs, dried	43·4	
7	Chicken roast	29·6	
8	Beef, frozen, raw	20·3	
9	Duck, roast	22·8	
10	Goose, roast	28·0	

It is seen that the hydrolyzed protein from shark flesh has a much higher protein content than that of many common food materials.

General Properties of the Product

The final product which is cream-white in colour is soluble in water having the natural taste and smell. It is found that the nutritional value of 1 lb. of fish albumen is equivalent to the egg white of 122 eggs. In the powder form it is found to have very good keeping qualities. This product was tested on patients in several hospitals in Calcutta and the results were extremely satisfactory. It has been found particularly useful in all cases of mal-nutrition, tuberculosis, duodenal and ventricular ulcers and for patients during convalescence. Since the whipping power of this product is more than 22 eggs, in food industry it can replace egg albumen in the preparation of all products such as ice-cream, whipped cream, butter cream, salad cream. To obtain foam equivalent to one pound of fish albumen, at least 22 dozen eggs are required.

It can also be used in Plastic Industry, colour binding, fire extinguishers, paint industry, leather industry, wool impregnation and in conjunction with rayon fibres.

Test Reports on the use of the Product on Patients

This product was sent to various doctors in Calcutta as well as to the S. C. B. Medical College Hospital, Cuttack, for testing. Reports of satisfactory progress have been received in cases of malnutrition and tuberculosis.

It is clear from the reports that the product will play an important role in meeting the protein deficiency in our country where the number of casualties due to mal-nutrition and wasting diseases is high. It is hoped that the product, which is at present wasted, will be produced on a large scale and utilized for the benefit of the country.

We express our gratitude to the Superintendent and the staff of the S. C. B. Medical College Hospital for their kind co-operation in analysing the product and testing it on patients.

RETROSPECT AND PROSPECT OF FRUIT PRESERVATION INDUSTRY IN INDIA

By

S. Ranganna and C. V. Paul

(*Messrs Earl Brothers, Bangalore*)

The authors have surveyed various factors which have contributed to the progress of the fruit and vegetable preservation industry. A strong plea is made for giving adequate protection to this industry in the form of supply of raw materials like sugar at subsidized rates, provision of good quality tin plate and containers, and necessary technical advice.

THE history of the Fruit Preservation Industry dates back to the beginning of the 19th century, but it was only in the second quarter of the 20th century that the canning industry first made its beginning in India. About 20 years have elapsed since then. Naturally, the question arises as to how far the industry has progressed. During these years, the industry had the support of the Government, co-operation of the enterprising manufacturers and assistance of qualified technologists, as well as an abundant supply of raw materials. In spite of this, the industry has not been able to produce fruit and vegetable products which are within the reach of the common man. It has up to this day remained an industry catering only to the needs of the upper classes.

This calls for a survey of the various factors which have been an impediment in the progress of this industry.

1. *Raw materials:*

(*a*) *Fruits and Vegetables:* The availability of the proper variety determines the quality of the product, while the extent of supply determines the cost of production. So far, no effort has been made to develop proper varieties of fruits and vegetables for canning and no encouragement given to growers in this direction. At present, the growers have no assurance of sales of their produce. For example, when Messrs Earl Brothers, Bangalore, started their Factory two years ago, the maximum quantity of strawberries available was only 5–6 lb. per day in the peak season. At present when sufficient encouragement has been given to the growers, 200–300 lb. per day of this fruit are being regularly received. Besides, there have been requests from various growers for taking contracts for regular supplies which we are not able to accept on account of huge stocks of finished goods which are remaining unsold due to high cost of production.

(*b*) *Sugar:* In spite of repeated requests made by the Industry for sugar at subsidized rates, no action has been taken by the Government in this regard. Instead, the Government thought it wise to export sugar to a foreign country by granting a suitable subsidy, the cost of subsidy being met by taxing sugar used both by the industry and by the public. Added to this, the quality of Indian-made sugar is not very satisfactory. The sugar supplied to the industry contains dirt, dust and often a good proportion of extraneous matter.

2. *Containers:*

(*a*) Poor quality of tin plate combined with its high cost has been mostly responsible in hampering the progress of this industry. The price of the tin plate has been going up with every tin quota that is released periodically. The cost of a base box of tin plate which was Rs. 36-2 in 1952 increased to Rs. 49-12 in 1953, an increase of 37·7% within a period of one year. Further, the charges of fabrication have also gone up considerably. Moreover, packing and freight charges from Madras to Bangalore works up to 22–25% of the cost of the containers.

The method of allocation of tin quota to various factories by the Government has been a matter of serious concern to all the fruit and vegetable processors in India. In their present method of allocation for each quarter, no tin quota is made available until the season is either well in advance or is almost over. This delay together with the time taken by the tin can fabricators and delays occurring in transporting them to factories have the net result that by the time the cans reach the manufacturers, they will have completely lost the season.

(*b*) *Glass containers:* While the above is the position with regard to tin containers, the position of glass containers is in no way better. At present, no manufacturer in India has been able to produce leak-proof bottles. If we have bottles, we do not have caps. The caps have to come from England and other foreign countries, because of the rubber lining inside the caps. When these caps come from foreign countries, Indian glass manufacturers are not able to fabricate bottles to suit the caps. While the imports of caps are permitted, those of bottles are prohibited on account of the protection granted to the indigenous glass industry. The prices are so prohibitive here, that the foreign bottles cost only 25%–50% of the price of the Indian-made bottles. While the imports of empty bottles are prohibited, imports of foreign products packed in glass jars are being allowed into India, which are being sold at prices lower than even our cost price.

3. *Quality and Standards:*

Even though the industry enjoyed a certain measure of protection, no effort was made by the Indian manufacturers to produce quality products and establish themselves in the trade. In his effort to compete with the price of the foreign-made products, the Indian manufacturer completely let down the quality and has been producing poor-quality products. This could have been easily prevented, if the Government had strictly enforced Food Laws, and dealt with the manufacture of low quality products severely. While this is the case with the Indian-made products, the foreign products are in no way better. While the Indian standard for jams requires a minimum of 45% fruit (fresh weight basis) in the finished jams, standard in foreign countries, *e.g.*, in England, the fruit content is as low as 20% in case of Marmalade, 22% in case of Black Currant Jam, 25% in case of Raspberry Jam, 37.5% in case of Strawberry Jam and is in no case above 40%. Although these standards are below the Indian standards and the manufacture of such products in India is liable for legal action, imports of such foreign products are being freely allowed. Further, it has been stipulated that for export of any product to foreign countries, sugar content and other manufacturing details have to be declared on the label, while foreign products are finding free entry into India without any such declaration. As regards the quality of foreign products, they are in no way better. Cut out tests carried out in our Factory showed that black currant jam manufactured by one of the concerns in Australia was full of barks and twigs of the fruit. Orange juice canned in the same country had a bitter taste and three out of the four cans purchased from the market bulged within a few days' storage. Pineapple canned in Malaya was much smaller in size and tasted insipid. Jams manufactured in England appeared to be mere pectin jellies, with a very low fruit content and added colour and flavour. In spite of all these apparent deficiencies, foreign products still find a good market in India on account of good containers, attractive, coloured labels and cheap price.

Reorganization of the Industry: Now that the country is envisaging a 'Five-Year Plan' and that this industry is on the verge of collapse, every effort should be made to help the industry by reorganizing the entire set up with a technique best suited to our peculiar environments. Some of the measures are suggested for the purpose in the following pages.

1. *Protection:* As an immediate measure, this industry should be given all-sided planned protection, for a period of three years. During this period, imports of all the foreign products, that could be manufactured in India, should be banned.

2. *Food Laws:* While the industry enjoys protection, the Government should strictly enforce the Food Laws and

adopt stringent measures in cases of any infringement of these laws. As regards the foreign-made products, it should be insisted that any product coming into India should strictly conform to Indian Food Laws and declaration made on the label to that effect.

3. *Supply of Sugar:* When the country could afford to subsidize the price of sugar for export, the same benefit to the indigenous industry, which is in dire need of it, is fully justified and should be given.

4. *Supply of Containers:* As regards the tin containers, the Government should fix the price of the tin plate for a definite period. Further, the present method of quarterly allotment of tin plate should be changed to yearly allotment by asking the manufacturers to formulate their manufacturing schedule on a yearly system. Further, the idea of keeping apart the imported tin plate for the exclusive use of the canning industry is a point worth consideration. With regard to glass containers, immediate steps should be taken to develop rubber-lined caps. As regards the prices, the Government may ask the glass industry to supply glass containers at reasonable rates.

5. *Development of Horticulture and Technical Aid to the Factories:* Not all fruits are available in each and every region, but the manufacturer is always induced to add a variety to his list. So, there is every possibility of the manufactured products being of inferior quality. This could easily be avoided by carrying out a survey of the various raw materials in each region and accordingly, restrict the manufacture of the products. For purposes of developing proper varieties of fruits and vegetables, promoting their cultivation and their utilization as a long-term measure, India should be divided into agricultural regions. In each of these regions, a laboratory should be set up, the personnel of which should consist of agricultural scientists and technologists. The work of these laboratories will consist in carrying out surveys of potentialities of the region concerned, development of proper varieties and their utilization and finally the supervision of the fact-

ories in the region concerned. The work of these laboratories should be co-ordinated by a central laboratory like the Central Food Technological Research Institute.

6. *Regulated Supply of Raw Materials:* To provide a regulated supply of raw materials to the industry, an organization represented by the manufacturers, the growers and the Government should be set up. Under this, the grower should be provided with financial assistance, with the stipulation that he shall supply the produce at a fixed price to the manufacturer in the region concerned. By doing so, not only the industry is assured of supply of raw materials at regulated prices, but also the grower gets a resonable price for his produce either in seasons of glut or scarcity.

7. *Publicity:* So far, no effort has been made for creating taste among the Indian public for canned foods. This can best be accomplished by a joint effort of the Government, the Food Preservers' Association and the manufacturer.

A well-integrated plan for the sound development is the only hope of this industry, and so long as the Government does not sponsor the entire range of measures, this industry cannot be saved from the slump from which it is suffering.

TECHNICAL AID TO THE FRUIT AND VEGETABLE PRESERVATION INDUSTRY

By

(*Messrs G. G. Industries, Agra.*)

This paper deals with such subjects as the development of experimental farms, establishment of regional laboratories, fabrication of machinery and supply of technical information to processing units in the country. Developments in these fields would go a long way in promoting the fruit and vegetable preservation on sound and scientific lines.

THERE are 572 units engaged in the Fruit and Vegetable Preservation Industry in India. Barring a few exceptions, most of the units are of small or medium size. Consequently, they are not in a position to carry out scientific investigations on their own for the improvement of the quality of their products. As this industry is paying a cess, it is natural to expect that the Government will render technical aid to the industries in all possible manner.

The following are some of the heads under which technical aid would be most useful to the industry:

(*a*) Experimental Farms,
(*b*) Regional Laboratories,
(*c*) Fabrication of indigenous machinery and equipment, and
(*d*) Technical literature.

(*a*) *Experimental Farms:* Suitable varieties of fruits and vegetables are not available to the industry. The Central and State Governments should establish Experimental Farms in different regions, with qualified and experienced Horticulturists in-charge who would evolve suitable varieties of vegetables and fruits required by factories in different regions.

For the sake of convenience, the fruit- and vegetable-growing areas may be divided into different regions. In each region, there should be an agency for co-ordinating the efforts of the growers, experimental farms and of fruit and vegetable preservers. Such a co-ordination will result in high standard indigenous products.

(*b*) *Regional Laboratories:* The Governments should also establish a requisite number of Regional Laboratories for research on Fruit Processing. The functions of the Regional Laboratory will be:

(i) To evolve new products from fruits grown in a particular region.

(ii) To devise methods for the utilization of wastes from regional fruits.

(iii) To help and solve the technical problems of canners and fruit preservers located in the area.

(iv) To examine the products of indigenous and foreign manufacture for the benefit of the public and fruit preservers.

(*c*) *Fabrication of machinery and equipment:* On account of the small size of manufacturing units in India, the Indian industry requires machinery with moderate output and such machines are difficult to obtain from abroad. Even the smallest food processing machines from foreign countries prove, in many cases, too large for the actual requirements of Indian processors and, in some cases, such machines are found uneconomical and costly. If machines suitable for small-scale production are fabricated in the country, they will be much cheaper than the imported ones and more economical in operation. The Central Government should give every encouragement to Food Engineers who would design different machinery required by the industry. Such machinery should be displayed in exhibitions and at convenient places as well as at various regional laboratories. This may also lead to the establishment of an important industry of the manufacture of food machinery to the advantages of the Indian Food Industry.

(*d*) *Technical Literature:* Useful work in this direction is being done by the Central Food Technological Research Institute and the All India Food Preservers' Association. The bulletins and booklets etc., issued by the C.F.T.R.I., Mysore, have been very helpful to the industry. The 'Indian Food Packer' published monthly by the All India Food Preservers' Association has also been serving the cause of the industry. In addition to these efforts, in order to meet the industry's requirements, it is suggested that a National Library of Technical Literature on Food Industries should be set up and the technical persons engaged in the industry should be encouraged to contribute freely to the creation of such an organization. The technical books should be easily accessible to all Food Technologists. Setting up of this library will greatly enhance our resources of knowledge on Food Industries, and will go a long way in ultimately improving the standard of our products.

In conclusion, it may be said that our food industry is still in a stage of infancy, but it has made a sound beginning. If it is to grow and develop into a full-fledged industry like its counterpart in foreign countries, the Government, industries, trade and consumers should rally round and play their parts in this endeavour of national importance. Then alone, Indian-made food products will be able to compete successfully with foreign ones in Indian and foreign markets.

SOME ASPECTS OF THE WORKING OF THE FRUIT PRODUCTS ORDER

By

P. H. Bhatt

(Development Officer, Fruit Products, New Delhi)

In this paper, the author refers to the analytical and testing work of 12,500 samples of Indian and imported food products, proposed to be carried out every year under the Fruit Products Order, 1948. This work will be of help to the Fruit and Vegetable Industry in India in improving the quality of its products. The author has suggested the formation of a Central Body under the chairmanship of the Director of the Central Food Technological Research Institute, Mysore, which will meet every year and recommend the study of general and specific problems of the industry to research institutions in the country. A few problems of immediate interest to the industry are suggested for investigation.

THE development of the processed and preserved fruit and vegetable industry is linked up with the Ministry of Agriculture, New Delhi. The re-centralization of the functions of the Fruit Products Order, 1948, has been made so that primarily the interests of the industry are looked after by the Central Government and the preservers benefited on a nation-wide basis. As the first step, arrangements have been finalized between the Ministry of Food and Agriculture and the Central Food Technological Research Institute, Mysore, to do the analytical work for the Fruit Products Order*.

1. Checking the samples, collected from markets in all parts of the country and from the manufacturers' premises, and taking necessary action in case of any contravention under the schedules of the Fruit Products Order; and

* The Fruit Products Order Testing Unit started functioning at the Central Food Technological Research Institute in April 1953.

2. Checking samples of all the imported fruit and vegetable products to ensure that their quality satisfies the requirement of the Indian Fruit Products Order.

The total number of samples to be collected and analysed will be about 12,500 per year. It is hoped that such technical aid will help the industry in checking products of inferior quality and improving the quality of their products.

Under the re-centralized organization, the country has been divided into five zones. There are 602 licence holders under the Fruit Products Order who are manufacturing various kinds of products. Although several manufacturers have been in the business for a number of years, their methods of production need improvement on modern lines. The manufacture of *murrabba, petha,* pickle, earthen pot vinegar, chutney, *achar, amchur* and mango leather forms a good part of the production of the Indian fruit preservation industry. The need for improvement of these products is beyond question. During our visits to various centres of production, it became apparent that there were various problems facing the industry which required close attention. A few problems of wider interest are as follows:

1. The use of hypochlorite in the bleaching of apples and other fruits in the manufacture of *murrabbas* and its subsequent washing.
2. The penetration of sugar in the manufacture of *murrabba* in relation to the inversion of sugar or use of simple sugar in conjunction with sucrose. (Vacuum concentration of syrup and its effect on quality of the finished product as well as the problem of utilizing the left-over syrup in the manufacture of crystallized fruits).
3. The adoption of slow or quick freezing methods prior to the manufacture of *murrabbas* in the destruction of cell-walls by the formation of ice crystals and creation of better osmotic conditions for more efficient penetration of sugar.
4. The effect of quicker cooling in the manufacture of *murrabba* on the colour and flavour of the finished product.
5. The retention of soluble sugars, vitamins and minerals of fruits or vegetables in the manufacture of *murrabba.*

6. The varietal studies, particularly of apples, regarding the suitability of specific varieties in the manufacture of *murrabba*, particularly in respect of browning and texture (varietal studies regarding the suitability of various fruits and vegetables need to be carried out especially as all the material available in the market seems to be fit for the processing and canning).

7. An alternative for earthen pots which are claimed to be the cheapest containers for retail sale. (The micro-flora of earthen pots and the desirability of their use in the industry requires to be studied).

8. The canning of some milk products like *Rasgulla* which has been tried with little success by some producers. (Asceptic canning at high temperatures as in the latest processes of milk canning may be tried with these products, as these have a good foreign market if proper colour and texture are preserved during processing).

9. The study of the indigenous micro-flora particularly with respect to thermophilic organisms and the optimum time and temperature required for processing of non-acid foods. (This study should be carried out especially for curried vegetables, where the presence of oil in the medium seems to encourage the resistance of some spores. It has been further reported by the Chief Director of Purchases that some pathogenic organisms seemed to have survived heavy processing in some of the canned vegetables. Specific tests regarding such organisms may be standardized, particularly in view of indigenous conditions).

10. The suitability of different varieties of green mango for brining, and their subsequent use in the manufacture of *chutneys* or pickles, the determination of right concentration of salt and acidity (natural and through fermentation), duration of fermentation and storage in relation to colour, flavour, texture and softness of the finished products.

11. Waxing oranges and other fruits for preservation during transport and application of this method with reference to conditions in Assam.

12. The use of heavy doses of artificial fertilizers in the field and their subsequent effects, if any, on the tin plate in canned pine-apples.

These are a few of the problems connected with some specific products, but there are others relating to different products, which need attention of research workers and technical personnel in the industry.

It is a matter of regret that there is hardly any or little co-ordination between the industry and research institutions. Regionally, we have various institutions either imparting technical education or doing research in the field, but even in the case of these institutions, there is little or no co-ordination with each other. It will be, therefore, desirable to have an All-India Body to discuss the general and specific problems of the industry and recommend the study of these to various institutions. This body may be constituted by selecting members connected with the different fruit products, technicians of high standing in the industry, members from the Central Food Technological Research Institute and other institutions and a member from the Directorate of Marketing and Inspection. This Central Body should meet at least once a year under the chairmanship of the Director, Central Food Technological Research Institute, Mysore, and

1. review the work done at the Central Food Technological Research Institute and other institutions regarding the preservation and processing of fruit and vegetable products;
2. suggest practical methods of utilizing research findings on an industrial scale;
3. discuss the problems of the industry in different States and determine, for each State, the order of priority to be assigned to the problems.
4. suggest in the case of certain problems of specific regional interest, ways of obtaining finance for research in conjunction with the State Governments or with individual concerns;
5. deal with regional problems by organizing research on the spot for specific products during the season, and
6. make recommendations for problems which may be studied in allied fields like horticulture, nutrition, etc.

FACTORIES ACT—HARDSHIPS OF THE POTATO COLD STORAGE UNITS

By

(*Messrs Farrukhabad Cold Storage Ltd., Farrukhabad*)

In this paper the author suggests that, in view of the peculiar needs of the potato cold storage units, the provisions of chapter VI of the Indian Factories Act should be relaxed, especially during the months April–October, when large quantities of potatoes are to be handled by each unit.

In the management of Cold Storage Units installed for the preservation of vegetables, particularly potato, the operation of chapter VI of the Indian Factories Act presents some difficulties. These relate mainly to working hours, rest and holidays for labour.

In order to preserve potatoes in cold storages, dealers and cultivators bring their produce during March and April and also during the early part of May. Deliveries of stored potatoes begin soon after the storage in May and last up to the end of October according to the best price fetched by potatoes.

During the period of storage and delivery, huge quantities of potatoes are handled throughout the whole day and the process of loading and unloading requires to be carried out as quickly as possible without any exposure to changing weather conditions. Hence, it is essential to have requisite labour arrangements all the day long to handle this work. Therefore it is inconvenient to follow the provisions of the relevant Sections of the Indian Factories Act in respect of working hours, rest and holidays for the workers during this period.

In England, the difficulties occasioned by the provisions of law embodied in the aforesaid Sections were realized as early as 1937. In the Factories Act, 1937, the protection and restriction as to hours of work, rest, holidays, etc., were confined to young persons and women only. Part VI of that Act embodies the provisions of law in this behalf. Adult male workers are not accorded any special protection under that Act. Even women workers and young persons are not given this protection in fish, fruits and vegetables preservation industry (*vide* Section 94 of the Factories Act, 1937, of England). As a matter of fact, this exemption was dictated by considerations of expediency in respect of this particular industry.

Exemption from the operation of the aforesaid chapter of the Indian Factories Act in respect of labour employed for loading and un-loading potatoes and other food materials during the season seems to be the only solution. This exemption cannot be said to be motivated by any consideration of profit, but is only dictated by the urgent and peculiar needs of the industry. Other industries, similarly placed, have also been given certain exemptions in view of their peculiar requirements.

MICROBIOLOGICAL AID TO FRUIT AND VEGETABLE PRESERVATION INDUSTRIES

By

D. S. Johar and J. C. Anand

(Central Food Technological Research Institute, Mysore)

The authors have drawn attention of food processors to the maintenance of strict sanitary controls in food processing factories. Examination of sugar and samples of fruit and vegetable products has revealed that spoilage in most of the products has been mainly due to bacteria and spore-forming organisms. The importance of hygienic methods in processing and adequate measures to destroy the harmful organisms are pointed out in this paper.

THE problems facing the food bacteriologist are: (1) to detect and prevent contamination of food with undesirable organisms, (2) to sterilize canned foods without impairment of quality, (3) to improve sanitary conditions in food manufacturing plants, and (4) to control micro-organisms by refrigeration, freezing, desiccation or by means of inhibitors.

The role of micro-organisms in food industries can be both constructive and destructive. In the first category may be included the industries relating to the manufacture of food products like cheese, food yeast, bread, cakes, wines, vinegar, concentrated proteins from vegetables, pre-digested foods, etc., in which the activities of fungi and bacteria are utilized. Proper selection and development of pure strains of micro-organisms under standardized environments ensure good quality of the final product.

Harmful organisms in foods cause a variety of changes, *e.g.*, rancidity development, darkening, disintegration, decomposition with emission of putrid odours and development of different metabolic products resulting from enzymatic activity. Although some of the micro-organisms causing spoilage are relatively harmless, there are others which are highly pathogenic. The ingestion of food infected with the pathogens may be sometimes fatal.

Prior determination of the nature and extent of the microbial load on raw materials can help in determining their keeping quality, the appropriate processing and storage techniques, and devising of suitable means of preservation of the finished products.

This paper deals with the microbiological standards of certain Indian foods like fruit and vegetable products, vinegar, sugar, etc. The probable origin of different types of spoilage organisms associated with these products and the remedial measures are also indicated.

Data regarding the microbiological examination of 375 samples of different fruits and vegetable products received from the Central Fruit Products Order Laboratory* and from the trade are given below:

Name of the Product	No. of samples	Samples not conforming to Fruit Products Order	Nature of the organism
Tomato products	51	18%	Gas formers
Canned fruits	39	13%	Facultative flat, sour thermophiles and other spoilage organisms
Canned vegetables ...	77	20%	do
Jams, jellies, and marmalades	19	10%	Osmophilic yeasts and mould species
Preserved and crystallized fruits	24	65%	do
Juices, squashes, cordials, and syrups	93	13%	Osmophilic yeasts
Pickles	37	28%	*Debaromyces* and Mould species

The above figures may not give an accurate idea of the microbiological standard of the factory conditions of their manu-

* This Laboratory was transferred to the Central Food Technological Research Institute on 1st April 1953.

facture especially as the observations are based on a small number of samples. The results, however, are indicative of the insanitary conditions existing in Indian food processing factories, which are apparently responsible for the poor keeping quality of the products. Some of the major types of spoilage associated with these products and the methods of checking them are briefly mentioned below:

Tomato Products

The tomato products examined included preparations like Tomato Ketchup, Tomato Purée and Tomato Paste. These products showed the presence of gas formers like *Lactobacillus lycopersici* and *Lactobacillus gayoni*. Some of the samples were found to be below the standard on account of higher counts of these organisms and positive fermentation test at 37°C in Dextrose Nutrient Agar. The presence of yeasts was also confirmed in two samples. Great progress has been made in other countries in the reduction of the number of these organisms, mainly through the use of sound fruit and by maintaining strict hygienic control in all stages of manufacture. The quality of the products can be improved greatly by adopting sanitary methods of production. Considerable success in the prevention of post-process spoilage can be achieved by filling the products hot in bottles, heated in hot water, and sealing immediately. Otherwise, the final temperature of the product filled in the bottle before sealing is lowered, resulting in the product being exposed to atmospheric contamination.

Canned Vegetables

Among the canned vegetables that were examined, about 20% were below the microbiological standards that are laid down under the Fruit Products Order. The heavy spoilage in canned vegetables was found to be mostly due to faulty seams and underprocessing. Any difficulty arising from bacteriological causes may be due to one or more of the sources liable to contamination *viz.*, the raw products, ingredients, plant equipment and cooking water. Thermophiles, high temperature resistant organisms, are the frequent cause of spoilage. They are usually present in food materials, and accumulate in plant equipment to a concentration sufficient to cause spoilage of the finished products.

The growth of thermophiles is very rapid. Based on the finding that a bacterial colony will become double in size every 20 minutes, a blancher tank with a count of 200 thermophilic spores per cc. of liquid, or 8×10^8 per 1000 gal. will have under optimum growth conditions (131°F and ample food), a total population of 15×10^{15} per 1000 gal. at the end of 8 hours. Fewer than 10 spores before retorting in can No. 2 are known to cause spoilage. Two methods for the prevention of thermophilic build up in the plant are: (1) to maintain equipment temperatures above or below the growth range, and (2) to prevent the accumulation of dirt, slime or scale deposits. In India, where the canneries do not operate all the 24 hours of the day, thorough washing of the plant with steam or hot water at the close and start of each shift will be found most helpful in overcoming this difficulty.

Murrabbas (Preserves) and Crystallized Fruits

The spoilage in indigenous products like *Murrabbas* and crystallized fruits is usually due to yeast belonging to the *Zygosaccharomyces* species which can tolerate high concentrations of sugar unlike other types of organism. These products have been associated with this type of yeast fermentation to such an extent that consumers have developed preference for this fruity odour and taste. The flavouring compounds that are usually present in these products are alcohol, esters and aldehydes formed as a result of the activity of the yeast. The slightest evidence of fermentation, on the other hand, is forbidden by the Fruit Products Order according to which the product should retain the flavour of the original fruit. The fermentation as detected in the finished product starts in the post-processing stage. Proper sealing of the finished product in sterile containers can help, to a great extent, in preventing the fermentation. To meet the demand of the public which have developed a preference for the fermented products, conditions for their preparation have to be standardized by adopting suitable measures.

It is yet to be determined whether the yeast fermentation in the preserves has got any deleterious effect on the health of the consumer. No health hazards have been observed in other indigenous products like *Halwas* and *Mahjoors* which have undergone a similar type of fermentation and are frequently used by Indian *Hakims* and *Vaids*. On the contrary, they are sometimes claimed to have beneficial effects, probably due to the synthesis of the B group of vitamins by the osmophilic yeasts. 'Khamirs', sugar-*cum*-herb pastes, with a total soluble solids content of 60–70%, undergoing vigorous gaseous fermentation, are said to have very beneficial effects. In the light of this experience the permissible level of yeast in such products should be decided.

Quality of Vinegar

The common defects observed in the samples of vinegar analysed in the laboratory were low acidity, total soluble solids, sedimentation, turbidity and, in some cases, incomplete fermentation. Most of the samples were not comparable with foreign vinegars as regards even their analytical figures. It is evident that no systematic procedure is being followed by the industry and vinegars of indifferent quality are produced. A systematic study of the various analytical data seems desirable in order to fix suitable standards in regard to the quality of vinegar. The present specification of acidity limit as 4% alone is not altogether sufficient if quality control is to be enforced rigidly with the ultimate idea of improving the quality of the product.

Quality of Indian Sugar

Sugar is an important raw material for the Canning Industry. Almost all types of micro-organisms may be found in raw refined sugar. The thermophilic types, however, are considered most dangerous since they are spore-forming and can withstand higher processing temperatures than most other bacteria. Of the three groups of thermophilic bacteria associated with sugar, sugars made in India are found to harbour flat sour type of organism which produces acid and little or no gas. An analysis of 34 samples of sugars collected from different Fruit Preservation Factories in various parts of the country revealed that 59% of the samples contained flat, sour and hydrogen sulphide forming anaerobes and thus would be unsuitable for canning purposes according to standards established by the National Canners' Association (U.S.A.). In one sample, flat sour type was as high as 1175 as against the limit of 125 per 10 gms. Before purchasing sugar for the cannery, it is necessary therefore to analyse the sugar for the above types of organism to avoid spoilage in canned products.

This short review has been presented mainly with a view to

guiding the industry and apprising it of the general defects observed in food products, the causes of spoilage and, wherever possible, the remedial measures. Our infant industries will thrive better if they keep in view the importance of microbiology in the manufacture of food products.

PRESERVATION OF FRUIT JUICES

By

N. Thandavan

(*Messrs A. P. V. Engineering Co. Ltd., Calcutta*)

Dealing with methods of preservation of fruit juices, the author has stated that de-aeration followed by pasteurization or heating of fruit juices before packaging considerably enhances their keeping quality. Other advantages ascribed to this method of preservation are the retention of the natural flavour, colour, appearance and nutritive value of fruit juices.

RAPID scientific advances made in the preserved fruit juices industry both in the processing methods and the output of the processed products are comparatively recent, dating from 1925. Various reasons can be assigned for this. Fruit juices have a universal appeal because of their excellent flavour, pleasing appearance and food value. They are available in conveniently-packed, 'ready-to-serve' forms, and are cheaper than juices pressed from fresh fruits. The last but not the least reason is the maintenance of consistently high quality of the products through improved methods of preservation.

As is well known, any weak solution of reducing sugars, if left to itself at ordinary temperature, soon starts to ferment. Fruit juices are no exception to this rule. The primary object of preservation, therefore, is to prevent the spoilage of fruit juices through fermentation, moulding or souring, caused by yeasts, moulds, or bacteria for the growth of which fruit juices act as very favourable media. The methods employed for preservation should be capable of retaining, in the finished product, as much of the natural flavour, colour, and appearance of the juice as possible. These tend to change rapidly due to various enzymatic and oxidative reactions taking place freely in the complex fruit juice. Retention of the orginal nutritive value of the fruit juice is also important. Further, the methods of preservation employed should not result in the development of cooked flavours.

The several methods of commercial preservation of fruit juices at present in vogue can be classified into three categories, viz., (1) preservation by incorporation of chemical reagents, (2) freezing and (3) heat treatment.

The most common chemical agents used for preservation which are permitted by Public Health Laws in most of the countries are benzoic acid (sodium benzoate) and sulphurous acid (sulphur dioxide or SO_2). Benzoic acid, the active principle when sodium benzoate is the preserving agent, owes its action to the formation of a complex compound with the proteins of the yeast. It acts effectively only in juices of high acidity, when added to an extent of 0.1% of sodium benzoate (1000 p.p.m.). Even a proportion of 0.2% is not effective in low acidity juices. Its optimum preservative effect is at a pH range of 2–4.5. Clear juices respond better to benzoic acid than turbid ones. Benzoic acid, though effective against fermentation in juices packed in bulk, has many disadvantages. It is incapable of stopping the growth of moulds on the surface of the liquid in containers. The preservative cannot be re-extracted from the juice and it imparts an irritating flavour. Loss of vitamin C in fruit juices during storage and consequent browning which are due to oxidation by the dissolved oxygen is not prevented by benzoic acid.

Sulphurous acid, as a preservative, is added in the form of either sulphur dioxide, or potassium metabisulphite, or bisulphite. It is effective against moulds, but presents certain difficulties with regard to prevention of fermentation, since some strains of yeast are resistant to sulphur dioxide. It is also more effective in acid media. But one difficulty is the loss of sulphur dioxide due to its combination with certain constituents of the juice. Points to its credit are retention of vitamin C, prevention of browning and its easy removal from the juice by the application of vacuum or heat. Juices preserved in bulk during the working season can be bottled as straight juice after the removal of sulphur dioxide.

Freezing methods would seem to offer an ideal way of preservation especially for juices which are susceptible to injury to flavour, by heating. But, because of the necessity of defrosting prior to use and marketing, freezing is used mainly for extending the operation of canning factories. It has not been commercially quite successful for retail distribution. The juices are chilled and frozen as soon as possible after extraction, but some require de-aeration before freezing. It may be stated that all micro-organisms are not killed by freezing and, consequently, the juice should be made sterile before freezing. If allowed to thaw and stand at room temperature the frozen juice is perishable by moulding or fermenting in a day or two. Hence, the juice is to be kept under refrigeration till it is ready for use. All these considerations do not make freezing attractive as compared with other methods.

For the production of quality juices, de-aeration and subsequent pasteurization appear to be the choice method. Fruit juices in general, and citrus ones in particular, deteriorate in colour and flavour on exposure to air. Air is present in the intercellular spaces of the fruits and always a certain amount of aeration takes place during the process of extraction of the juice. The dissolved and occluded oxygen is responsible for the oxidation and consequent loss in nutritive value and flavour of the juice. It is, therefore, necessary and advisable to minimize the exposure of the juice to air during the process of extraction, straining and other treatment and also to resort to the means of removal of the occluded air. De-aerated juice possesses better keeping qualities and can be filled into containers without the attendant trouble of foaming.

Fruit juices may contain 3–4 cc. of total gas per 100 cc. of juice. Complete de-aeration is not necessary and 90–95% removal is considered satisfactory. The old practice was to remove the oxygen by heating the juice in batches. But modern de-aeration methods depend on subjecting the juice to a vacuum high enough to reduce the partial pressure of the gases above the juice to practically zero. The degree of de-aeration would depend on the extent of vacuum employed, time, and surface of contact between the liquid and vapour. Commercial de-aerators are based on these principles.

Three general types of de-aerators are available. The juice is admitted in the form of a spray or a thin film and the surface of contact is increased by spreading the juice over baffles. One type consists of a stainless steel column in which is placed an array of trays made of porcelain or stainless steel. The APV design consists of an outer stainless steel vessel and an inner perforated cylinder designed to spread the juice in thin films during its passage through the vessel. The top of the vessel is closed by an armour plate glass cover, thus facilitating visual inspection of the processing conditions. A third type comprises a small vacuum chamber in which juice is sprayed upon a rotating plate and employs the centrifugal force for throwing the juice to the sides. Any de-aerator of good design should be capable of easy dismantling and opening up for the purposes of cleaning. Vacuum can be created by pumps, or preferably, by a two-stage steam jet ejector. In continuous processing, the juice is removed by a positive pump capable of working against vacuum. For small capacities, continuous operation becomes difficult and, consequently, it will be necessary to use two or more de-aerating vessels to maintain a steady supply of juice to pasteurization and filling machines. The vacuum in the system can be relieved either by air or by an inert gas.

The preservation of fruit juices by heat with prior de-aeration has come to the forefront in recent years and is the most important method. Pasteurization effects the destruction, through heat, of micro-organisms causing spoilage and must be so carried out as not to impair the flavour. The time of heating is inversely proportional to the temperature of pasteurization. Yeasts are killed in a few minutes at a temperature of 50°–60°C. While some types of mould require a temperature of 80°C for 20 minutes for destruction. Since moulds are aerobic organisms, their growth can be effectively prevented by the elimination of oxygen from the head space of the container. It is, therefore, possible to preserve fruit juices by heating at lower temperatures, and by maintaining the product sterile in sealed containers. Heating can be done in a water-bath or, alternatively, steam can be used. A simple batch pasteurizer can be a shallow tank or vat containing water heated by a closed coil or by admission of steam through a sparger pipe. The tank has a false bottom and juice in bottles or tins in wire baskets is immersed for a pre-determined length of time. After pasteurization, the baskets are taken out and cooled quickly to about 38°C. It is important that every part of the can should reach the desired temperature and the transfer of heat should take place as quickly as possible. This can be achieved by agitation or rotation of the containers. Large factories use continuous pasteurizers in which the tins are carried through a water-bath by roller conveyers and cause the cans to rotate on their own axis. A machine of this category is 'Thermoroto' manufactured by The Thermal Engineering Corporation, Richmond, Virginia. In Thermoroto which contains also a cooling system, the temperature of citrus juices can be raised from 70°F to 180°F in 90–100 seconds. This rapid processing helps to preserve the colour and flavour of the fruit juice, and eliminates prolonged exposures to high temperature, besides ensuring uniform and thorough heat penetration.

The above methods of pasteurizing, which may be regarded as ordinary, if not carried out with care, may cause the development of an undesirable cooked flavour in the juice. It is obvious that either a lower temperature or a shorter period of heating should be able to eliminate this defect. This is achieved by 'flash pasteurization' which consists in heating the juice to a high temperature in a thin film for a few seconds, followed by immediate cooling. Usually, temperatures ranging from 85 to 90°C (185°F–195°F) and holding times ranging from 30 to 12 seconds are employed. The heat exchangers used are either of the plate type or of the coiled tube type. In the former type, the juice and the heating medium, usually hot water, are run in counter current flows between stainless steel plates. The same frame also contains a regenerator and cooling section. Tubular pasteurizers are available in different designs. One design uses a spiral coil of flattened tube, the spiral coil assisting considerably to increase the rate of heat transfer. In the Mallory Flash Pasteurizer the juice is given a high velocity by pumping it through a coil of small diameter, thus reducing the thickness of the stagnant film.

The APV Standard Combined De-aeration and Pasteurization Plant has a nominal continuous capacity for processing 400 gallons per hour of natural strength fruit juice containing fruit cells and is constructed throughout in polished stainless steel of the molybdenum-bearing quality, which has the maximum corrosion resistance. The plant consists of a float balance tank, de-aerator and foam trap, plate type pasteurizer, holding tube assembly, necessary pumps and inter-connecting pipework, auxiliary vacuum producing equipment and hot water circulating system. During operation, the float-controlled balance tank serves to secure a constant head of juice and also receives back any under-heated juice rejected by the manually-operated Flow Diversion Cock. The juice is sucked from this tank into the de-aerator by virtue of the vacuum created in the latter by a two-stage steam jet ejector. The juice is extracted from the de-aerator by an all-stainless steel pump suitably designed to work against vacuum, which pumps the juice into the paraflow plate type heat exchanger. This, along with the holding tube assembly, forms the important part of the whole plant. The primary aim in the use of a 'paraflow', is (1) to secure high rates of heat transfer and consequently quick heating, (2) to work to close terminal temperature differences, which results in better temperature control, and (3) to lessen the danger of overheating. The high heat transfer efficiency of the paraflow is due to the patented design of the stainless steel plates which consist of a series of inter-locking corrugations of special shape. These corrugations have carefully worked-out angles to direct the flow of liquid over the plates by a series of controlled changes of direction and velocity which help to break-up the viscous, heat-insulating film formed between the flowing juice and the metal surface. The plates are one-piece, polished, stainless steel-pressings of great strength. Another advantage of the paraflow is the ease with which the plates can be opened up for cleaning and inspection by merely releasing the tightening screw. In the paraflow, the juice is heated from 60°F to 195°F, initially by the hot juice and finally by hot water fed at a temperature of 200°F. The juice is then held for the required time in the holding tube assembly before re-entering the pasteurizer, cooled initially by heat exchange with the incoming juice and finally by cold water circulated at about 2½ times the actual juice rate. By this arrangement it is possible to attain a final temperature within 10°F of the inlet temperature of the cooling water. Hot water which is the heating medium is obtained from a standard APV hot water system. The plant also includes a stainless steel instrument-panel upon which is mounted a recording thermometer showing the pasteurizing temperature and having electric contacts arranged to close an alarm bell circuit if the temperature rises above or falls below that pre-determined for pasteurizing. A suitable relay and alarm system is provided and mounted at the back of the panel. The different components of the plant are assembled to form a compact unit occupying an actual floor space of 18′ × 9′ only. Allowing for working space for gangways and barrels, the aggregate space requirement of a plant of this type is approximately 25′ × 14′. For operation of this plant, 450–700 lb. of steam at 90/100 lb. per square inch and approximately 1000 gallons of cooling water per hour are required.

Thus, the new type of de-aeration and pasteurization epuipment, useful for the preservation of fruit juices comprise the following features:

1. Elimination of oxygen and other occluded gases and consequent retention of the nutritive value of fruit juices, and prevention of discolouration.
2. Destruction of enzymes which are detrimental to appearance, flavour and keeping quality of the juice.
3. Prevention of the settling of the suspended pulp and the consequent formation of cloud in fruit juices.
4. Economy in floor space, ease of operation and quickness of processing.
5. Consistency and reliability of results.
6. Quality of product.

The writer is thankful to Mr H. Pickard, Managing Director of the A. P. V. Engineering Co. Ltd., for permission to present this paper. Special thanks are also due to Mr J. Thompson, Manager of the Chemical Department, for his valuable assistance and suggestions in the preparation of this paper.

FRUIT PRESERVATION IN MYSORE

By

B. P. Mascarenhas

(*Fruit Preservation Expert, Government of Mysore*)

In this paper the author has indicated the vast potentialities of the Mysore State in respect of raw materials (fruits, vegetables, sugar, etc.,) and containers (glass, enamelled and glazed wares), and has referred to the proposed establishment of a canning factory in Bangalore.

THE fruit preservation industry is of great importance to the economy of the Mysore State. Side by side with the Grow More Food Campaign, concerted efforts should be made for preserving fruits according to known scientific methods.

All the conditions favourable for starting fruit industries are available in the Mysore State. These include the availability of raw materials like fruits and vegetables, tinplate, bottles and sugar, cheap water and power, labour and, last but not the least, technical personnel and advice which are easily available on account of the Central Food Technological Research Institute which is located in Mysore.

1. *Fruits and Vegetables:*

Mangoes, ash gourds, woodapples, plantains, oranges, pineapples, guavas, tomatoes, gooseberries, limes, jambolana, etc., are available in large quantities in the Mysore State. The acreages under mangoes, plantains, oranges and other fruits in the different districts of the Mysore State will be seen from Table below:

Acreage of different fruits in Mysore State *

District	Area under Fruit Crops in Acres				
	Mango	Plan-tain	Oranges	Other fruits	Dist. Total
Bangalore	6,555	2,049	26	3,935	12,565
Kolar	12,749	447	...	270	13,466
Tumkur	2,972	1,231	79	2,045	6,327
Mysore	1,115	2,226	5	266	3,612
Mandya	1,686	4,285	...	997	6,968
Hassan	2,680	3,512	2,345	2,446	10,983
Shimoga	921	250	...	15	1,186
Chikmagalur (Kadur) ...	2,603	2,453	2,400	838	8,294
Chitaldrug	983	3,683	...	2,628	7,294
Total ...	32,264	20,136	4,855	13,440	70,695

It will be seen from the above Table that Bangalore, Kolar and Hassan are the three districts which are best suited for the supply of fruits for Fruit Preservation Industry in the Mysore State.

* The Season and Crop Report (1946-47), issued by the Revenue Department, Government of Mysore.

The different seasons in which fruits and vegetables are available in large quantities in markets will be seen from Table below:

Periods of availability of fruits and Vegetable

Commodity	Season	Producing areas
Fruits		
1. Oranges	Nov. to April	Chikmagalur and Hassan Dists., Coorg.
2. *Mosambies* (Sweet lime)	Aug. to Jan.	Chickmagalur Coorg and Kadur and Sathukudi.
3. Grapes (*Deccan*) ...	June to Sept. Dec. to March	Bangalore, Hoskote. Devanhalli Taluks.
4. Mangoes (*Neelam*)	April to June	Srinivasapur, Chintamani Mulgage, Bangalore, Bangalore, Mysore, Tumkur Dist. Krishnagiri, Hosur.
5. ,, (*Totapuri*)		
6. ,, (*Happus*)		
7. ,, (*Piari*)		
8. ,, (*Malgova*)		
9. Guavas	July—Nov.	Bangalore Taluk.
10. Papayas	Throughout the year	,,
11. *Chickoos*	April—Sept.	,,
12. Banana Yellow	Throughout the year	Bangalore, Mysore, Hassan.
13. ,, green		
14. Sour Limes	June—Sept.	Bangalore, Tumkur and Mandya Districts.
Vegetables		
1. Carrots (English) ...	Aug.—Feb.	Bangalore Taluk
2. Tomatoes	Aug.—April	Bangalore District
3. Cabbages	Nov.—April	Bangalore Taluk
4. Cauliflower	Jan.—June	do
5. Cluster Beans ...	July—Dec.	Bangalore, Devanhalli Anekal, Hosakote, Kengeri, and Nelamangala Taluks.
6. French Beans ...	April—Nov.	
7. Broad Beans	April—Nov.	

2. *Containers*—Tin-plates

In regard to the tin-plate position it is likely that the Government of India will accord a high priority.

3. *Bottles:*

We are fortunate in having the Mysore Glass and Enamel

Works in Bangalore and this company will be able to supply our requirements.

4. *Sugar:*

The supply position has improved at present and Mysore is proud to have a Sugar Company at Mandya which will be able to supply the sugar requirements of the industry.

5. *Transport:*

Transport plays a very important part in the working of any factory. It is absolutely essential to have a first-class transport system.

6. *Labour:*

The availability of machine-minded labour in an industrially advanced State like Mysore is a feature of great importance, as it will ensure the satisfactory working of factories from the very start.

7. *Water supply and disposal of cannery waste:*

Although bacteriological purity of water is a *sine qua non* for a cannery, other factors such as taste, dissolved solids, metallic contamination and acidity or alkalinity of water must be considered. The water in Bangalore is suitable for canneries.

The disposal of cannery waste has to be ensured by running the screened wastes over land and taking care to avoid the production of offensive odours or the pollution of adjacent water supplies by percolation of the wastes through the soil. Furrows can also be used as receiving channels for the effluent, thus providing a greater surface area for absorption.

8. *Technical aid:*

Modern canning technology is far removed from the hit-and-miss methods adopted in the early days, and today the industry has become a highly specialized one. The place of a laboratory in a modern cannery is no longer a luxury, but an essential part of the plant. We are very fortunate in having the Central Food Technological Research Institute in Mysore to guide us.

It is proposed to start a canning factory on a Joint-stock Company basis at Krishnarajapuram, Bangalore. The site is fourteen acres in extent and has several buildings which can be easily converted to suit the requirements. The factory will be close to Krishnarajapuram Railway Station and there is also a railway siding on the premises.

In Saklespur and Chickmagalur, varieties of citrus fruits are often not harvested by coffee planters as they do not find an easy market. Lakhs of rupees worth of citrus and other fruits such as goose-berries and wood-apples thus go to waste. It is very essential to take steps to utilize these fruits as a part of the programme of the reconstruction and reorganization of industries in Mysore.

FRUIT AND VEGETABLE PRESERVATION INDUSTRY OF ASSAM—ITS PRESENT AND FUTURE

By

L. K. Handique

(*Department of Agriculture, Assam, Shillong*)

The author has drawn attention to the various handicaps facing the fruit and vegetable growers in Assam. On account of the partition of India and inadequate transport facilities between Assam and the rest of the country the once flourishing fruit and vegetable trade of Assam is greatly hampered. The solution to this problem, it is pointed out, is to establish some fruit and vegetable preservation factories in this part of India.

ASSAM, the North Easternmost State of the Republic of India, is full of natural resources. Practically all varieties of fruits such as mandarin orange, lemon, pineapple, plum, peach, sand pears, papaya, banana and vegetables like potato, tomato, peas and beans are found in this picturesque part of the country.

The oranges and pineapples of Assam have an all-India fame. The smooth-skinned orange of Khasia and Jaintia Hills and the gigantic pineapples of the Upper Assam areas are comparable to the best of oranges and pineapples available in any part of India.

The area under orange cultivation is about 20,000 acres at present. Presuming that about 60% of the area is in fruiting stage, the total annual production, at 200 *maunds* per acre, is estimated at 24,00,000 *maunds* of fruits. The total acreage under pineapples is about 6,000 and the total annual production about 6 lakh *maunds*. Before the partition of the country, these fruits used to be exported to almost all the important cities and towns of the eastern and northern India. There was a big volume of trade in pineapples, oranges and potatoes with the neighbouring areas, now forming a part of Eastern Pakistan. But, after the partition, acute transport difficulties have arisen, and as a result, export trade in fruits and vegetables received a temporary set-back. Assam is now connected with the rest of India by the newly constructed rail link which is the only means of land communication with the rest of India. But, even this often goes out of action, especially during the monsoon season. Thus, even the restricted markets in the Indian Union are lost to the State. The riverine communication which is easy and less costly passes through Eastern Pakistan, and whenever any trade deadlock arises between India and Pakistan, the river transport gets blocked and the trade virtually comes to a standstill. The consequences of all these difficulties have been seriously felt by fruit growers in the State.

Though every endeavour is being made to improve the present transport conditions, some permanent and durable solution should be found to market the abundant supply of these perishable commodities. This can only be done by the development of the preserved fruit and vegetable industry in the State. For this purpose, the Government of Assam initiated a scheme of fruit and vegetable preservation by opening a Fruit Technological Laboratory at Gauhati. The main objects of this Institution are: (1) to investigate and work out recipes for the various products, utilizing the fruits and vegetables abundantly grown in this area, (2) to impart training in fruit technology, and (3) to foster the development of the fruit and vegetable preservation industry on sound and scientific lines.

Work is being carried out in this Laboratory for the last three and a half years. Scientific data have been collected for the preparation of the following products: (*a*) squashes and juices of orange, pineapple and lemon, (*b*) jams of pineapple, orange, plum and sand pear, (*c*) guava jelly and orange marmalade, (*d*) canned pineapple, sand pear, plum, papaya and peas, (*e*) curried vegetables, (*f*) candies of ginger and orange peel, and (*g*) tomato products. Work on the dehydration of potato has also been started. Four students have been trained in fruit technology in the advance course (nine months), 13 students in the short course (three months) and 348 ladies in the 15 day course. From the technological point of view, the Laboratory has achieved a great success, but the idea with which it was started, *viz.*, the scientific and systematic development of the preserved fruit industry, is yet to be achieved. Some result has no doubt been obtained in this direction as is evident from the fact that, prior to the establishment of this institute, there was only one fruit preserving concern manufacturing a small volume of squash in the State, whereas now there are six licensed units. However, the volume of production of all these units is so small that it hardly solves the problem of dealing with the surplus and unmarketable fruits in the State.

There is great scope for the development of the Preserved Fruit and Vegetable Industry in the State of Assam. Although the establishment of highly mechanized factories may not be feasible due to the communication difficulties, it is quite possible to develop the industry on a cottage scale, using mechanical appliances as far as possible. A fairly big factory at Gauhati with feeder units located in the important fruit growing areas will meet the situation to a large extent. Orange and pineapple juices can be extracted and preserved in barrels in the fruit-growing areas and can be transported to Calcutta and other places.

The difficulties that have been experienced in the development of this industry on a sound and economic basis are: (1) lack of private capital, (2) want of marketing facilities, (3) high cost of production due to prohibitive cost of sugar, bottles and cans, and (4) high railway freight for transporting the finished products to distant places. Private capital is shy in the beginning as the industry is a new one in the State and people hesitate to invest until a steady progress is observed by them. Internal market for the products being very limited, a big volume of the produce will have to be exported and for this purpose a good export market will have to be created.

In consideration of all the difficulties enumerated above, State help seems to be necessary in the initial stage. This can be done by (*a*) providing cheap finance to enterprisers at a nominal rate of interest, (*b*) supplying sugar to the fruit preservers at *ex-factory* rate, (*c*) lowering the cost of bottles and cans, and (*d*) allowing adequate concession in railway freight to transport the finished goods.

The climatic and soil conditions of Assam are suitable for increasing the cultivation of fruits and vegetables to a large extent and, if the surplus fruits and vegetables are utilized by the Preservation Industry, Assam can meet the demand of the fruits and vegetables products of many other States in India.

POTATO SEED TRADE OF BIHAR

By

Sri Prabhudatta **Mukerji**

(Messrs Kisan Cold Storage and Refrigeration Service, Ltd., Patna)

In this paper the author has drawn attention to the need for improving potato seed trade in Bihar by ensuring cultivation of high-yielding seed varieties and sale of good quality seed potatoes by recognized agencies. A strong plea for the Government to take appropriate measures in this direction is made.

SINCE long, Bihar was the home of good quality potato seed which was supplied to the whole of northern and eastern India. Among the potato-growing districts in Bihar, Patna ranks first, and many growers in this area specialize as seed growers. The usual custom is to get the hill potatoes from Darjeeling during the sowing season (October-November) and plant them in other States to get much higher yields than from any other type of potato seed. A flourishing seed trade has thus developed, and, along with it, a large number of scientifically planned Cold Storages for the preservation of potato seeds have been established in this State. The total capital invested in Cold Storages in this State is over 50 lakhs of rupees.

But, at present, this industry is faced with multifarious difficulties and, unless timely action is taken, the entire seed trade and the Cold Storage Industry in Bihar will be jeopardized. Unscrupulous people in and outside the State have started taking advantage of the good name of Patna seeds and are adulterating these with inferior varieties. Generally speaking, the grower is being cheated.

The main difficulty faced by Cold Storages is the lack of proper quality seeds which can be stored and sold with confidence to the numerous purchasers in northern and eastern India. Here again, the grower does not necessarily get the good and unadulterated *Darjeeling Katua* seeds with the result that the potatoes he obtains on harvesting in March are not of the genuine *Katua* variety. They are seldom true to type or free from diseases. Consequently, the quality and yield of the seeds deteriorate rapidly. Unless this problem is tackled with vigour and foresight, the confidence of customers in the *Katua* seeds may be lost.

The Government of Himachal Pradesh have taken a bold step in arranging, in recognized plots, the proper cultivation of potato seed by recognized seed growers. The Government are receiving full co-operation from cultivators and those interested in seed potatoes. This procedure has ensured a bright prospect for potato cultivation and the potato seed trade. It is therefore suggested that the Bihar Government should either arrange its own cultivation of Darjeeling Red varieties on a sufficiently large scale or make available suitable lands to Cold Storage establishments and other organized agencies who may undertake the cultivation of genuine varieties. This would ensure the quality of the potato seeds stored and supplied to numerous customers all over India. In this venture, the co-operation of the Central Potato Research Institute will be of great advantage. Suitable steps have to be taken to lay down certain essential principles of potato cultivation to improve the crop and maintain the quality, and to see that the principles are followed by recognized growers and stockists.

There is another factor worth mentioning in connection with the preservation of potatoes, both for seed and table purposes, *viz.*, the use of D.D.T. powder. Although the D.D.T. powder keeps away insect pests, it has no effect on the spoilage of potatoes due to high temperatures. Moreover, D.D.T.-sprayed table potatoes are definitely inferior as an article of food. They not only take longer time to boil, but also develop an unpleasant odour. Authorities on potato storage have declared that spraying of table potatoes with D.D.T. should be abandoned.

These steps are suggested in the best interests of potato seed cultivation and trade in Bihar.

A PLEA FOR DEVELOPING AND MODERNIZING FRUIT PRESERVATION AS A COTTAGE INDUSTRY THROUGH COMPREHENSIVE TECHNICAL AID

By

P. V. Surya Prakasa Rao

(Government Fruit Products Research Laboratory, Kodur)

The author has put forth a strong plea for the development of fruit and vegetable preservation industry in India on a cottage-industry scale, using modern scientific techniques. The small-scale units may be developed side by side with large-scale factories already existing in the country. The importance of this method of tackling the problem of utilizing local surpluses during glut periods of production to the national economy is stressed.

Fruit and vegetable production is widely dispersed throughout the length and breadth of our country. The plains and plateaus, the hills and valleys, the coastal areas and interior uplands, all enjoy a variety of climates and grow a multiplicity of fruits and vegetables. Our forestes and even our scrub jungles produce a wealth of wild fruits, herbs and roots, which are rich in food and medicinal values. On the other hand, our means of transport and channels of utilization of these protective foods are as yet poorly developed as compared with our needs. As a result, valuable food material to the tune of 25–50 per cent of our production, and perhaps much more of what is grown for us in forests, jungles and elsewhere are lost. And, this is so at a time when our *per capita* consumption of fruits and vegetables is much below par and when we are straining ourselves to conserve and maximize our output of food! Loss of fruits and vegetables due to wastage and spoilage occurs almost continually at all stages, from the point of production to that of actual consumption, *viz.*, during picking, assembling, packing, transport, storage and distribution. In addition to this, a certain amount of loss is also occasioned through pre-harvest drop and damage due to enzymic-*cum*-microbial spoilage.

Obviously, the huge volume of national produce, which is going to waste is not such as cannot be collected and made available at a few chosen centres to feed and sustain large, mechanized preservation units all round the year. The fact that the loss is huge does not necessarily mean that only huge factories are needed to process them. Could we then escape the conclusion that the wastage can be stemmed by universal home preservation and by a network of modern small-scale preservation units judiciously dispersed all over the country, and more especially in important producing regions, pooling centres, along distributing channels and in consuming areas?

Consequently, it becomes clear that, in any scheme designed to stop the stupendous loss of food material in our country, small-scale or cottage-scale preservation units have an important place. The cheap man-power abundantly available in the country-side almost all the year round and the trained personnel being increasingly made available by institutes like the Central Food Technological Research Institute, the polytechnics, laboratories and universities are important factors for the success of these industries. The level of daily production capacity of a small-scale unit may be of the order of 50–200 lb. of different types of products.

There is another factor which is of importance in any consideration of the question of fruit preservation as a cottage industry. We have in the country a vast number of people engaged in home and cottage-scale preparation of pickles, chutneys, dried fruits, vegetables, *Murrabbas, Sherbaths* and a variety of sweets and sweetmeats. Preservation of these is an art and a profession which is handed down from generations and in which we can boast of many an expert and connoisseur. The basic practices followed in the preparation and preservation of these products are so remarkably simple, sound and scientific that they have remained essentially the same and have stood the test of time. We have a tremendous reservoir of experience, skill and knowledge in this art, accumulated over many years and spread on the widest possible scale in the country. These faculties have to be rationalized or reorientated in the light of modern scientific knowledge and attuned to the latest scientific techniques. It is exactly for this purpose that all that the modern technical aid can offer should be commissioned and exploited. We have already a few cottage industries in our country and it is necessary to build up the fruit and vegetable preservation industry according to our needs. This is an important and a worthy task for science and technology to accomplish.

In this context, it is gratifying to find that a high priority has been accorded to small- and cottage-scale industries in our National Plan in recognition of their great importance and eminent suitability to our social and economic conditions. The plan has also laid down certain principles of policy for the Central and the State Governments to follow for the development of these industries. Broadly speaking, these may be stated as follows: (1) organization of village co-operatives, rural workshops, research, training, demonstration and production centres; (2) provision of finance, credit, controlled and uncontrolled raw materials, and other aids for the production and marketing of goods; and (3) elimination of unhealthy competition between large- and small-scale industries by (*a*) reservation of spheres of production, (*b*) imposition of a cess on large-scale industries and (*c*) non-expansion of the capacity of the large units. It is a happy augury, too, that the Central Government and some of the State Governments have already started taking steps to implement the above policy.

I have so far endeavoured to show the importance of and the imperative necessity for developing fruit and vegetable preservation as a cottage industry and the value and faith our National Plan places in industries of this category. I shall now try to indicate the various possibilities that exist for such a development and the great role which technical aid can play in this process.

(*a*) *Product Development:*

(i) A variety of sweets and sweetmeats are prepared and consumed in our country on a colossal scale by people belonging to all age groups from different economic and social strata. It should be easy to produce and introduce 'fruit sweets' containing one or more cheap, nutritious and popular fruits and vegetables like mango, banana, papaya, guava, jack, cashew-apple, palmyrah, country fig, tomato, carrot, pumpkin, peanuts, coconut kernel, etc., with honey and refined jaggery. Fruit products like the familiar *halwas* with raisins, nuts, etc., are extremely popular. Such products which are suited to the palate and pocket of the Indian populace should be developed and standardized. Intensive efforts should be made to introduce them in schools, canteens, cafetarias and similar agencies.

(ii) The country produces annually 770 millions of bottles of aerated waters, a large majority of which are synthetic. We need not quote figures to prove their universal presence and popularity these days. Syrups and carbonated beverages with fruit and vegetable juices are equally popular.

Encouraging indications have been obtained in this direction at our Laboratory at Kodur from preliminary trials with lime, cashewapple, *Jaman* and passion fruit juices. There is a vast and almost unlimited field here to seize and exploit. Clarified cane juice or jaggery syrup and tender coconut water seem to hold high promises, the former as cheap substitutes for the refined white sugar and the latter as an excellent refresher and a blending agent with fruit and vegetable juices.

(b) Standardization and simplification of processess, recipes, etc.

All the existing useful methods and recipes and those newly developed should be standardized and simplified so as to be capable of application on the widest possible scale. Tables, charts, ready reckoners, simple general formulae, etc., have to be provided to simplify the calculations involved and to ensure accuracy and uniformity in the composition of products. Preservatives and chemicals to be used should be made available in the form of tablets or pellets of convenient standard weights.

Simplification of the process. Methods of hygienic control of various processes, premises, equipment and personnel and of maintaining adequate standards of sanitation and quality should be simplified and made cheap with the help of modern aids like antiseptics, disinfectants, detergents, etc. The ultimate goal in all these matters is to make the entire process of preparation and preservation safe, even in the hands of an ordinary worker.

(c) Container Development:

Packaging. Ours is a plastic age and plastics have revolutionized the economics in many a sphere and transformed the fortunes of several industries. Fruit preservation is, however, yet to come under their magic spell. Fruit preservers in the country know to their cost the very unsatisfactory position of containers both of tin and glass. Some efforts seem to be urgently called for to alleviate the distressing situation.

(d) Equipment Development:

Simple, small and efficient tools and appliances, capable of being fabricated from indigenous materials at a low cost by village artisans, should be devised and standardized. For instance, it is possible to make an orange juice reamer (made of red cedar wood) which could be fitted to the rear wheel of a bicycle and worked satisfactorily like the familiar dynamo lamp. It should be easy to make reamers after the fashion of the various types of improved spinning wheel.

In view of the increasing electrification of rural areas, we should develop small-scale preservation equipment and outfits including heaters and driers which can be operated by electric power.

Suitable appliances have also to be designed for simple hand-extraction of oils from citrus peels, fruit seeds and stones, for husking seeds of cucumber, melon, pumpkin, etc., and for the utilization of other by-products and wastes.

(e) Integration of small-scale and large-scale industries:

Modernized 'cottages' of preservation, suitably located in a country-wide network of production and distribution, appear to be best suited for the production of semi-processed goods like preserved juices, pulps, and slices of mangoes, citrus fruits, pine-apples, jack-fruits, cashew-apples, mushmelons and passion fruits for subsequent absorption and manufacture into final, finished products by large mechanized units. They can, thus, very usefully play the role of small 'feeder' units and sustain themselves over a longer period of the year. In this way, the two units, *viz.*, the cottage industries and the large-scale factories can work in a harmonious, co-operative and complementary partnership, salvaging the enormous wastage of produce occurring all along the country's production and marketing line.

Except canned fruits, products of almost all other categories lend themselves to preservation as semi-processed articles and are being actually preserved as such. A common, integrated programme of production, as suggested above, appears to be full of possibilities in minimizing unhealthy competition between large- and small-scale establishments and in promoting their common good. Here is another line of interest for the technologist.

I have broadly indicated certain possibilities on which action should be taken as early as possible. There are several other ways in which science and technology can be of great help in improving the general standards and techniques adopted by the Cottage Industry and in maximizing the utility, popularity and quality of preserved products and minimizing their costs. Also, the useful results have to be disseminated and popularized on the widest possible scale, by modern methods of propaganda and publicity, through demonstration centres, model preservation 'cottages', mobile canteens, cafeterias, etc.

The great benefits that Science and Technology can confer are not the monopoly of any one type of industry. Given the necessary goodwill and co-operation of all concerned, there is no doubt that fruit preservation can be organized and developed as a cottage industry on modern lines to the advantage of all. It is to be hoped, therefore, that these two requisites will be forthcoming in an abundant measure as a result of the deliberations at this Symposium.

TECHNICAL PROBLEMS IN PACKAGING

By

T. M. Rama Aiyangar

(Messrs The Metal Box Company of India Ltd., Calcutta)

In devising a suitable pack, the factors to be considered are: causes of deterioration, remedies, consumer preference and consumer purchasing power. There should be a greater appreciation by food industries of the fundamental fact that the manufacture of the product and the packaging of it are one continuous operation. The standardization of the pack for any particular industry or group of industries will be a step in the right direction.

THE Metal Box Company of India, Ltd., has, for the best part of the past two decades, been trying to place packaging on a sound and scientific footing. Although the measure of its success has been considerable, experience indicates that there has not been adequate appreciation of the part played by packaging in most of the industries, and especially in the food industry. This Symposium, therefore, is most timely and is bound to contribute to the rapid progress of the Indian Food Industry. We are very grateful to the organizers for giving us an opportunity to participate in this Symposium which holds out so much hope for the future.

In the ultimate analysis, the aim of all food packaging is to preserve the product in its natural or modified form, until it is consumed. It may be emphasized that *the production and packaging of a processed food is one continuous operation*. The container has got to be so designed as to hold and retain the product in its 'factory-fresh' condition until it is consumed. The scientific basis for the production of foods should be extended to their packaging.

In designing the package, many points have to be carefully considered.

1. The factors contributing to the deterioration of the pro-

duct in storage have to be determined, first in the laboratory, and later, under field and commercial conditions. For example, it is common knowledge that, during processing, the preservation of the attractive colour of certain fruits and the discolouration due to sulphur in certain vegetables can be effectively prevented by using cans suitably lacquered inside. Similarly, the deterioration of roasted and powdered coffee can be arrested by replacing air with an inert gas and packing the product in airtight containers.

2. The type of pack has to be very carefully chosen. In a large country like ours, the product has to be transported over long distances by different types of transport. It is, therefore, essential that the container should be strong enough to withstand all transport hazards and changes of climate. A knowledge of these conditions and the evolution of a scientific basis for determining the most suitable pack are problems that deserve careful study.

3. The manufacturer must carry out an intensive survey of consumer preference and consumer purchasing power. These should determine the size of his pack. In this connection, it should be borne in mind that the world trend is towards tamper-proof packs so that the consumer can be confident that the product is in the same condition as when it left the factory. Today, the consumer demands the guarantee of quality and it is the duty of the producer to take this into account.

4. The employment of mass production techniques has proved that manufacturing costs could be reduced considerably. Nowhere else, the cost problem is as important as in this country on account of its present low purchasing power. The success or otherwise of any food industry will depend whether or not its products, however good and essential, are sold at a price that the consumer can pay. When a manufacturer of a food product contemplates employing mass production techniques, the package has to be so designed as to be capable of being filled, closed and wrapped at speeds commensurate with the rate of production of the product. The lay-out of the factory, the choice of filling, closing and wrapping equipment, the provision of suitable conveyers, etc., are all technical problems of fundamental importance and must be worked out in close collaboration with the technical personnel of the container manufacturers.

Once again, as the landed cost of the container will depend

on the speed at which it could be produced, the standardization of the pack for any particular industry or a group of industries as a whole will be a step in the right direction. However, the tendency, desirable in certain cases, to evolve packs very different from those in the market for attracting purchasers must be toned down to marketing circumstances. In the present stage of the development of food industries in this country, this is a very important matter affecting their very existence, and therefore, the technical and commercial personnel and individual members of the associations should select packs which are suitable to manufacturers of containers and to the industry as a whole.

5. In addition to the functional aspect of the package, it is also important that the outward appearance of the finished pack should be properly evolved. Labels and decoration must be so designed as to attract the attention of the buyer. There is large scope for improvement in this direction.

6. Governments are enforcing laws and regulations concerning the manufacture and sale of food products in the interest of public health. Such laws and regulations also apply to packaging and labelling. A manufacturer has, therefore, to bear these requirements in mind when deciding the package.

We should like to repeat that the product and its pack must always be considered together, for the quality of the product depends entirely on the quality and suitability of the package used, and that as much scientific thought and effort must be devoted to the evolution of the package as to the manufacture of the product.

TANNERY BY-PRODUCTS FOR THE MANUFACTURE OF EDIBLE GELATINE

By

Y. Nayudamma

(Central Leather Research Institute, Madras)

In this paper the author has said that the basic raw materials to the gelatine manufacturer are the by-products of the Tanning Industry. Maximum co-operation between leather and gelatine industry is therefore very essential. Only the best hide and skin offals in a well-preserved state are useful for the manufacture of gelatine. These raw materials should be explored to the full for the manufacture of edible gelatine in India.

BONES, hides and skins are the raw materials used in the manufacture of gelatine and glue. India produces about 19 million hides (cow and buffalo) and 37 million skins (goat and sheep) per year. During the processing of hide to leather, 5%–10% of the material are obtained as trimmings or cuttings and these form an important raw material for the manufacture of gelatine and glue. This raw material is being utilized to some extent at present and glue is made in India on a cottage scale as well as in a few factories. The manufacture of gelatine, however, has not progressed. In the year 1951–52, glue and gelatine worth about 2.5 million rupees were imported into India. In the same year, 5,500 tons of the raw material were exported from India. Gelatine is being imported at Rs. 4,000 per ton, *i.e.*, at ten times the price of raw material. This is certainly a matter of concern. In the interests of national economy, therefore, every effort should be made to conserve the raw materials and exploit them to the full.

Preparation of gelatine: Pieces of skin are simmered in water. When the soup cools, it sets into a firm jelly but not always, and this is one of the difficulties met with in the turning of skin into gelatine. In the very act of turning skin into gelatine, the gelatine is degraded, a change leading to the decrease in power of setting to a firm jelly and the viscosity of its solution. This degradation is due to the action of heat or to the growth of micro-organisms.

Raw hide is a suitable medium for the growth of micro-organisms. If the raw material is already degraded by bacteria, the gelatine produced from it will also be degraded. The raw material for the gelatine manufacturer is a by-product to the tanner. The ignorance or indifference of the tanner regarding this degradation will result in the waste of valuable raw material for gelatine manufacture.

The gelatine manufacturer is thus forced to rely on the tanner for the quality of his raw materials and it would be in his interest to get acquainted with the nature of his raw materials, the processes that precede and their effects on the raw stock before he gets them. It is to the advantage of the tanner to find out ways and means for maintaining his by-products in good condition for high grade gelatine manufacture and for getting a higher price for his material. Maximum co-operation between the leather and gelatine industries, which are so closely connected, is thus essential.

Composition of Hides and Skins

The terms 'hide' and 'skin' are identical. Hide is the skin of a big animal. The chemical constituents of skin are: water, fats, mineral matter and fibrous and non-fibrous proteins.

Histologically, the skin is divided into two distinct and superimposed layers. The top layer is the epidermis which is very thin. Underneath the epidermis is the main layer of the skin called the corium which constitutes about 98% of the skin thickness. Underneath the corium is the adipose tissue or flesh.

Collagen fibres constitute the major part of corium. These white fibres are composed of small fibrils which are again made up of more minute micelles. Collagen fibres are present in bundles encased in a net-like sheath of reticular fibres. The ensheathed fibre bundles are wavy and inter-weave with one another at an angle.

Like all proteins, collagen is a polypeptide formed by the linking together of a number of amino acids. The amino acid composition of collagen is known from X-ray evidence and electron-microscopic work. It is considered that collagen fibril, in its natural state of hydration, is essentially a smooth cylinder or ribbon. Helical and spiral configurations are also proposed.

The cohesive forces that operate in the net-like structure of collagen are (1) ionic (-CO H_3 N-) (2) ion-dipole (-CO—H_2 N-) (3) dipole-dipole (including hydrogen bond -CO—HN-) and (4) van der Waal's forces. The cohesion of this net-like structure depends upon external influences. When the bonds of forces of cohesion which are not originally very resistant are overcome, the structure of collagen is loosened. A characteristic property of collagen is that it has a shrinkage temperature around 65°C. (It shrinks to about 1/3rd its original length in contact with water at 65°C). The shrinkage temperature may be said to be the internal viscosity or plasticity of the fibrous protein. Shrinkage may be due to the rupture of certain cross bonds between polypeptide chains with subsequent local orientation of parts of these chains into thermodynamically more probable space arrangements. Further breaking of cross bonds leads to transformation of collagen into gelatine. In acid or alkaline solutions and especially on heating, break-down (hydrolysis) of the polypeptide chains takes place; in other words collagen is turned into gelatine. This important reaction is indeed responsible for the name 'collagen' derived from Greek, meaning 'glue former'. Collagen-gelatine transformation is in the map a structural rather than a chemical transformation. The gelatine solution when cooled sets into a jelly. Original random structure moves towards a more ordered form. Jelly is merely a tangle of long-chain molecules.

Another important property of collagen is that it swells in acid or alkali solutions and has an isoelectric point around pH 5.0. An understanding of the chemical properties and molecular structure of collagen and the control of the configuration of collagen fibre is very necessary for the tanner as well as for the gelatine manufacturer.

Raw Materials—Tannery Treatment

The skins of 'fallen' (dead) or slaughtered animals are flayed. As they carry with them a vast number of micro-organisms the skins are 'cured' to avoid putrefaction by bacteria. Curing is accomplished by dehydration of the skin either by evaporation (drying in the shade or sun) or by osmotic action of strong solutions of salts (brining and wet salting) or by a combination of drying and salting (dry salting).

The cured skins reach the hide godown or a tannery. Here, the skins are rounded or trimmed to cut away unwanted portions such as tails, pates, etc., which have no value in leather making. These are collected and dried and sold to the gelatine manufacturer. The tanner should see that this stock is properly dried. Impurities and high alkalinity of salt, high relative humidity and sun-drying result in a 'hard cure', hard to rehydrate as the soluble proteins of the skins get denatured and cemented and the fibres get stuck. Certain salt-tolerant micro-organisms cause trouble. Once colonies of bacteria are established, their growth takes place very rapidly. Hence, addition of effective antisceptics is helpful.

The trimmed hides are soaked in water to remove salt, dirt, etc., and to rehydrate the skin bringing it to its original condition.

The soaked and washed hides then receive unhairing treatment. This is done by immersing the skin in suspensions of hydrated lime, or in lime in admixture with sharpeners, such as sodium sulphide, red arsenic, sodium cyanide, etc., to expedite the depilatory action. The main objects of liming are to loosen the epidermis with the hair and condition the corium, by removing soluble proteins, saponifying natural fats, by adequate opening up of the fibre structure, plumping and water uptake of collagen and activating the ionic groups by breaking up salt links through hydrolysis.

At this stage the loosened hair, the saponified fat and the flesh are removed by mechanical means; and the 'pelt', as it is called at this stage, is again trimmed. The limed pelt is at times split. The limed trimmings, bellies, split hides which would not repay tanning and the fleshings are collected. Lime water is sprinkled on this material and the material dried in the sun and sold to gelatine and glue manufacturers.

In the case of limed stock, care should be exercised to see that the stock does not contain arsenic or cyanide that might have been used in unhairing. For edible gelatine manufacture, the raw materials should conform to certain standards of purity. Only the best hide and skin offal should be utilized. Pates and trimmings of calf skin are claimed to be excellent for the manufacture of edible gelatine. Another source that may be mentioned is the raw hide pickers discarded after use by textile mills.

Edible gelatine is produced in various grades invariably blended from several batches to get uniform product in powder flake or sheet form.

It is to be remembered that conditions under which gelatine is made must confirm to very high standards of hygiene. A clear understanding of the functions of different operations of gelatine manufacture made possible the abandonment of the rule-of-thumb methods and the introduction of laboratory control.

The raw material used to make hide gelatine contains salt, dirt and other impurities. The material should be purchased on its nitrogen and grease contents. An effective check has to be kept on the presence of arsenic, copper, zinc, lead and cyanide etc., in all materials. Good potable water is a necessity. Bacteriological tests on the raw materials, on the finished product and at different points in the plant have to be carried out. Speed and cleanliness are of paramount importance.

The edible gelatine is graded on the basis of bloom test (jelly strength and viscosity) gold number, colour, odour, low So_2 content, low metallic content, low bacterial count, low ash content and a constant isoelectric point, pH or acidity. To supply, a product which will have the same properties depends entirely upon the analytical control.

Uses: Gelatine finds application as a fining agent, stabilizer, protective coating, in confectionery and household cooking. Gelatine is one of the easiest proteins to digest and its cleavage products are completely absorbed by the human system and is a valuable addition to the diet.

The prosperity of the hide gelatine industry is dependent on the care exercised by the tanneries in handling its raw materials. Hides and skins are liable to be easily exposed to conditions which will materially reduce their value of the gelatine matter. It is in the interest of both the tannery and gelatine industries to understand each other's problems, pool their experience and share their knowledge to ensure that this valuable raw material is exploited to the full.

THE MANUFACTURE OF EDIBLE GELATINE IN INDIA

By

H. C. Bijawat

(*National Chemical Laboratory, Poona*)

The manufacture of edible gelatine would be a very profitable industry on account of the abundance of raw materials such as hides, skins and bones in India. There is, however, no indigenous production of high quality gelatine and our requirements are met by imports. A pilot plant for the production of edible and photographic gelatines was designed and installed at the National Chemical Laboratory, Poona. The process was leased out to a firm in Northern India and the Laboratory was assisting the firm in the lay-out and designs for a plant with a rated capacity of ½ ton of gelatine per day.

GELATINE, an albuminoid protein, is derived from collagen which comprises the major part of the organic matter of bones, skins and connective tissues of animals. Animal hides, skins and bones, therefore, constitute the principal raw materials for the world's most richly endowed country in respect of these raw materials, possessing an estimated 250 million cattle and 58 million sheep and goats. Our annual production is upward of 25 million cow hides, 6 million buffalo hides and 25 million skins. We are the world's largest exporter of hides and skins.

The gelatine manufacturer generally uses hide cuttings and trimmings from tanneries, and certain slaughter house wastes such as sinews, tendons and bones. Estimating the available tannery discards at 5%–10% of the hides handled, there is a plentiful supply of raw materials available for the gelatine industry.

The question naturally arises as to why, with this wealth of raw material, we make no edible gelatine. In fact, we export the raw materials and import the finished product at a high price. Yet, we could produce gelatine not only for the domestic market, but also for export instead of relying, as we do, on foreign sources for almost all our requirements of high quality gelatine. The answer lies in the circumstance that, besides the necessary raw materials, the successful operation of a gelatine plant requires proper climatic environment, particularly as regards temperature and humidity. High temperature combined with high humidity which prevail in most parts of India during summer render the manufacturing process troublesome and expensive. Recourse to full-scale air conditioning would make the finished product non-competitive because of the necessity of handling very large quantities of wet materials and hundreds of thousands of cubic feet of air.

One solution of this difficulty would be to combine the manufacture of gelatine with that of glue which is, in fact, an impure or degraded gelatine. During two or three of the worst summer months, the production of gelatine could be suspended and glue alone made, as this is not so adversely affected by humid heat. This slack time could be advantageously used for plant maintenance. Such a procedure would require a simple switch-over in operation without calling for additional equipment or facilities.

There are over a dozen plants in India producing animal glue, and a few have attempted to make edible gelatine. But, on account of unsatisfactory practice and neglect of proper sanitary standards, the product is essentially a glue rather than an edible gelatine. Consequently, almost all the high-grade gelatine required in India for edible, pharmaceutical, photographic and lithographic purposes is imported, principally from the United Kingdom, Belgium, and Switzerland.

Work at the National Chemical Laboratory, Poona

With a view to fostering the development of an indigenous gelatine industry, an investigation was undertaken at the National Chemical Laboratory, Poona, to work out the details of manufacture under the peculiar conditions prevailing in India, and to explore the economics of the process. The work was carried through from a laboratory to a pilot-plant scale. Contrary to the predictions of a section of foreign opinion, it was found that the hazards of unfavourable temperature and humidity, though very real, were not insuperable. With due care and vigilance, the production of a highly satisfactory edible gelatine from hides and bones was found to be entirely within the realm of possibility and, what is more, the same gelatine proved to be admirably suited to the preparation of light-sensitive photographic emulsions. Several hundred-weights of the gelatine were prepared and tested.

With hide trimmings and cuttings as the raw material, the price of the finished product was found to be competitive with the prevailing market prices of foreign gelatines. Gelatine produced exclusively from bones was at a price disadvantage for reasons that will be discussed later.

This demonstration of the production and economic feasibility of the indigenous production of quality gelatine elicited immediate response from an industrial concern which undertook to install a commercial plant in Northern India to be designed and operated on the basis of the data and experience acquired through our pilot plant investigations. It is hoped that this plant will be the precursor of several more in the near future.

Raw Materials

(*a*) *Hides and Bones*. The principal raw materials for the manufacture of gelatine are skins or hides, connective tissues, cartilage and bones. The bulk of these materials is obtained by the gelatine manufacturer from tanneries and slaughter-houses, where they constitute waste or by-products. It is important for the tanneries and slaughter-houses to be aware and appreciative of the fact that these 'wastes' are in fact a basic raw material for the gelatine manufacturer, and proper preservation of these could mean substantial profits. Once putrefaction and degradation set in, nothing can be done to restore the gelatine-making value of the stock.

To check putrefaction and hydrolytic break-down of proteins, the simplest method is to sprinkle lime water over the hide stock several times a week and to turn it over regularly. This also prevents the accumulation of bacteria. Alternatively, salt may be sprinkled between the layers of stacked hides. Another method, to be recommended only for the highest grade of material, is the complete desiccation of the stock. This is expensive, and has been used only when materials have to be transported over long distances from the tannery.

In order of gelatine-making value, the best materials are hide stock, green bones, and ossein.

Among hide stock, calf skin, although somewhat high in mucinous substances, yields the best and clearest gelatine. Kip stock, or skin from almost mature calves, ranks next, and then come hides from mature cattle. Skivings or tanned hide cuttings can, after proper treatment, be used for gelatine extraction. Chrome-tanned hides are easier to deal with than tannin-tanned hides.

Another useful source of gelatine, of special interest in India, is worn loom pickers discarded by textile mills.

Skins from other animals such as sheep, goats, deer, rabbits, pigs, dogs and horses have been used, but except possibly sheep and goat skins, these sources are of small importance in India, and do not yield a particularly high grade gelatine.

Bones vary greatly in their gelatine-making value. Green bones from mature animals yield the best gelatine. The soft bones of the head, shoulder, feet and knuckles give more gelatine than, for instance, thigh bones. In general, flat bones are richer in gelatine than tubular bones. Bones must be carefully graded and selected for the best results.

(*b*) *Water*. The water requirements of a gelatine plant are quite large, being of the order of 100 gallons per pound of hide stock. For the best gelatine, the water used must be low in total salt content especially as the presence of salts in wash water inhibits swelling of the hide stock and results in low yields and quality. Salts present in the water used for extraction find their way into the finished product, and reduce its clarity. It is therefore not sufficient that the water is merely soft.

If a high concentration of bacteria exists in the water, it must be sterilized. If chlorine is used for this purpose, the amount must be kept to the minimum, since it tends to harden the hide stock and render extraction difficult.

(*c*) *Air*. Air, used for drying the wet gelatine jelly, is also needed in large quantities, to the extent of about 2,50,000 cubic feet per pound of dry gelatine. Special care must be devoted to the proper conditioning and purification of this air. Bacterial spores must be removed by the use of bacterial filters; we have found that several kinds of liquefying bacteria entering with the air cause liquefaction of the jelly in the drying chamber.

Process—Hide Gelatine

(*a*) *Washing*. The hide stock as received must be thoroughly washed to remove adhering blood, hair and dirt, if from the slaughter-house, and lime or salt (used as preservatives) if from the tannery. This can be done in a rotary wooden or galvanized iron drum type washer.

(*b*) *Liming*. The skin consists essentially of a thin outer layer called epidermis composed mainly of albuminous matter, covering a thicker layer of intertwined fibrous matter known as the corium. The corium consists chiefly of collagen, from which gelatine is obtained.

The washed hides are limed in cement pits, the idea being to remove the albuminous and mucinous matter which are alkali-soluble, and to plump the hides. The temperature, pH, duration of liming and the concentration of liming liquor are all important factors in determining the yield and quality of gelatine. Optimum values for these must be worked out for the climatic conditions prevailing at the factory site, and for the particular kind of hide stock used. Some stocks require longer liming than others, and if a variety of hide stock is to be used, it is well to grade and classify the hides according to the different liming treatments they require.

In general, liming is best done with a dilute (3–4°Bé) lime solution for a period ranging from 6 to 8 weeks. To prevent the accumulation of bacteria, and to expose fresh surface to the action of the liming liquor, it is advisable to change the liquor two or three times during the liming period, and simultaneously, to turn the hide stock over.

(*c*) *Deliming*. After the hides have been satisfactorily limed, they must be washed free of lime liquor, dissolved albumins and mucins, and salts. This is done either in a drum type washer such as previously used, or in a wooden paddle washer which consists essentially of a wooden trough in which is mounted, on a horizontal axis, a rotating wooden shaft fitted with paddles.

Dilute hydrochloric acid is added to the wash water after a while to neutralize the lime, and to aid in the swelling of the stock. About 12 lb. of 28% HCl are needed to delime 100 pounds of hides. The pH of the stock, after this treatment, should be adjusted to about 5.0, as this is the optimum pH for the next step. The hydrochloric acid used should be low in iron which will discolour the finished product, and it must be free from other impurities such as arsenic.

(*d*) *Extraction*. In this step, the collagen of the hide stock is hydrolyzed to gelatine by heating the stock in water under carefully controlled temperature. The reaction may be represented thus:

$$\underset{\text{Collagen}}{C_{102}H_{149}O_{38}N_{31}} + H_2O \rightarrow \underset{\text{Gelatine}}{C_{102}H_{151}O_{39}N_{31}}$$

Gelatine is among the higher hydrolysis products of collagen, but if the extraction step is drastic, either as regards time or as regards temperature, progressive hydrolysis of the collagen results in break-down into proteoses, peptones, polypeptides, amino acids and finally ammonia. Consequently, it is of prime importance to conduct the extraction step as rapidly and at as low a temperature as possible.

In practice, several batch extractions, each of about 4 hours duration, are made at several progressively increasing temperatures in the range of 55°–80°C. The best gelatine is obtained from the lowest temperature extract.

The residue, after the last extract, is heated to boiling with water, and the extract so obtained is processed as glue.

Aluminium is particularly suitable for the fabrication of the extraction vessel. Ordinary steel vessels must not be used as they impart colour to the solution.

(*e*) *Clarification and filtration*. The gelatine extracts contain in suspension a number of impurities such as albuminous and mucinous matter, greases, lime soaps and organic material which must be filtered out in order to obtain a clear and high quality product. Filtration of gelatine solutions can be a troublesome problem unless a proper filter press is used in conjunction with an effective filter aid. We have experienced considerable difficulty when using a conventional wooden plate and frame filter press. More suitable to this work would be a type 304 stainless steel leaf filter, operating at about 60 pounds pressure, with paper pulp as filter aid.

It has been observed that on concentration, the once clarified extract again develops turbidity and colour. A little aluminium sulphate and lime are added, which serve as precipitants for the suspended matter, and the solution is again filtered. This should give a solution of good clarity.

(*f*) *Concentration*. The dilute gelatine extracts containing, on an average, 2–4% gelatine are concentrated to about 15% strength under vacuum. Here again, it is important to keep both the time and temperature of evaporation low, and for this reason long tube vertical vacuum evaporators are recommended. The material of construction may be type 304 stainless steel or monel metal (70% Ni, 30% Cu). Mild steel equipment must be avoided.

(*g*) *Chilling and setting*. The older procedure, which we adopted in our work for reasons of simplicity and availability of equipment, is to spread the concentrated solution in aluminium trays, and store the trays in a refrigeration chamber maintained around 40°F, where exposure to cold causes the solution to set to a jelly. This procedure, involving the manual handling of large quantities of sticky solution and storage of the material in a damp and soggy room where bacterial contamination is most likely to develop, is not particularly satisfactory. Very often, liquefying bacteria render whole batches of gelatine useless in the refrigeration chamber.

Modern factories employ an endless conveyer belt running through a refrigerated compartment for chilling and setting of the jelly. For small factories in India, this may be an expensive installation, and the older process, operated with scrupulous regard to clean and sterile conditions, may still be advisable.

(*h*) *Drying*. The chilled jelly is cut into strips by means of wires, and laid out on chicken-mesh screen trays, which are then stacked on trolleys and wheeled into a counter current type tunnel dryer. The condition of the air used for drying is important. Air, filtered, if necessary, through a bacterial filter, is heated by steam coils to such a temperature that its wet bulb temperature is below the melting point of the jelly being dried. The air rate and rate of addition and withdrawal of trolleys should be so adjusted as to give a product of uniform moisture content and achieve maximum heat economy.

For excessively humid air, dehumidifying equipment may be necessary.

The final product from the dryer will be in the form of thin, clear, transparent sheets of gelatine containing 10–15% moisture. These may then be sold as such or in flakes or granulated form.

The yields of gelatine obtained in our pilot plant averaged around 28% on the weight of dry hides. This overall gelatine yield is made up of three extracts taken at temperatures of 55°C, 65°C and 80°C. The average yield of glue (extracted at the boiling point) was about 23% on the weight of dry hides.

BONE GELATINE

The preparation of bone gelatine differs somewhat from hide gelatine in the initial stages. The analysis of fresh bones is on the average, as follows:

Water	51%
Fat	15.7%
Ossein	11.4%
Mineral matter	21.9%

Ossein is a protein consisting mostly of collagen and to a small extent of osseomucoid and ossalbuminoid. The inorganic matter of bones is mainly composed of calcium phosphate (about 85%) and calcium carbonate (about 10%).

In all cases, the bones must first be degreased. They may or may not then be decalcified prior to extraction of the ossein.

The bones as received from the slaughter house are first disintegrated in a hammer or roller mill to ½–¼ in. size. They are then thoroughly washed of blood and dirt in the same type of prewasher as was used for the hide stock.

Degreasing, which follows, is done by boiling the bones with water in steel digesters under a pressure of 50–60 lb. per sq. in. taking care to adjust the pressure and period of boiling so as not to progress to the stage of extraction of gelatine. The water is run off and cooled. Fat is skimmed off the top, and the recovery is 70–75% of the fat contained in the bones.

Alternatively, the bones may be degreased by solvent extraction, using solvents such as benzene, carbon tetrachloride, carbon disulphide or trichlorethylene. Although this process removes all but 1% or so of the fat contained in the bone stock, it is expensive, and almost none of these solvents is manufactured in India. Moreover, the fat obtained by steam extraction is clear in colour and of faint odour. Solvent-extracted fat is brownish and has an unpleasant odour. For Indian conditions, therefore, degreasing by autoclaving is advisable. The grease so recovered is a valuable by-product and, after suitable refining, has a ready market.

The degreased bones may now be directly extracted for gelatine if decalcification is not desired. Prior to digestion, it is useful to treat the bones with an N/200 solution of caustic soda to dissolve out mucoid and albuminoid matter, and then to wash them thoroughly. Extraction is done in stainless steel digesters at a pressure of 20–30 lb. per sq. in. One extraction or more may be made. The gelatine extract is now processed in exactly the same manner as extracts from hide stock. The residue after extraction may be dried, ground and sold as fertilizer.

Bones may be decalcified by acidulation with dilute hydrochloric acid, followed by neutralization of the leach acid liquor with lime. This results in the precipitation of dicalcium phosphate, which is a widely saleable neutral fertilizer containing about 40% P_2O_5. The ossein obtained after decalcification is extracted as above and, being more porous than undecalcified bones, is more readily extracted and gives a superior gelatine.

For acidulation, approximately 1.25 tons of 31% acid are required per ton of bones, and this acid must be free of impurities. In India, the cost of hydrochloric acid is extremely high, being about 3½ annas per lb., whereas the best yield of gelatine that may be expected from green bones is of the order of 10–12%. Thus, the HCl alone accounts for almost 50% of the cost of total raw materials.

Under these conditions, the preparation of gelatine from bones is not an economically favourable proposition, and this has been confirmed by our pilot plant trials.

Specifications of Edible Gelatine

In sheet form, the gelatine must be clear, transparent, free from colour and air bubbles.

Edible gelatine must conform to the specifications, to be acceptable as a food product. To maintain and ensure a uniform and standardized quality, flake or granulated gelatines may be blended. The physical properties generally tested are melting point, viscosity and jelly strength.

The amount of ash, and its composition should be determined. The metallic impurities in the ash should be within prescribed limits. The U.S. Food Laws specify the following limits.

Arsenic	max.	1.4 parts per million
Sulphur dioxide	,,	350 ,,
Zinc	,,	100 ,,
Copper	,,	30 ,,
Lead		nil

The bacterial count must be below 30 per gram for a good gelatine. The pH should be in the range 5–6.

Photographic gelatine should contain no grease or mucinous matter, and be free from colour.

The following table gives comparative figures in respect of melting point, viscosity, ash, and moisture for samples of gelatine prepared in this Laboratory and those of imported German gelatine.

Gelatine sample	Melting point (°C)	Viscosity (in relation to water)	Ash (%)	Moisture (%)
NCL sample 1*	30·4	3·21	1·34	9·13
NCL sample 2*	30·7	3·38	2·37	8·50
NCL sample 3	29·6	2·69	1·98	8·50
NCL sample 4	29·1	2·11	1·42	9·00
German sample 1	30·0	3·52	2·13	11·80
German sample 2	29·8	3·45	1·47	13·24

* Pretreatment of hide stock with $CaCl_2$ prior to liming.

Applications of Gelatine

Edible gelatine finds a variety of uses in articles of daily consumption, and its popularity stems from three main properties: (1) its ability to form stable jellies, (2) its being a protective colloid, and (3) its easy assimilability by the human digestive system.

Almost everyone is familiar with the dessert jellies made from gelatine. Large quantities of gelatine are used in ice-cream manufacture. The addition of a small quantity of gelatine (about 1 lb. per 50 gallons of ice-cream) stabilizes the ice-cream against formation of large ice crystals, and against separation of cream and sugar on prolonged standing, and imparts improved body and texture. In the United States, where the manufacture of ice-cream is a multimillion dollar industry, gelatine finds a large outlet in this direction. It is also used for various types of confectionery, such as marshmallows.

Abroad, gelatine is used as a thickener for cream, jams and fruit preserves, but in India, its animal origin might preclude, to a large extent, its use for this purpose.

Gelatine, when added to an infant's diet, has been found to aid in the digestion of milk.

In medicine, pharmacy and bacteriology, gelatine finds varied applications such as for making capsules, for transfusion (as a substitute for blood plasma), for suppositories, in chap and sunburn ointments, and for the preparation of nutrient media for the growth of bacterial organisms.

Gelatine is used in the photographic industry for the preparation of light sensitive emulsions that are applied as a coating on raw film base, photographic papers and plates. Motion picture production is among the major industries of India, and the present estimated annual demand is above 200 million feet (25 million sq. ft.), which is all met by import. It is now proposed to put up a factory near Krishnarajasagar Dam in Mysore State for the manufacture of raw film. In the initial stage, it will produce 19 million square feet of raw film base annually. In addition, a complete unit is to be installed for coating, perforating and packing the film base. Future plans call for doubling the capacity of the factory.

The establishment of photographic film manufacture in India should be the green light for the simultaneous development of an indigenous gelatine industry. Investigations in this laboratory have shown that if proper care is exercised with respect to the choice of raw materials and cleanliness in manufacture, the production of photographic gelatine can easily be undertaken by the manufacturer of edible gelatine. The same factory can therefore produce all grades of gelatine, including edible, pharmaceutical and photographic.

Besides the domestic market, our abundance of raw materials and low labour costs should induce us ultimately to look for export markets, particularly in the Middle Eastern and South East Asian countries which also depend largely on imports for high grade gelatine. In our progressive march towards industrial advancement and self-sufficiency, we must utilize as much of our raw materials wealth for the indigenous production of finished products as our financial resources and the limitations of overall planning permit.

The work of my colleagues, Dr H. K. Joshi, Mr M. M. Uppal, and Mr G. V. Potnis, on the gelatine pilot plant at the National Chemical Laboratory, Poona, is gratefully acknowledged.

VEGETABLE OIL REFINING INDUSTRY

By

C. S. Srinivasan

(*Messrs The Mettur Chemical and Industrial Corporation Ltd.,*

Mettur Dam R.S.)

The author has described the methods of refining vegetable oils as practised in India, and put forth the plea that by the adoption of modern continuous or semi-continuous centrifugal refining methods a large proportion of refining losses could be avoided.

INDIA is one of the largest oil-seeds producing countries in the world, the annual production being over 7 million tons of oil-seeds. About 11.4 lakh tons of oil were produced from the quantity available for crushing in 1951–52, and of these, 9.34 lakh tons were available for human consumption in India. In addition to the oil, 3.57 lakh tons of ghee and 12,860 tons of butter were also available. Still, the per capita availability of fats and oils in India was only 10.2 lb. per annum against the minimum nutritional requirements of 39.2 lb. Great leeway has to be made by getting increased yield of oil-seeds per acre by the use of fertilizers, by developing the oil-crushing industry, developing the commercial expression of non-edible oils from the neglected resources of oil-bearing plants such as *Kamla, Karanja, Kusum, Neem,* etc., and making such non-edible oils available to replace a part of the large tonnages of edible oils utilized in the soap industry.

Of the 9.34 lakh tons of vegetable oils available internally for edible purposes, about 2 lakh tons were refined, and a good part of it was hydrogenated in addition. There are about sixty factories in India engaged in the refining and hydrogenation of vegetable oils with an employed productive capital of Rs. 25 crores. This paper will indicate how by adopting modern refining techniques, oil refineries can save more of refined oils for edible purposes and will also indicate the phases in which technical aid is required by oil refineries for achieving greater efficiency and cheaper working costs.

Refining Methods

Crude vegetable oils produced by expression of the oil-seeds or by solvent extraction contain non-glyceride constituents or impurities in varying amounts, free fatty acids being the chief ones. The other minor impurities are proteoses, peptones, pentosans, phytosterols, phospholipins, mucilaginous substances, xanthophyll, chlorophyll and carotenoid pigments, and traces of hydrocarbons, ketones, etc. Most of these impurities have to be removed since they render the oil dark-coloured, cause it to foam or smoke, and affect the stability of the oil. Several refining methods are adopted in the western countries, but the most common method adopted universally is refining by means of alkalies. Again, whereas continuous centrifugal refining methods have displaced batch refining methods in the United States and other advanced countries, most of the vegetable oil refineries in India are still adopting the batch refining methods.

Batch caustic soda refining is carried out in open kettles equipped with cone bottoms, heating coils, and variable speed mechanical agitators, in which separation of the neutral refined oil and soapstock is effected by prolonged gravity settling. An excess of 5–25% alkali over that required theoretically is always necessary for reducing the free fatty acid content to the minimum and this excess alkali and the phosphatides and other surface-active materials in the oil combine and form a heavy emulsion with soap and water, which entangles a lot of neutral oil. The by-product obtained is called 'the foots' or 'soap stock', and represents the refining loss. Even with the most careful selection of the lye and careful treatment of the oil in the kettle, refining losses have been found to be over two times the non-glyceride content of the oil, due to entrainment of neutral oil with the soapstock.

The semi-continuous method of alkali refining employs a centrifuge of the De Laval or Sharples type. The oil is treated with the alkali in the kettle as in the normal gravity settling system, but immediately after the 'break' is observed, the entire charge is run through a soapstock separator which gives an efficient and a continuous separation of soap from the neutral oil by virtue of a centrifugal force many times that of gravity.

In the continuous centrifugal refining process, oil and lye are fed through proportioning pumps into a mixer, and after proper coagulation, the mixture is fed to soapstock centrifuges which separate out the oil and soap. The additional advantage in the continuous type is the reduced time of contact between oil and alkali, and thereby reduced chances for the alkali to saponify the neutral oil. The refining loss by the continuous centrifugal caustic soda refining method is claimed to be only about 1½ times the 'Wesson loss' or absolute refining loss estimated on the basis of the non-glyceride impurities in the oil and hence the theoretical minimum to which the refining loss can be reduced.

More recently, the continuous caustic soda refining process has been improved upon in the Clayton continuous soda-ash-caustic-soda process. In the Clayton process, refining is carried out in two stages and with two reagents. In the first stage, the oil is largely neutralized, and phosphatides and other gums are removed by treatment with a 20° Bé soda ash solution; in the second stage, neutralization is completed, and colour bodies are removed by treatment with 20° Bé caustic soda solution. The Clayton process effects a substantial saving in refining loss over the continuous method in which caustic soda is used alone. The refining loss by this process is only slightly in excess of the 'Wesson loss' and is less than the refining loss by batch process by 40–50°.

Substantial savings can be effected by a change-over to the semi-continuous, and better still, to the continuous Clayton process of vegetable oil refining by the yield of more of the valuable neutral refined oil and less of the cheaper by-product soapstock. The cost of installing the centrifugal soapstock separators will be paid off within a very short period by the savings effected by the yield of more of neutral oil. Taking an instance, the installation of a continuous caustic soda refining equipment for an oil refining plant of twenty tons per day capacity might cost 1–1½ lakhs of rupees. If 6,000 tons of oil of average 3% F.F.A. are refined every year, batch refining would yield a maximum of about 5,550 tons of neutral oil, and the continuous caustic soda refining a minimum of 5,700 tons of neutral oil. Over and above this 150 tons of extra neutral oil, about 20 tons of neutral oil will be recovered by centrifuging the wash-waters. The value of the recorded neutral oil would be over Rs. 80,000 and the annual return on the investment would be about 75% or more.

Many vegetable oil refineries in India have not yet changed over to the continuous or semi-continuous refining system due to the threat to the very existence of the oil refining and hydrogenation industry from prejudices and wrong ideas. The industry was not therefore willing to invest more on plant equipment without being assured of a bright future, even if it was for a change-over to the modern and more efficient technique. The recent dispelling of popular misconceptions by scientists of the National Institutes and the appreciation by these institutions and the Government of the oil refining and vanaspati industry as an essential food processing industry are encouraging signs, and will greatly help in the development of the industry.

It is to be noted that in converting soapstock containing neutral refined oil into soap, oil refineries are losing a lot of refined oil. This is wasteful because crude vegetable oils would do for soap-making and also because neutral oil in soapstock gets the same cheaper value as the combined fatty matter in the soapstock. By a change-over to centrifugal refining methods, vegetable oil refineries in India can save over 6,000 tons of oil for edible purposes and thereby make available more of fat products for raising the per capita consumption to the nutritional requirements for a healthy living in the country.

The term 'Refining' in an oil refinery refers only to the process of the removal of the free fatty acids, but as applied to refined oils available in the market as such or as hydrogenated oils, includes the processes of decolourization and deodorization of the oils also. In regard to the process of bleaching vegetable oils, natural or activated Fuller's earth, and activated carbon are being used as adsorbents for the pigments in oil. Formerly, a good portion of these requirements was being met by imports. Now, though a part of our requirements is being met from indigenous production, the quality of the same has to be improved to the standard of imported materials. Also, the possibility of activating the bentonites available in plenty in Kashmir, Bihar and other places and meeting the entire demand for the oil-bleaching materials is being studied. Recently, the Ministry of Commerce and Industry was investigating if chemical industries making hydrochloric and sulphuric acids could try to undertake manufacture of activated bentonites. It is desirable that such industries are furnished with available technical information on the subject of activation of Fuller's earth or bentonite, and also with the information on the qualities and quantities of bentonites available and the scope for uniformity of the raw material in quality. The possibility of making in India good activated carbon from coconut shells and other seed hulls should also be studied in the National Laboratories and technical assistance given to the existing small-scale industries which are badly in need of the same.

Generally, the final process carried out in an oil refining plant is the deodorization. This process consists in removing the odoriferous substances, in the oil by low pressure steam stripping in high vacuum. In the United States, condensing low pressure Dowthern vapours are used for maintaining the temperature of the oil as well as of the stripping steam. In the oil refineries in India high pressure steam is used for maintaining the temperature of the oil at operating temperatures ranging from 360° to 420°F, and open steam, superheated or saturated, is blown into the oil for the stripping. Though the effect of the use of low pressure superheated steam or of saturated high pressure steam in the deodorizing of oils is practically the same, information on the keeping qualities of products of the two systems, and the advantage of either system, is meagre. The National Laboratories in India can undertake studies of these problems, and other problems such as recovery of nickel from the spent catalyst, enrichment of refined and hydrogenated oils with vitamins, and keep oil refineries better informed. The collection and publication of all available useful information on the refining and hydrogenation of edible oils by a Central Organization is also desirable.

PROBLEMS IN COFFEE TECHNOLOGY AND RESEARCH

By

C. P. Natarajan and D. S. Bhatia

(*Central Food Technological Research Institute, Mysore*)

The authors have dealt with recent developments in coffee technology and the manner in which they could be adopted under Indian conditions. Problems dealing with processing, packaging, and brewing of coffee are discussed. Specific lines of research on coffee both in its fundamental and applied aspects and also the development of by-products industry are briefly outlined.

COFFEE is an expensive commodity and consequently the coffee trade tends to fluctuate with the purchasing power of the consumers. Before World War II, the coffee production in our country was in excess of domestic consumption and export formed an important outlet for the excess produce. Now that the internal consumption has gone up, the gap between the production and consumption seems to have been filled up. The average domestic consumption has increased from 8,841 tons in 1938–1941 to 17,700 tons in 1950–51. This increased demand has apparently resulted in the current high price of coffee.

Acreage under coffee in India has increased from 1,83,003 acres in 1939–1940 to 2,28,586 acres in 1950–51 (2), but there has not been a proportionate increase in production. The production cost in plantations is reported to be increasing and although varieties with higher yields are replacing the old plantations, the consensus of opinion seems to be that the present high price of coffee may continue for some time to come. An alternative to tide over the present situation and also as a long-range policy, seems to be to devote greater attention to better utilization of the existing production of coffee. Special emphasis should be laid on conducting research on problems relating to processing, packaging and utilization of by-products.

Processing

This is a field in which there is great scope for improvement in our country. The relatively new development in processing equipment is the Raoeng Cylinder Pulper which removes the mucilaginous coating of coffee berry in one single operation under water pressure. Fermentation is considered unnecessary and drying is speeded up. De-pulping of *robusta* coffee without fermentation has been successfully applied in Africa using water pressure process. (7) Already, experiments have shown that fermentation can also be speeded up by controlled activity of pectic enzymes. A chemical method using alkali has also been reported. Perfection of non-fermentation methods may change the entire economic picture of coffee processing. How far these methods affect the cup-quality of coffee is yet to be seen. Systematic work should be undertaken with a view to cutting down the cost of processing coffee.

Roasting

Numerous improvements have recently been made in the constructional design of coffee roasting equipment. Continuous and closed cycle roasters are some of the recent developments in coffee roasting machinery (3). The Indian Coffee Industry is not of such a magnitude as to permit immediate use of continuous automatic roasting equipment; but, in any case, we have to standardize the roasting procedures adopted in our country. People have to be educated with respect to proper roasting in order to minimize shrinkage and at the same time to develop the typical aroma for which we cherish the coffee beverage.

No factual data are available with regard to consumer preferences for one type of coffee or another. Consumer perferences for various blends of different types must be ascertained and it should be possible to evolve a generally acceptable blend of plantation and cherry types of coffee.

Packaging

A great deal of work has been done in other countries on packaging of roasted coffee (1). One of the recent developments is the introduction of vacuum-packed and pressure-packed cans. Attempt has also been made to pack coffee under vacuum in flexible containers, thus effecting a considerable saving in container cost. 'Cup brew coffee bags of cellulose' containing 10–

12 gallons of coffee are now being marketed in the U.S.A. In India, at the present time, coffee is being packed under CO_2. The cost of the container is high and we need simpler and cheaper methods of packaging coffee. The moisture in packed coffee should not exceed 7% during storage, otherwise the quality will be adversely affected. Investigations should be undertaken to study the effect of antioxidants on the retention of aroma during storage of coffee.

Coffee Brewing

Very few people realize the importance of accurate measurements, proper grinds, correct temperature of water and adequate time of brewing in preparing good coffee. It is hardly realized that proper storage of the brewed decoction is very necessary to preserve the aroma typical of freshly brewed coffee. Consumer education on these aspects is seriously lacking and the Indian Coffee Industry could render useful service to the public through visual aids and extension work.

Steeping and filter methods are commonly adopted in Indian homes for making coffee. On account of its lower cost, brass filter is generally used. It has been recently reported that contact with brass affects adversely the flavour of coffee and it is therefore recommended that brass filters should be tinned on the inside if good coffee is desired (4). Further improvements in the design of filters should also be considered in order to get maximum extraction with minimum loss of aroma.

The importance of grind of the powder for making good coffee is generally not appreciated in our country, whereas standard grinds of coffee as shown in the following table have been adopted in the U.S.A.

Grind designation	Amount of Coffee retained on		Amount of coffee passing through 28 mesh	Tolerance on amount passing through 28 mesh	
	10 and 14 mesh	20 and 28 mesh		Not less than	Not more than
	%	%	%	%	%
Regular ...	33	55	12	9	15
Drip ...	7	73	20	16	24
Fine ...	0	70	30	25	45

Sieves referred to are Tyler standards corresponding to U.S. standard sieves 12, 16, 20 and 30 mesh.

No grind designations have, however, been defined by the Indian Coffee Industry. The coffee powders sold in the market are of varied particle sizes and are generally finer than the 'Fine' as specified by the U.S. standards.

Consumer Habits

Data regarding consumer habits have been compiled by the Pan-American Bureau for the United States of America (6). It has been found that 18% of the consumers drink only one cup a day, 22% 2 cups a day and 60% 3 or more cups a day. The lower age group, 18–29 years, drink mostly 1–2 cups while the groups drinking more than five cups a day are concentrated in the ages 30–49 years. The consumption has been found to be fairly uniform through different income groups. Differences in geographical areas and population centres have also been worked out. It would be interesting and useful to conduct such a survey in order to assess the coffee drinking habits in different parts of the country.

Organoleptic Tests

Appearance of the raw coffee bean is the main criterion by which coffee is adjudged for its quality in this country. Cup tests on brews are not normally performed to grade coffee for its aroma and taste. The industry should employ trained persons who could adopt standardized procedures for organoleptic evaluation of coffee. Such tests would be useful in developing blends from different types and varieties of coffee.

Some Problems for Investigation

1. It has been recently reported that roasted cherry husk gives more extract than the beans and that it can easily be admixed with coffee instead of chicory (5). Many practical difficulties have, however, been reported in utilizing this material. Attempts should therefore be made to work out a technique for roasting the whole coffee berry.

2. Generally, 25–30% by weight of coffee can be extracted in water. It would be worth developing some processing technique whereby it may be possible to get a higher extract from the coffee bean.

3. *Arabica* is rated superior to *robusta* coffee from the flavour point of view. It would be interesting to undertake a detailed

study of the varieties with respect to their aromatic constituents.

4. Recovery of aromatic principles from roast gases and their use for fortifying the flavour of roasted coffee would be a useful line of investigation.

5. During pulping, good part of sugars and other constituents are lost in the wash water and it would be worth exploring the possibility of recovering them economically.

6. Recovery of caffeine from cherry husk and plantation pulp may form a useful by-product industry.

7. The adulteration of coffee is more rampant now than ever and the need for simple and reliable methods for quantitative detection of adulterant is indicated.

8. Preliminary studies conducted by us have indicated that solubles from cherry husks could be used as a base for making soluble coffee. The coffee industry may consider the utilization of coffee husk on these lines.

The foregoing are some of the problems which could be profitably tackled through close collaboration between research institutions and the industry. The importance of developing a by-products industry using materials hitherto not commercially exploited is stressed in order to improve the general economy of the coffee industry.

References

1. Coonen, N. H., *Tea and Coffee Trade J.*, 1952, *102* (5), 58-62 79-80.

2. Indian Coffee Board, *Eleventh Annual Report*, 1952.

3. Kaufman, C. W., *Food Technol.*, 1951, *5* (4), 154-59.

4. Natarajan, C. P., Kantaraj Urs, M., Bhatia, D. S., and Anandaswamy, B., *Indian Coffee*, 1952, *XVI* (7), 133-35.

5. Natarajan, C. P., Bhatia, D. S., and Subrahmanyan, V., *J. Sci., industr. Res.*, 1952, *11A* (9), 410-411.

6. Pan American Bureau, Coffee Statistics, Release No. 15.

7. Wickinzer, V. D,. Coffee, Tea and Cocoa, Food Res. Inst., Stanford University, 1951.

NEED FOR DEVELOPING FERMENTATION INDUSTRIES IN INDIA

By

B. S. Lulla and D. S. Johar

(*Central Food Technological Research Institute, Mysore*)

There are at present more than fifty fermentation processes which could be industrially exploited. The necessary raw materials and the technical 'know-how' are available in India. The authors put forth the plea that fermentation industries should be started in the country for the manufacture of food products.

Micro-organisms play an important role in the economy of nature by participating in the cycles of transformation of essential elements—carbon, nitrogen, phosphorus, sulphur, etc.

It is the object of the science of microbiology to study and control these organisms for a variety of beneficial purposes. Preparation of alcohols and alcoholic beverages (wines, ciders, beers), protein-rich foods like compressed yeast, vitamins, enzymes, drugs, antibiotics and organic acids can be prepared by harnessing microbial activity. A number of industries, besides alcoholic fermentation, food and fruit preservation industries, could be economically started in this country, with the combined skill of fermentologists and chemical engineers.

The various fermentation industries yielding alcohols, acids, proteins, enzymes, vitamins, antibiotics, fine chemicals, etc., are indicated below:

Alcohols:

(*a*) Butanol-Acetone Fermentation.

(*b*) Sorbose from sorbitol.

(*c*) Amyl alcohol.

(*d*) 2–3, Butylene glycol.

ACIDS:

(*a*) Gluconic acid.
(*b*) Lactic acid.
(*c*) Citric acid.
(*d*) Tartaric acid.
(*e*) Oxalic acid.
(*f*) Gallic acid.
(*g*) Propionic acid.

PROTEINS:

(*a*) Compressed yeast.
(*b*) Anaerobic digestion of vegetable waste material.

ENZYMES:

(*a*) Diastase.
(*b*) Invertase.
(*c*) Protease.
(*d*) Pectinase.

VITAMINS:

(*a*) B-Complex.
(*b*) Folic acid.
(*c*) B_{12}.
(*d*) Ergosterol (Provitamin D).

ANTIBIOTICS:

(*a*) Penicillin.
(*b*) Streptomycin.
(*c*) Auromycin.
(*d*) Terramycin.
(*e*) Gramicidin.

FINE CHEMICALS:

(*a*) Nucleic acid.
(*b*) Sterols.
(*c*) Purine and Pyrimidine bases.
(*d*) Glutathione.
(*e*) Glycogen.

MISCELLANEOUS:

(*a*) Dextran.
(*b*) CO_2.
(*c*) H_2.
(*d*) Methane.

The success of industrial fermentation depends on the selection of the organisms giving the maximum yield. A suitable medium containing all the essential nutrients and optimum conditions for microbial activity must be established. The raw material employed should be cheap and easily available. Conditions, permitting the easy purification of the product obtained, should be maintained. Broadly speaking, the industrial fermentations are based on:

(*a*) Microbial growth on liquid medium.
(*b*) Microbial growth on semi-solid medium.

In the case of liquid medium, the organism is grown either in shallow trays containing culture medium, or in submerged conditions in deep fermenters. Example of the former type is the citric acid fermentation; of the latter, penicillin production.

In the case of semi-solid medium, two different techniques have been developed, especially for work on a large scale. One is the rotary drum method, and the other, quiescent or tray method. Both these methods have worked exceedingly well in the production of fungal and bacterial enzymes. It has been observed that suitable adaptations of the above techniques contribute to the success of a given fermentation process.

The basic raw materials used for the fermentation industries are generally carbohydrates derived mainly from the following sources: 1. Molasses, 2. Starchy cereals and tubers, *e.g.*, potato, tapioca, sweet potato, 3. Fruits and fruit products—grapes, oranges, 4. Flowers like the *Mahua* flowers, 5. Forest waste products, *e.g.*, waste wood, waste leaves, etc., 6. Agricultural waste products, *e.g.*, hulls and straw from wheat, barley, rice, baggase, cotton stem and pods, 7. Raw sugars—*gur*, jaggery, etc., and other sugars like lactose, 8. Industrial wastes like sulphite liquor from paper factories, 9. Municipal wastes, farm yard wastes, brewery slops and distillery wastes. A number of products like acetic, citric, gluconic acids, protein concentrates, vitamins and enzymes can be produced by the adoption of suitable fermentation techniques. Diastase, a costly enzyme which is used both in pharmaceutical preparations and for desizing starch in the textile industry, has been successfully produced in the Central Food Technological Research Institute, Mysore, by using the mould *Aspergillus oryzae* as the fermentating agent and wheat bran as the medium.

The above account indicates the lines on which fermentation industries can be developed in the country. Only a few fermentation industries such as breweries and distilleries have been developed to some extent in our country. All the raw materials for the industries mentioned above are available in plenty and can be utilized if fermentation industries are organized on sound scientific lines to prepare products of industrial, medicinal and pharmaceutical value which are now almost entirely being imported to meet the demand in the country.

UTILIZATION OF FRUITS FOR WINE MAKING

By

D. S. Johar and J. C. Anand

(*Central Food Technological Research Institute, Mysore*)

An attempt was made to find out cheap and minor fruits to serve as a suitable base for the preparation of wines, tonic wines, and other fermented beverages. It is found that Coorg plum, Coorg orange and cashew apple can be successfully used for the above purpose. Methods for the preparation of these wines and the cost of production worked out in the Central Food Technological Research Institute, Mysore, are briefly given in this paper.

INDIA is importing different types of wines, liquors and spirituous drinks to the tune of 16 lakh gallons. These imports, which are considered essential to meet the civil, military and pharmaceutical needs, cost the exchequer about 1.5 crores of rupees. A large quantity of medicated and tonic wines is also imported and consumed in the country. Recently, some breweries, distilleries and other establishments have started the manufacture of 'Indian-made foreign liquors', but, barring a few firms preparing Ayurvedic types of medicated wines, there is no factory for the preparation of fruit wines (2). Some fruit wines from raisins and local varieties of grapes are produced on a small scale by pharmaceutical concerns for incorporation in their patent medicines. The non-availability of the right quality of grapes and their high cost have also stood in the way of industrial exploitation of this fruit.

In an attempt to find some cheap and easily available raw materials to serve as a base in the preparations of tonic wines, different types of fruit extensively grown in South India were tried. It has been found that plums and oranges grown in Coorg and in the Nilgiris can easily be made use of for the preparation of good quality wines. The methods of preparation of the wines are briefly described below.

Coorg Plum Cider: Coorg plum fruit, locally known as

'Karvanji Hannu', is grown extensively in certain regions of the Coorg State. The fruit is very sweet and possesses estery odour somewhat resembling that of ethyl acetate. The fruit is pale red in colour when ripe and possesses a thick smooth peel. The fruit usually weighs 10–20 gms. It has a membraneous central axis containing, on either side, luculae with two seeds. The fruit consists of the following:

Juice	= 52%
Seeds and axis	= 8·5%
Peels	= 17%
Brix of the Juice at 245·°C	= 11·5%
Reducing sugars	= 9·3%
Vitamin C	= 2 mg./100 gm.

Method of preparation: The fruit is cut into two pieces and the juice extracted with a juice extractor. The juice is sulphited and inoculated with an active culture of *Saccharomyces cerevisiae* var. *Ellipsoideus Burgundy* grown in sterile plum juice. The fermentation is complete within 7–10 days when the clear portion of the wine can be racked, matured, bottled and pasteurized. The lighter type of wine prepared from the fruit has an excellent taste and pleasant bouquet. It is estimated that the cost of a 26 oz. bottle of Coorg Plum Cider will be about Rs. 2.

Orange Wine: Coorg is growing annually 5,000–7,000 tons of loose-skinned oranges (Mandarin). The fruit has a deep orange colour and is fairly big in size and possesses a refreshing taste and flavour. The main crop is picked from December to March and forms 80% of the total production of oranges in Coorg. The second or the monsoon crop is harvested from June to August.

As revealed from the survey of the orange-growing areas, at least 5–10% of the summer crop consists of undersized, deformed and slightly sun-burnt fruits, and fetch a very low price. These fruits can, with advantage, be converted into wine. Of the monsoon crop, which comprises 500 tons, hardly 40% reaches the market and only 15–20% to the consumer. The rest of the fruit is destroyed by fungal and bacterial rots on account of heavy rains during the harvesting season. It is estimated that 1,00,000 pounds of orange juice go to waste from this crop alone. This huge waste can be avoided if the fruit is utilized on the spot for wine making, before the rot sets in.

Analysis of the fruit:

Juice	... =	60-70%
Brix of the Juice at 22·5°C. ...	... =	10·5
Acidity as citric acid ...	... =	0·32%

Method of preparation of Orange Wine: The oranges are peeled and the juice is extracted with a juice extractor. The juice is filtered over aluminium sieves which hold back crude pulp seeds, etc. Sulphur dioxide at the rate of 75 p.p.m. is added to the juice. To every 40 lb. of the juice, 10 lb. of sugar and 14 lb. of water are added to raise its sugar level to 28° Brix. It is then inoculated with actively fermenting starter, prepared from one pound of sterile orange juice inoculated with wine yeast. The fermentation is complete within 12–15 days when the clear wine can be racked, matured, bottled and pasteurized. It is estimated that the cost of 26 oz. bottle of orange wine will be about Rs. 2.

Cashew Apple Cider: The annual production of the cashew apples in India, which are a by-product of the cashew nut industry, is about 2,00,000 tons (3). The cashew is grown mostly in the Western Ghats, Madras, Mysore, Malabar and Cochin. It is estimated, on the basis of the production of cashew-nut, that about 55,000 *maunds* of the fruit go to waste. A small fraction of the available quantity is said to be used for distillation of cashew liquor and vinegar manufacture. This fruit can also be profitably used for wine making.

Method of manufacture: The fruit is steamed at 5 lb. pressure for 5 minutes, as recommended by Jain, Bhatia, Anand and Lal (1) to get rid of the excess of tannins. By this process, the tannin content of the juice is reduced from 0.34% to 0.07%, which is essential for all the fruit wines. The juice is then expressed in a basket press and sulphited with 75 p.p.m. of sulphur dioxide which is added in the form of potassium metabisulphite.

The average composition of the fresh juice which has a pale yellow colour and which forms 50–60% by weight of the fruit, is as follows:

Degree Brix	=	13·5 %
Total sugars (mostly invert) ...	=	12·0 %
Acidity as citric acid	=	0·25%
Tannins	=	0·34%
pH	=	4·2

It is then inoculated with a fermenting starter of pure wine yeast in plum juice. After about 10 days, the fermentation is complete and the wine settles down. The clear portion can be removed, bottled and pasteurized. The cashew cider has a pleasant aroma and taste. It is estimated that the cost of a 26 oz. bottle of cashew cider will be about Rs. 2.

The average composition and the cost of preparation of these wines are summarized in the Table below:

Name of the product	Alcohol by vol.	Total Citric acid	Volatile acids as acetic acid	Tannins	Approximate cost per 26 oz. bottle
Plum Cider ...	5·5 %	0·24%	0·062%	0·045%	Rs. 2 0 0
Orange Wine ...	12·21%	0·32%	0·082%	0·048%	Rs. 2 0 0
Cashew Apple Cider ...	5·84%	0·30%	0·084%	0·07 %	Rs. 2 0 0

Similar work on the assessment of the suitability of other fruits, especially minor fruits, for the preparation of wines and fermented beverages is in progress at this Institute.

To meet the demands of wines and tonic wines, there is at present no organized wine industry in the country. On the other hand, there is abundance of raw material which is cheaply available and which can be used in the preparation of tonic and medicated wines. A substantial quantity of waste products in the fruit preservation and sugar industries can also be turned to good account by the manufacture of tonic and medicated wines which are now being imported. There is large scope for the development of wine industry in India and it is hoped that the experiments carried out in the Central Food Technological Research Institute, Mysore, will give a lead in the establishment of this new industry.

References

1. Jain, N. L., *et al.*, Cashew Apple Products, *J. sci. and industr. Res.*, 1951, **10A**, (5), 209.

2. Report and Recommendations of the Food Ind. Panel No. 3, 'Fruit Wine Industry in India', Ministry of Industry and Supply, Government of India.

3. Report on the Marketing of Cashewnuts, Directorate of Marketing, Delhi, 1944.

PROBLEMS OF A SMALL-SCALE INDUSTRY—*PAN SUPARI*

By

Sri M. K. Krishna Chetty

(*Messrs Asoka Betelnut Factory, Coimbatore*)

In this article, the present status and possibilities of future developments of the Pan Supari Industry which is at present being run mostly on cottage-industry scale have been described. Difficulties of this industry and the nutritive value of Pan Supari are also referred to.

In India and in most of the eastern countries down to Malaya, almost every one, irrespective of caste or creed, uses *pan supari* in some form or other. Betel chewing is a ritual with the Hindus, and *pan supari* is offered for welcoming guests at marriages and other religious functions; it is taken after meals and as a digestive after heavy feasts and is also offered when guests leave the house. Even in the Moghul times, offering of *pan* to guests was given top priority. Special receptacles of gold, silver, brass, bidriware, lacqueur, mat, for keeping *pan* leaves, arecanut, *chunam* and spices have been developed. In the South, the ingredients are sold separately, like *pan* (betel leaf), arecanut (ordinary or scented) and *chunam* (slaked lime). The consumer makes his own *beeda* by adding *supari* and *chunam* to the leaf. In the North, *katha* (catechu) is used with *pan*. In Banaras and Lucknow, *pan beeda* is sold wrapped in silver leaf. In aristocratic houses they even use gold leaf to cover the *pan beeda*.

Cultivation of Betel Leaf and Arecanut: Pan leaves are cultivated in different parts of India and the size, quality and taste vary from place to place. Different varieties of *pan* are known to exist, like *Desi Pan, Sanchi Pan, Kapuri Pan, Banarsi Pan, Bangle Pan, Mittha Pan,* etc. Similarly, arecanut is used in many ways in the different parts of India. The nuts are allowed to dry whole after ripening and then cut into pieces or into fine slices like shavings. This process is mostly followed with imported nuts. Nuts grown in Mysore and Malabar are treated in a different way, by boiling the unripe nut and then cutting into different shapes and these go by the different trade names. The best variety of *supari* is grown on the Mysore plateau and the chief market for the arecanut trade for this kind of *supari* is at Shimoga in the Mysore State. This *supari* is suitable for conversion into powder, which, with the addition of spices, make the scented *supari,* which has become extremely popular.

Thamboola Amritham (Pan Supari Nectar): The Central Food Technological Research Institute has evolved a process for extracting in liquid form the essential properties in betel leaf, arecanut, *chunam* and other spices used in *pan*. The author has tried the mixture on his many *pan*-chewing friends, but none of them has taken kindly to it, because the liquid in the bottle when once opened could not be kept long and people who are used to chewing the *pan* with the saliva do not get the same pleasure in swallowing an ounce of *Thamboola Amritham*. Further, the extract in liquid form is not convenient to carry.

Alternative to Thamboola Amritham: It is, therefore, desirable that some new process should be found by which the whole *beeda* could be squeezed into a solid form like chewing gum or lozenges. This finished product should contain all the ingredients used in the scented *supari* with the addition of calcium and the betel juice. The Central Food Technological Research Institute could usefully take this up and make experiments to see how far they could succeed. Such a product could be packed and labelled for use in this country and for export outside India.

Benefits of betel chewing: From time immemorial the chewing of *pan supari* in Southern India has been followed with religious sanction and medical advice. Women during their confinement are allowed to take large quantities of betel leaves, arecanut and *chunam*. They swallow the chewed mixture with the saliva which helps digestion, kills germs in the system and replaces the calcium that is lost during and after confinement.

Import of arecanut: India is not self-sufficient in arecanuts and about 20 per cent of the country's requirements are imported from Ceylon, Malaya, etc. The imported variety is the round raw, sun-dried whole nut, which is almost exclusively used by consumers in Northern India, Bombay, etc. This nut is quite different from the boiled South Indian arecanut. The fluctuations in the Indian arecanut market depend on the quantity that is imported, and the policy with regard to the import of arecanut is guided by the Indian Central Arecanut Committee at Kozhikode.

In the preparation of scented *supari,* spices are used, some of which like cardamom are grown in India. For cloves, we have to depend on imports from Zanzibar and other places. To give an example, I will give you the present price of this article compared to the pre-war price.

Cloves are now being sold in the Madras market for a maund of 24 lb. at Rs. 220, whereas the pre-war price was only Rs. 14.

This is a great hardship to the manufacturer of betelnut powder. Government should carefully watch the situation and take measures to arrest the tendency of rising prices of this commodity.

Export: India does not export raw arecanuts to other countries. There is, however, a potential export market for processed or scented *supari* in Ceylon, Malaya and other countries where Indians have migrated and settled. The high import duty (in some cases up to 100%) imposed in these countries is a serious handicap to the expansion of Indian trade in this commodity. The matter deserves to be treated at Government level if the scented *supari* industry is to flourish either as a cottage-scale or a large-scale industry.

* * * * *

Dr Girdhari Lal proposed a vote of thanks.

DISCUSSION

(*4th Feb.* 1953)

Shri K. D. Malaviya (*The Chairman*): We have just heard a series of comprehensive and interesting papers on the technical problems facing the fruit and vegetable preservation industry. I am happy to note that this industry is keen on improving the quality of its products and emphasizing the need for setting up suitable specifications. It is now open for the House to discuss this important issue.

Dr Parpia (*Messrs Pure Products and Madhu Canning, Ltd., Bombay*): My firm as well as others are indeed anxious to have standards for different fruit and vegetable products. Unfortunately, however, the canners' organizations in our country do not possess the necessary facilities to develop the standards. I personally feel, for instance, that standards for processing, for retorting operations or for grading syrups are badly required for the industry. It will be of great help, therefore, if the Government through an institution like the Central Food Technological Research Institute, Mysore, take up this question and formulate specifications which will be followed by factories in India. Such standards are already available in countries like the U.S.A., and we may have, of course, to modify them to suit our particular requirements. This work should start as early as possible, for it will take quite a few months. The standards so evolved may be enforced after a specified period, after giving the factories enough time to correct themselves.

Dr Lal (*C.F.T.R.I., Mysore*): I should like to clarify certain points raised in Dr Parpia's paper and make a few suggestions for the industry. Dr Parpia suggested subsidies for the industry for its healthy progress. Through the efforts of the All-India Fruit Preservers' Association as well as of the former Indian Institute of Fruit Technology, some progress in this direction was made. This point was placed before the Government, but somehow the Government had difficulties in providing subsidies to different organizations. About the Fruit Products Order and Army specifications, I would add that they were based on two different lines, because the functions of these two organizations were formerly different. The specifications of the Fruit Products Order were based on just the minimum standards of quality and we did not want to have very hard and rigid rules. The manufacturer will realize the implications of standards in due course and will adopt them for the general good. The F.P.O., on the other hand, wanted to bring the sanitary and other conditions up to the mark and the question of quality came afterwards. Ultimately, through the efforts of Government-sponsored institutions we believe that the industry will make good headway in this direction.

With reference to the Army Specifications, I should like to state that there has not been a full agreement on the subject of these specifications. What I would suggest is a closer co-operation in future between the Food Ministry and our Institute for laying down the standards. We shall be very happy indeed if this institute is actively associated with this work.

Shri P. M. Mathur (*Department of Industries, U.P.*): While we are discussing the question of setting up standards, it is important to remember that we have in this country a number of cottage-scale industries as well as large factories for fruit and vegetable preservation. We have to develop both types of this industry in order to consume all the raw materials we have in this country. It may not be possible to lay down common standards. So, we may have to split them into two sets: one for cottage-scale and the other for large-scale production.

As to the standard of quality, it is imperative that we have to enforce existing laws and regulations and see to it that only graded products come to the market.

Shri V. Sane (*Government Hill Fruit Research Station, U.P.*): While speaking about standardization, I feel that we are not taking the picture as a whole. As one of the speakers mentioned in his paper, only quality raw materials will give quality products. It is high time that we bring about a liaison between the grower, the marketing agent and the manufacturer so that the whole preservation industry will function as a complete unit instead of working only at one end. We have to consider this broad problem very seriously and encourage the grower to grow suitable varieties for canning, help the marketing agent to get over the bottle-neck of transport especially in the hill areas and thus ultimately enable the manufacturer to produce quality products.

Shri V. Balu (*C.F.T.R.I., Mysore*): While discussing the quality of products and the enforcement of food standards, I would stress that a human approach is very essential. A certain amount of respect for moral standards will have to be developed so that industrialists may give the best products to the consumer. Whatever food standards are evolved and whatever arrangements are made to enforce the laws, much will ultimately depend on the adherence to a code of moral standards. In the initial stages, even at the sacrifice of a certain amount of profit, the workers in the factory as well as the industrialists should pay regard to this factor of moral standards.

Shri K. D. Malaviya (*The Chairman*): I should like to ask if Dr Weber, who is amongst us, would care to make a few remarks on this question of standards or on the fruit and vegetable preservation industry in U.P., with which he is connected.

Dr F. B. C. Weber (*F.A.O. Expert with the Government of U.P.*): It was my intention just to listen, but having heard several interesting views, I should like to make a few remarks. Of course, I have my limitations in this matter, since I have been in India only for 4 months, and furthermore, in Uttar Pradesh only.

As an outsider, I feel that the Fruit Products Order (1948), gives minimum requirements, which are reasonably adapted to the possibilities of the young fruit preserving industry in India and the economic conditions of the bulk of the population.

I do not expect improvement of the present condition of the fruit preservation industry by the application of foreign standards. As long as there exists a local surplus production of fruits on the one hand and scarcity or under-consumption of fruits on the other, nothing much will be gained by the introduction of higher minimum standards. However, I do feel that international standards should be adopted for export business.

In Uttar Pradesh there are plenty of apples, pears, peaches and apricots and the supply of the raw materials to the industry is essentially a problem of quality, quantity, continuity and distance.

One of the main complaints is that the quality of the fruit is generally poor. But we must remember that the quality of fruits will not be improved unless ways are found for using the unmarketable fruits to make the orchards and the fruit growing business economically sound.

In U.P. a major problem is transportation by rail. I won't go into details here, but I feel sure that it can and will be solved by co-operation with local railway authorities.

As regards small-scale fruit industries referred to in the discussion, the most difficult problem of this industry seems to be that of water supply and the quality of the water; other problems, so far as I can see, are such as will be solved, at any rate in U.P., in due course.

An important Government Service both to the industry and the consumer is, of course, offered by the Central Food Technological Research Institute, Mysore, but in the light of my experience I venture to say that the influence of the Mysore Institute is hardly felt, for instance, in Uttar Pradesh. The distances in India are so great as to make daily contacts with the Mysore Institute almost impracticable, if not impossible. The local problems, *i.e.*, those of local importance and State-wide scope should be studied and solved in local institutes of which one should be established in each State as a part of the Government machinery, at any rate in such States which have the benefit of a food and fruit preserving industry. Such a Fruit Utilization Institute will have to deal with each and every problem of local and State-wide importance: teaching and training, elementary research, advice to the industry, advice to the State Government, statistics, rural industrial planning, horticultural-industrial planning etc., and avoiding duplication of research and leaving all the problems of all-India importance to the Mysore Institute. There should be constant interchange of views and data between the State Institutes and the Mysore Institute.

'Eat More Fruit' campaigns are of utmost importance and community canning centres should be made an integral part of the community projects in which India excels. A food industry, organized on a State-wide and nation-wide basis and a National Board having representatives of the Indian Fruit Processing Industry, would only then be the real counterpart of a well-planned and organized Government service.

Shri K. D. Malaviya (*The Chairman*): Ladies and Gentlemen, on your behalf, I should like to thank all the contributors to the discussion and of papers for their valuable suggestions. On this question of quality a lot more can be said, but serious note will be taken of what has already been said. It is the sense of the House that the manufacturers should indicate the standards to suit their working conditions so that the Government may take further action in the matter through its competent bodies.

DISCUSSION

(*5th Feb.* 1953)

Mr M. Shankaraiya (*The Chairman*): The papers that have been presented by Mr Chauhan (Messrs Parle Products, Bombay) and Mr Bhaskara Rao (Britannia Biscuit Co. Ltd.,) mention a difficulty regarding the availability of citrus oil. They contain also references to other difficulties such as lack of analytical data on Indian wheats, oozing of fat, packaging materials, etc. Mr Bhasker Rao has informed us that Australian wheat flour is best suited for biscuit manufacture.

Dr D. S. Bhatia (*C.F.T.R.I., Mysore*): I would state in connection with the point regarding the analysis of Indian wheats, that in the Lyallpur Laboratories, we had a testing unit for cereals. Unfortunately, that type of unit does not now exist anywhere in the country. I am sure when we get the necessary equipment here, we will try to conduct the tests for different kinds of cereals produced in different States and we will be able to evolve standards in this respect.

Mr R. Bhaskar Rao (*The Federation of Biscuit Manufacturers' of India, Delhi*): I mentioned about the Australian wheat as the one preferred for biscuit manufacture on account of the elastic properties of its gluten. The Government could allot Canadian wheat for bread-making and Australian wheat for biscuit manufacture.

Dr D. S. Bhatia (*C.F.T.R.I., Mysore*): As to the oozing of fat and packaging difficulties, I think I agree with Mr Bhaskar Rao that the addition of mono-glycerides will not stop the oozing of fat. It does not seem to depend either on the amount of fat, but rather seems to be linked with the melting point of the fat used and the ratio of certain other components admixed with it. We have prepared in this Institute a shortening of 41° m.p., which we intend trying out in factories and then test the biscuits prepared with it for shelf life. So far, in the laboratory, we have had encouraging results.

Regarding the packaging materials, I understand that the Government want to lay down specifications for packaging materials suitable for biscuit manufacture under Indian conditions. I also understand that the Government would induce some of the Indian paper manufacturers to make paper according to these specifications. The wax paper now made is defective as it contains very tiny holes. The wax paper manufacturing firms are not able to make much progress because standards have not been prescribed for wax-paper. If manufacturers of biscuits and confectionery should tell them their exact requirements and suggest standards and should a guaranteed off-take be ensured, the firms will be able to manufacture wax-paper according to requirement.

Dr G. Lal (*C.F.T.R.I., Mysore*): I should like to ask the representative of Messrs Metal Box Co., a question with regard to packaging materials. This concern deals mostly with tin containers. Does it contemplate doing anything in the line of other packaging materials such as paper packaging?

Mr T. Rama Iyengar (*Messrs The Metal Box Co., of India, Calcutta*): At the moment, our plans are that we should concentrate on tin, but in England, and particularly in South Africa, we have developed the paper group and the cork materials group, and, in fact, we have recently developed cork-paper compositions which are supposed to have better quality and which can be had at cheaper prices than tin containers. Our biggest problem is that, even in the matter of tin containers, the scale of operations is insufficient to think of further expansion. We have to think in terms of mass production, and unless there is scope for paper and other materials, or at least there is indication for future expansion in this country, there is no possibility of expansion in this direction in India for the time being. But, should that be a point which will mean the expansion of the industry in this country, we shall not hesitate to make available the knowledge and technique in this line.

Mr H. C. Bijawat (*N.C.L., Poona*): Referring to the paper presented by the representative of Messrs Mettur Chemical and Industrial Corporation, I would state that the National Chemical Laboratory, Poona, has done some work on industrial carbons and that it would go into the question in detail. In this connection there is a paper published in the *Journal of Scientific and Industrial Research,* on the recovery of spent nickel, and information on this point will be gladly given if the firm contacts the National Chemical Laboratory.

Dr M. Srinivasan (*C.F.T.R.I., Mysore*): I should like to make a small observation. It is appropriate that the last paper to be read at the Symposium was on the *Pan-supari* Industry. *Pan* *supari* is associated with auspicious occasions and it rounds them off. It is a hint for guests to leave and for those remaining behind to ruminate and chew the cud. We have been interested for some time past on the rationale of *pan* chewing. Arecanut, one of the three constituents of *pan,* contains an alkaloid arecoline. The constitution of this alkaloid bears a close resemblance to nicotinic acid. We have tried *in vitro* experiments to convert, if possible, arecoline to nicotinic acid, but without success. We are contemplating rat-feeding trials to find out if this conversion can be brought about in the animal body.

Sri M. Shankaraiya (*The Chairman*): In my remarks, after the presentation of papers, I wanted to suggest the appointment of a Committee of Experts to go into the issues raised in the course of the discussion and the papers read. There are some papers which have been taken as read and the suggestions contained therein have also to be taken into account. I understand that all the suggestions and recommendations will be considered by the committee and published in the proceedings of the Symposium for the benefit of the food industries. The proposals will have to be dealt with by research institutions, State Governments and the Central Government. I should like to see the suggestions with reference to particular industries, such as Fruit Preservation, Biscuits, Confectionery, etc. This Institute would be of help to a great extent in solving some of the difficulties of the industry.

Thank you, gentlemen. It is now my duty to declare this Conference closed.

APPENDIX

CONCLUSIONS OF THE SYMPOSIUM

The Symposium records its thanks to Shri K. D. Malaviya, Deputy Minister for Natural Resources and Scientific Research, New Delhi, and Shri M. Shankaraiya, M.L.C., for their encouraging words of advice and the active interest they took in the discussions of the Symposium. Members of the Symposium hope that personal contacts and co-operation between producers and consumers, industries and research organizations, and scientists and Government departments, to which the Minister referred, will continue on an increasing scale.

Quality Control. The Symposium welcomes the suggestion from the industry for laying down standards for improving the quality of Indian food products and recommends that the Government, in co-operation with the industry, should prescribe suitable standards for raw materials, sanitation in factories, thermal processing and quality of finished products, and also set up machinery for their implementation and continuous improvement.

Biscuit and Bakery Industry. The Symposium observes that the Biscuit and Bakery Industry is faced with many special technical problems, investigations on which should be carried out either by the Industry or by the Central Food Technological Research Institute, Mysore, in co-operation with the industry.

In particular, a good deal of experimental work requires to be carried out in biscuit manufacture, on the utilization of (i) substitutes as well as new raw materials like soyabean flour, groundnut flour and tapioca starch, (ii) fats of higher melting point, (iii) various sweetening agents and (iv) indigenous spices as flavouring materials.

The Symposium requests the Council of Scientific and Industrial Research and the Indian Council of Agricultural Research, to initiate research projects for the study of Indian wheats for biscuit-making and *Chapati*-making. The Symposium also requests the Ministry of Food and Agriculture and the Defence Science Organization to start schemes to improve the quality (palatability, storage life, etc.,) of Service Biscuits.

The Symposium observes that statistics are not available regarding the bread-makers, small-scale biscuit-makers, pastry cooks, etc., in the country and recommends that systematic survey should be carried out for collecting these statistics.

In order to take maximum advantage of the progress made in the processing of wheat and wheat products in countries like United Kingdom, United States of America, Canada, etc., the Symposium recommends that steps should be taken for deputing representatives of the Industry and the Government departments concerned on study tours under the Colombo Plan in consultation with the Wheat Boards of the countries.

The Symposium notes that there is a real need for developing varieties of cereals for specific technological purposes and recommends that a close collaboration between cereal breeders and cereal technologists, which is practically non-existing at present, should be brought about as early as possible.

Barley Products Industry. The Symposium notes that the efforts of Barley Products Industry are hampered on account of inadequacy of local grain supplies as also of the lack of grading of this grain. The Symposium recommends that a State-aided Central Body similar to the Australian Barley Marketing Board should be established in order to deal with these problems as well as to acquaint the farmers with requirements of millers, decorticators and maltsters with respect to the varieties and quantities of barley, as well as correct methods of harvesting, storage and grading of the grain.

Confectionery, Cocoa and Chocolate Industries. With regard to the confectionery industry, the Symposium notes with satisfaction the formation of a Technical Committee by the Indian Confectionery Manufacturers' Association for laying down minimum quality standards for confectionery products. In this connection, the Symposium recommends that (i) investigations should be carried out to find cheap indigenous anti-oxidants and suitable moisture-proof packaging materials for the confectionery and (ii) technical aid and encouragement should be given for the manufacture, in India, of products such as corn syrup, citric and tartaric acids, essences and essential oils, fast edible colours, etc., required by the confectionery industry.

The cocoa and chocolate industry depends entirely on foreign sources for supplies of the cocoa bean. The Symposium recommends that, concomitantly with the facilities now granted for importing this bean, attempts should be made to grow, on a plantation scale, disease-resistant, high-yielding and good quality cocoa plants in suitable areas in the country so that the industry may become self-sufficient in respect of this raw material in due course.

The Symposium observes that the Indian Sweets Industry is scattered all over the country and confined to small producers, who do not possess the necessary scientific and technical knowledge. The Symposium recommends that a thorough study should be made of the composition, economical methods of processing, packaging and storage of selected types of Indian Sweets which lend themselves to large-scale production.

Fruit and Vegetable Preservation Industry. At present, large quantities of fruits and vegetables go to waste in various parts of India, mainly due to lack of storage facilities and quick means of transport. The Symposium recommends that steps should be taken to provide cold storage facilities at marketing centres and to improve and cheapen transport facilities from producing to processing centres and from processing to marketing centres.

In order to foster the growth of the fruit preservation industry the following measures of encouragement are recommended:

(*a*) the industry should be given planned protection for a period of three years, particularly, with respect to sugar which should be supplied at subsidized rates, and the tin plate of which the price should be fixed for a definite period and allotment made to the industry on yearly basis, (*b*) the provisions of the Fruit Products Order should be strictly enforced both in the case of indigenous products and foreign products imported into India, (*c*) in the interest of quality, the industry should utilize the services of persons who have received specialized training in various branches of fruit technology, (*d*) in order to foster greater co-ordination between fruit and vegetable industry and research institutions, an All-India Body under the Chairmanship of the Director, Central Food Technological Research Institute, Mysore, and consisting of representatives and technicians from the industry, members of the C.F.T.R.I. and other similar institutions, and the Directorate of Marketing and Inspection, should be established, (*e*) a comprehensive study of all the organisms found in Indian canned foods should be carried out preferably at the Central Food Technological Research Institute, Mysore, and (*f*) side by side with the development of large-scale fruit preservation factories in the country, encouragement should be given for the development of small-scale units for utilizing local surpluses of fruits and vegetables during glut seasons of production.

The Symposium takes note of the difficulties of the fruit growing industry in Assam and recommends that encouragement should be given for starting fruit preservation factories in order to utilize large quantities of fruits grown in that State.

The Symposium notes that cold-storage industry in the country has developed to a stage when the formation of an All-India Cold Storage Owners' Association is indicated to bring about a planned development of the industry.

The Symposium wishes to bring to the notice of the Fruit Preservation Industry that there are possibilities of an export market for mango and mango products. It recommends the establishment of quick freezing pilot-plants for mango and mango pulp which will go a long way in developing this industry in India. This will also prevent the wastage of a good proportion of mangoes grown in the country.

The Symposium recommends that attempts should be made for the manufacture, in India, of high quality edible gelatin which is now imported for various purposes including the preparation of jams and jellies. In order to get the best raw materials for the purpose, maximum co-operation between the leather and gelatin industries may be secured.

Engineering Industry. The Symposium recommends that State Governments should give full encouragement to Food Engineers for the design and fabrication of different types of machinery required by the food industries.

Packaging Industry. The Symposium recommends that Indian Forest departments should be requested to include in their afforestation programmes the cultivation of such types of trees as would be suitable for the manufacture of light and strong packing cases for various food industries.

INDEX